A Coterie Press Book

By William Taylor

With Photographs by Peter Darley

1965: Jim Clark & Team Lotus
The UK Races

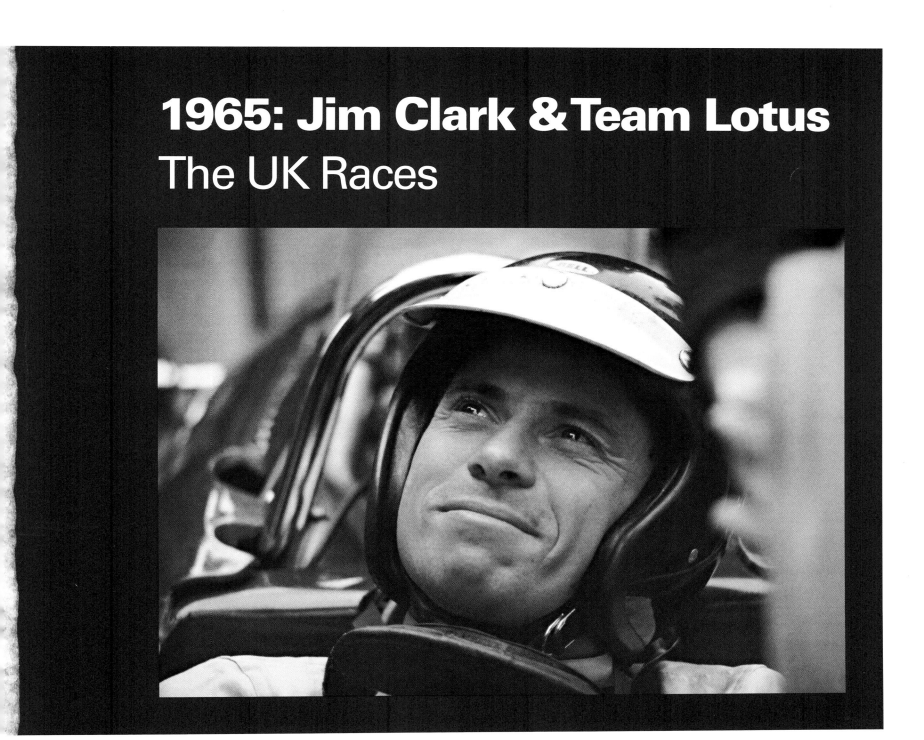

Contents
1965

A Coterie Press Book

1965: Jim Clark & Team Lotus - The UK Races

First British Edition July 2009

Published in the UK by Coterie Press Limited
22-36 Hastings Street, Luton, Bedfordshire LU1 5BE
Contact Tel: +1 303 933 2526 (Head office USA)
Fax: +1 303 904 9294 (Head office USA)
coterieltd@aol.com

www.coteriepress.com

USA Office
5 White Birch
Littleton
Colorado 80127

ISBN: 978-1-902351-36-0   Standard Edition
ISBN: 978-1-902351-37-7   Publishers Edition

The Author wishes to extend his special thanks to:
Peter Darley, Jack Sears, Bob Dance, Clive Chapman,
David Hobbs, Ed & Sally Swart, David Long, John Elwin,
Martin Hadwen at motorracing-archive.com, Terry Clark.

AUTHOR: William Taylor
EDITOR: David Long
EDITORIAL ASSISTANTS: Jo Taylor & Sandy Lardinois
CREATIVE DIRECTOR: William Taylor
DESIGN: Scott Wilson Design
PHOTO RETOUCHING: Susan Roushey & Olivia Taylor
PRINTED BY: Colorprint
ORIGINATION BY: Coterie Press

Foreword
Jack Sears

Jimmy and I had three things in common - farming, motor racing and flying. When we first met in 1960 our farms grew arable crops. He had sheep as an additional enterprise, I had beef cattle and pigs, and we often discussed the merits of our respective farming systems. Before Jimmy started motor racing his father had frequently said to him, "*take your stick and dog and go up to the hill and look after the sheep!*"

Jimmy did as he was told but his great farming friend Ian Scott-Watson introduced him to the world of motorsport when he was not working on the farm. Ian was astounded at Jimmy's speed in his saloon car and decided that Jimmy should race it. Success followed success and, to the delight of all his friends and racing enthusiasts, an embryo World Champion emerged.

My first duel with Jimmy was in 1963 at Brands Hatch when we were driving Ford Galaxie 500s which that year had dominated saloon car racing whilst beating the Jaguar 3.8 MK II contingent on every occasion. It was the first time Jimmy had driven this huge car but he got the measure of it very quickly and led into the first corner with me tucked in behind him. I hung on to his tail for the first five laps before a puncture caused me to retire and Jimmy went on to win. After the race I asked him what he thought of the car. He replied, "*Terrific, I have never had so much fun in my life!*"

He never raced a Galaxie again but in 1964 he was entered in the British Saloon Car Championship by Colin Chapman. Driving a Team Lotus-Cortina he spent every race trying to pass my Galaxie. Whilst he would 'tailgate' me through corners the Galaxie had more 'grunt' out of the corners and he never succeeded. However, he was supreme in his class in every race and went onto to win the BTCC that year. Soon he proved to be a consistent winner in every type of car he drove.

In 1965 Colin Chapman invited me to become Jimmy's teammate in the Team Lotus Cortinas contesting the British Saloon Car Championship. I regarded this as a great honour and was determined to learn about Jimmy's technique on the track. I never managed to beat him but would follow his line through the corners and improve my laps times that way. In March 1965 we travelled together to Miami, picked up a hire Galaxie and set off for Sebring to race the Team Lotus Cortinas in a three hour race. Colin Chapman's words were ringing in our ears: "*Make sure you beat the BMWs.*" Jimmy won of course and I was second.

On the way to the race, in the Galaxie, Jimmy was driving when we were stopped for exceeding the 55mph speed limit on the Interstate. After we paid the $50.00 fine the policeman asked us where we were heading and on hearing our destination was Sebring he said, "*I guess you are race fans*" to which we replied "*Yes!*" Two months later Jimmy won the Indianapolis 500 and I often wonder if the policeman, on seeing a picture of Jimmy in the newspapers, did a double take and exclaimed, "*Well I'll be darned if this isn't the guy I fined for speeding a couple of months ago!*"

I enjoyed being his teammate very much. Not only did I learn from him but his personality was so likeable that it was always such a pleasure to be in his company.

Jack Sears. May 2009

Introduction
William Taylor

More than four decades on, 1965 for Team Lotus still stands as one of the single most successful and significant years in the history of motorsport for an individual team.

That year, the last of the 1.5 litre formula, Team Lotus won nine of the 15 major Formula One races; in fact they won nine out of the first ten F1 races of the season - they did not take part in the race at Monaco - the results only tailing off once Clark's sixth GP win at the German Grand Prix in August had secured both the Drivers' and Constructors' World titles for Colin Chapman's Team Lotus.

Of course by missing Monaco the team was to provide the racing year's biggest story - and its largest prize fund - namely Jim Clark's sensational win in the Memorial Day, Indianapolis 500 race. The first victory for a non-US team was also the first for a rear-engined car at the Brickyard, with Lotus taking the first five places on the grid, along with first, second and fourth places in the final results. By no means is it an exaggeration to say that the win by Team Lotus at Indy changed the face of motor racing in the USA forever.

The start of the 1965 season had seen Team Lotus victorious in the Tasman Championship, with Clark taking four wins in the seven-race series based in Australia and New Zealand. With a Formula 2 Lotus 32 modified to new 32B specification (with a 2.5 litre Coventry-Climax FPF engine) he took pole position and posted the fastest lap at the four meetings he won at.

In Formula Two the competition was much tougher but, running under the Ron Harris Team Lotus banner, the British cars from Cheshunt won the two major series - the British Autocar Championship, with two wins in five races, and the European/French Championship with three out of four. Elsewhere Francesco Ghezzi in a Lotus 32 was placed second in the Italian championship after securing one win in the three-race series.

The previous season had provided an easy win for Clark in the British Saloon Car Championship: throughout 1964 he had been very much the fastest thing on four wheels, and more than occasionally on three. In 1965, however, Jimmy's battles with the American 'big bangers' resulted in several unscheduled comings-together and more than a few retirements. These races provided much entertainment for the crowds but, together with other commitments leading him to miss a number of races, left the door open for Roy Pierpoint's Weybridge Engineering Ford Mustang to steal the title from Team Lotus Racing. Even so, Clark and Sears managed to break the class lap record at every event they attended as well as scoring a brace of outright wins over the American muscle. Sears also took a class win in the Championship, finishing fourth overall.

In the European saloon car series the Alan Mann Cortinas were even more impressive, winning the overall title with four victories, and in the USA, Team Lotus Racing with English Ford Line (Dearborn) contested several races with an extensive fleet of cars and drivers. So many of them, indeed, that at times even Colin Chapman didn't know quite who was driving, where and when.

So this book is not about the big wins of the year, the famous victories in F1 and Indy, about which so many words have been written already. Rather it covers a season of racing with Team Lotus in Britain, where the prize funds were considerably smaller but the competition always fierce and the wins – when they came - no less important and no harder to achieve than the big ones. More than anything the story told in **1965: Jim Clark & Team Lotus** shows the company building its reputation and laying the foundations for a future as one of the leading race and road-car manufacturers. It was, for everyone, a real year to remember.

William Taylor. June 2009

Chapter One
Brands Hatch
13th March

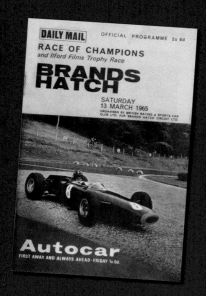

"SPENCE WINS FIRST EVER RACE OF CHAMPIONS"

The first Formula 1 race of the 1965 European season
went to Mike Spence in the works Lotus Type 33 when he
won a race new to the F1 calendar, the two-part
Race of Champions at Brands Hatch....

Above right
Jim Clark, Bruce
McLaren and Colin
Chapman wait on the
grid before the start of
the Race of Champions.

Timetable

Event: Daily Mail Race of Champions Meeting
Date: 13th March 1965
Location: Brands Hatch
Circuit Length: 2.65 miles

Time	Race	Laps	Distance	
1:30 pm	Daily Mail 'Race of Champions' Part I	40	105.94 miles	
3:10 pm	The Ilford Films Trophy Saloon Car Race	20	52.97 miles	
4:20 pm	Daily Mail 'Race of Champions' Part II	40	105.94 miles	

Brands Hatch, Long Circuit – Existing Lap Records

Formula 1	Jim Clark	Lotus-Climax	1m 38.8 sec.	96.56 mph.
Formula 2	Graham Hill	Repco-Brabham	1m 43.4 sec.	92.26 mph.
Formula 3	Brian Hart	Lotus-Ford	1m 45.6 sec.	90.34 mph.
Sportscars over 2000cc	Hugh Dibley	Repco-Brabham	1m 42.6 sec.	92.98 mph.
Sportscars under 2000cc	Frank Gardner	Brabham-Ford	1m 44.0 sec.	91.73 mph.
Saloon Cars over 2000cc	Jim Clark	Ford Galaxie	1m 54.4 sec.	83.39 mph.
Saloon Cars 1301cc to 2000cc	Jackie Stewart	Lotus-Cortina	1m 55.6 sec.	82.53 mph.

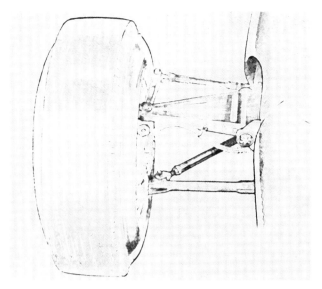

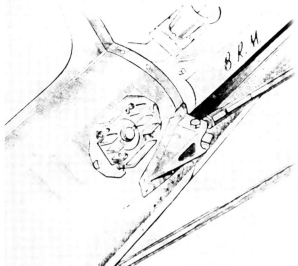

A Full Complement In The Paddock

Billed as many thought rather grandiosely as the 'Race of Champions', the first European Formula 1 race of the 1965 season nevertheless attracted all the leading teams and every recent World Champion with the notable exception of Phil Hill. The American was sadly without a GP ride for the whole of 1965, although his form in the latter half of the Tasman series must have left some team managers wondering if they had made the right decision. Innes Ireland and Trevor Taylor were similarly out of the running, BRP having pulled out of racing at the end of 1964.

With a particularly strong field at Brands, however, the organisers had even managed to persuade Ferrari to attend – thus ensuring there was a car for John Surtees, the current World Champion. Unfortunately, arriving late on Thursday evening, just in time for the practice session the following morning, the car in question promptly blew its engine at which point (in typical Ferrari fashion) it became apparent that the team had forgotten to bring any spares. To remedy this a call was made to Modena asking for the necessary parts to be flown over. These duly arrived albeit only just in time for the second practice session, having been put on a flight which itself ran into technical problems.

In the event Surtees managed to post an almost respectable time of 1m 37.3sec.. Sufficient to put him seventh on the grid, but more than two seconds slower than the front-runners, it was, even so quite an achievement given that – in the resulting rush to rebuild the car – the fuel injection had been incorrectly set thereby causing the engine to lose around 1,000 r.p.m.

at the top end. Despite spending most of the test session making adjustments, the mechanics proved unable to make up the loss.

Meanwhile at Lotus, Jim Clark and Mike Spence had been furnished with a pair of Type 33s, a Type 25 travelling with them as a spare which was still running an older-style 'high level' exhaust together with experimental Goodyear tyres. The Type 33s were chassis numbers R9 and R10, Clark as team leader was driving the newer car with which he had previously won the first GP of the season in South Africa. A third Type 33 was also present at Brands, R8 having been driven by Moises Solana in the '64 Mexican GP before being sold to Dickie Stoop. Stoop wanted it for Paul Hawkins, although as a late entry, Hawkins was posted as a reserve driver and was only allowed to compete in the second part of the two-race event after two cars had retired in the first.

Clark, as ever, was comfortably the fastest driver during practice, putting in a time of 1m 34.9sec. to take an easy pole position at 100.53mph and – as an indication of how rapidly improvements were being made in Formula 1 at this time – shaving a full 3.6 seconds off his 1964 lap record. The achievement also won him 100 bottles of Champagne from the Evening News as it was the first ever official 100mph lap of Brands Hatch. (In a true battle of the newspapers, the Daily Mail was race sponsor whilst the Daily Sketch also got in on the act by sponsoring a 'Miss Motor Racing' beauty competition held over the course of the weekend.) Teammate Mike Spence, in only his ninth Grand Prix, showed that he had really got the hang of Formula 1 by following up his

Race of Champions
For Formula 1 Cars
Entry List

No.	Entrant	Car	Engine	C.C.	Driver
1	S.E.F.A.C. – Ferrari	Ferrari 158	Ferrari V8	1497	John Surtees
3	Owen Racing Organisation	B.R.M. P261	B.R.M. V8	1498	Graham Hill
4	Owen Racing Organisation	B.R.M. P261	B.R.M. V8	1498	Jackie Stewart
5	Team Lotus	Lotus 33 (chassis R10)	Climax V8	1496	Jim Clark
6	Team Lotus	Lotus 33 (chassis R9)	Climax V8	1496	Mike Spence
7	Brabham Racing Organisation	Brabham BT11	Climax V8	1496	Dan Gurney
8	Brabham Racing Organisation	Brabham BT11	Climax V8	1496	Jack Brabham
9	The Cooper Car Company	Cooper T77	Climax V8	1496	Bruce McLaren
10	The Cooper Car Company	Cooper T77	Climax V8	1496	Jochen Rindt
11	R.R.C. Walker	Brabham BT11	B.R.M. V8	1498	Jo Siffert
12	R.R.C. Walker	Brabham BT7	Climax V8	1496	Jo Bonnier
14	Scuderia Centro-Sud	B.R.M. P578	B.R.M. V8	1498	Masten Gregory
15	Scuderia Centro-Sud	B.R.M. P578	B.R.M. V8	1498	Ludovico Scarfiotti
16	Reg Parnell	Lotus 25 (chassis R3)	B.R.M. V8	1498	Richard Attwood
17	Reg Parnell	Lotus 25 (chassis R7)	B.R.M. V8	1498	Mike Hailwood
18	John Willment Automobiles	Brabham BT11	B.R.M. V8	1498	Frank Gardner
19	John Willment Automobiles	Lola T55	Ford 4-cyl	1498	Jo Schlesser
20	D.W. Racing Enterprises	Brabham BT11	Climax V8	1496	Bob Anderson
21	Ian Raby (Racing) Ltd.	Brabham BT3	B.R.M. V8	1498	Ian Raby
22	Gerard Racing	Cooper T60	Climax V8	1496	John Taylor

Reserves

No.	Entrant	Car	Engine	C.C.	Driver
23	Sports Motors Manchester	Brabham BT14	Ford 4-cyl	1498	Rodney Bloor
24	Roy Winkelmann Racing	Brabham BT16	Ford 4-cyl	1498	Alan Rees
25	D.W. Racing Enterprises	Lotus 33 (chassis R8)	Climax V8	1496	Paul Hawkins
26	Gerard Racing	Cooper T71	Ford 4-cyl	1498	John Rhodes

"The steering wheel which Jim Clark used in his Lotus 25 during his fantastically successful 1963 championship season, and which he recently presented to Brands Hatch, is now in a place of honour in the pavilion. But there is just one problem, they have mounted it upside down!"

excellent fourth place finish in the South African GP with a lap time of 1m 36.1sec. thereby putting himself on the outside of the front row of the 3-2-3 grid.

In the pits with the Lotus team was Jimmy's girlfriend at the time, Sally Stokes. "*I used to sit on the pit counter and do the timing for Jimmy, (as did most of the wives and girlfriends) with the Heuer split timing watch that had been presented to Jimmy at the '64 Geneva Motor Show and he gave to me for my birthday. I had a large timing pad to record the 'running' times and subtract the lap times, lap by lap and I suppose I must have been reasonably good at it since one time at Brands they had an electric failure and the timing people came to Bette Hill and myself for the times to set the grid. None of us are perfect though and another time, I remember Colin being upset with me when I had missed a practice time. We used to record 10 at a time, and he said "The trouble with you girls, is that you are much better at adding than subtracting!" He was quite a joker.*"

BRM brought its US GP-winning car for Graham Hill and a second which had been built for Jackie Stewart to use in the South African round and now had the team's new, revised suspension set-up both front and rear. Hill's remained as before, making it the only driver/car combination which was truly capable of duelling with Jim Clark for fastest practice lap: on the day his time of 1m 35.6sec. put him on the middle of the front row. Jackie Stewart, still feeling his way around Formula 1, managed a steady 1m 36.7sec. to take the inside of the third row although his consistent speed in what was only his second race at this level, was an indication to all that he would soon be up with the front runners.

Contrasting with this, the more experienced Dan Gurney and Jack Brabham pairing at Brabham ran into trouble early in the first practice session. The latter recorded a time of 1m 36.6sec., a full one and a half seconds slower than Clark, but with his fuel injection playing up Gurney wasn't able to put in a time at all. His car still wasn't right in the second session either, although completing a lap in 1m 38.1sec. he secured a place on the outside of the fifth row. Brabham meanwhile could only find a tenth of a second improvement putting him neck-and-neck with Jo Bonnier's Rob Walker Brabham Climax at 1m 36.5sec.. Not for several years had the Swiss driver been as fast as Jack Brabham in what was essentially the same car, but a veteran of 10 seasons in Formula 1 he had somehow upped his game at the start of 1965 and the results were plain to see.

Working overnight the Brabham crew finally sorted out Gurney's car, and on Saturday morning an unofficial test session saw him post a stunning 1m 34.2sec. This naturally shook up the other teams – it was more than half a second quicker than Clark – and with both Gurney and Brabham running Goodyear rubber it looked like the tyre war which had started between the top two manufacturers in the Tasman Championship, had now arrived in Europe. (At this time most leading drivers were on Dunlop tyres and, until the new R7 became fully available, still using the yellow spot R6.)

At Cooper the team's hopes were riding on a heavily-revised version of the T77 spaceframe chassis, various suspension modifications being tried out in a bid to improve the handling of a chassis that, in its essentials

Above
Resting on the boot lid of Jimmy's Cortina in the paddock, Colin Chapman and the RAC Scrutineer discuss the finer points of a serious technical matter.

Above
Two different approaches to 1964 sportscar design. On the left from Italy an ISO Grifo A3/C and on the right a Series1 Lotus Elan.

Left
Colin Chapman's eldest daughter Jane tries Jimmy Clark's Type 33 for size.

Opposite page
Graham Hill wearing Dunlop overalls, knitted roll top and 'modern' style helmet is ready for the start of the race. Behind him Ian Raby takes the old school approach with nothing more than a Polo shirt for protection.

"The Club Lotus annual dinner dance took place at Bush House in the Aldwych in central London, on February 12th."

dated back to the start of the '64 season. Attempting to compete with a new breed of monocoque designs, the T73 had run in '64 and scored a couple of second place finishes in the hands of Bruce McLaren after being stiffened by riveting steel sheeting to the frame. The T77 was merely a revised version of the same design and with both McLaren and new boy Jochen Rindt still in the early stages of sorting it out, the Coopers were somewhat off the pace. That said, with Brands his first outing in the new car, Rindt ended up three tenths of a second and one place ahead of his vastly more experienced team mate.

The remainder of the field comprised a fairly varied selection of privateers, although several of these proved embarrassingly competent when it came to showing up the works drivers.

Bob Anderson, for example, driving a Brabham-Climax BT11 with a new fuel injection system, took his place on the outside of the third row with a creditable time of 1m 37.4sec.. Similarly Richard Attwood, in what was his first outing with the BRM-powered Reg Parnell Lotus Type 25, managed a decent 1m 38.1sec., while Jo Siffert in the Rob Walker Brabham-BRM BT11 was placed alongside Attwood after posting an identical time. Further back Mike Hailwood in the other Parnell Lotus 25 was positioned ahead of Frank Gardner in the Willment Brabham-BRM; also Ian Raby (Brabham-BRM), John Taylor (Gerard Cooper-Climax), Ludovico Scarfiotti and Masten Gregory in a pair of Centro-Sud BRMs. Bringing up the rear was Frenchman Jo Schlesser in the Ford Twin-Cam-powered Willment Lola, nearly ten seconds slower in qualifying than Clark.

A Race Of Two Halves
Race day dawned with the track bathed in warm sunshine, and a crowd estimated at nearly 40,000 squeezing into the Kent circuit for their first taste of F1 racing that year. The race itself was to be run in a two 40-lap format either side of a saloon car fixture, with the aggregate time across both being used to determine the overall winner.

Ferrari, still trying to deal with a car well down on top-end power, was forced into something of a panicky plug-change on the V8 engine immediately before the warm up lap started. With the cars lined up on the dummy grid there was a similar last-second panic at BRM when a breather pipe burned clean through on Graham Hill's car. Fortunately this was quickly fixed and, as the field moved forward to the main grid and waited for the flag to fall, Hill nonchalantly looked across and smiled at his children sitting in the stand, only raising his goggles into place at the very last second. As a result, at the flag he was momentarily caught unprepared and promptly out-dragged by the two works Lotuses either side of him. Thus Clark and Spence led the pack into Paddock bend for the first time, followed by Hill, Bonnier, Stewart, Surtees, Brabham and Rindt.

It was a perfect start for Team Lotus and, in an impressive display by the duo, both green and yellow cars began pulling away from Hill while behind him Stewart, Bonnier, Surtees and Brabham bunched up in a good old scrap. Masten Gregory's car sustained a broken half shaft on the second lap but this went almost unnoticed by most of the fans in the excitement of their first big race of the season. For his own part Dan

Above
Number two in the Team Lotus Formula 1 line-up, Mike Spence really began to make his mark during 1965.

Race of Champions
Grid – Part I

Pole Position

Mike Spence	Graham Hill	Jim Clark
Lotus-Climax	B.R.M.	Lotus-Climax
1 min 36.1 sec	1 min 35.6 sec	1 min 34.9 sec

Jack Brabham	Jo Bonnier
Brabham-Climax	Brabham-Climax
1 min 36.5 sec	1 min 36.5 sec

Bob Anderson	John Surtees	Jackie Stewart
Brabham-Climax	Ferrari	B.R.M.
1 min 37.4 sec	1 min 37.3 sec	1 min 36.7 sec

Bruce McLaren	Jochen Rindt
Cooper-Climax	Cooper-Climax
1 min 38.0 sec	1 min 37.7 sec

Dan Gurney	Jo Siffert	Richard Attwood
Brabham-Climax	Brabham-B.R.M.	Lotus-Climax
1 min 36.1 sec	1 min 38.1 sec	1 min 38.1 sec

Frank Gardner	Mike Hailwood
Brabham-B.R.M.	Lotus-B.R.M.
1 min 39.0 sec	1 min 38.8 sec

Ludovico Scarfiotti	John Taylor	Ian Raby
B.R.M.	Cooper-Climax	Brabham-B.R.M.
1 min 41.3 sec	1 min 40.6 sec	1 min 40.4 sec

Jo Schlesser	Masten Gregory
Lola-Ford	B.R.M.
1 min 44.0 sec	1 min 41.4 sec

"Lotus will have four new F1 cars for the 1965 GP season. Two V8s and a further 2 designed to take the hoped for Coventry Climax flat-16 unit. Colin Chapman is also building two new monocoques for Indianapolis. Brian Hart joins the Lotus F2 team, again to be run by Ron Harris. Lotus are developing a new factory at an airfield near Norwich."

Gurney, who had been fourteenth on lap one, was soon passing cars left, right and centre and by lap five was lying eighth and threatening everyone in the bunch ahead. Rindt, Anderson, Attwood, Siffert, Hailwood, McLaren, Gardner, Taylor, Raby, Scarfiotti and Schlesser pressed on behind.

Over the course of the next few laps Clark moved confidently away, pulling out a lead of several seconds over Spence who, in turn, was having little difficulty keeping ahead of Graham Hill. Hill's team mate, Jackie Stewart, was meanwhile being pushed along by the group behind him and was very soon in danger of catching the BRM number one.

On lap seven Brabham managed to force a way past Bonnier and set his sights on Stewart just before Gurney eased past Surtees whose Ferrari was still short on revs despite the last minute plug change. The next retirement came on lap ten when Bob Anderson's engine died at Clearways: leaping out of the car for a quick inspection he discovered a broken throttle linkage rod – at least it was a relatively short walk back to his pit.

Over the next few laps Gurney muscled his way past team mate Jack Brabham before disposing of the two BRMs. Brabham passed Stewart and Hill a couple of laps later, leaving the race order Lotus, Lotus, Brabham, Brabham, BRM, BRM although with Gurney rapidly shrinking the gap between himself and Mike Spence, that line-up would not last long. Further back Jo Bonnier continued to show the excellent form he had shown in practice and was holding off the reigning World Champion's Ferrari with apparent ease.

Gurney's next victim was Mike Spence and, after brief resistance from the Lotus number two, he was able to slip through on the inside at South Bank bend. Clark was now more than 20 seconds ahead however, so Gurney's progress through the field was to stop there. Whilst able to clip of a fraction of a second here and there, in the end he was quite unable to make much of an impression the race leader.

Finally, towards the end of the race, Surtees found some improvement enabling the Ferrari to dispatch with Bonnier and take on Stewart, eventually managing to steal sixth place from the Scotsman's BRM.

Jim Clark's resounding win – crossing the line a full 20.8 seconds ahead of Dan Gurney – left the Californian driver with an almost impossible task ahead of him. If an overall victory was to be his, he would have to win the second heat by a quite enormous margin. Certainly the the crowd didn't think this was going to happen, and many had already resigned themselves to another dominant win for Jimmy and Team Lotus before the cars had even been taken back to the pits.

Mechanics Race To Repair
The race regulations stated that, with the overall result being based on the addition of the race times from two separate heats, the mechanics would be allowed to work on the car during the interval. This gave each team approximately one hour to refresh/repair their cars, while spectators were treated to a quite different spectacle, namely the 20-lap 'Ilford Films Trophy' which comprised the first round of the BRSCC British Saloon Car Championship for 1965.

Above
Jim Clark and Team Lotus mechanic Dick Scammell chat before the start of the race.

Race of Champions
Results – Part I

Pos.	Driver	No.	Car	Laps	Time/Reason	Speed
1st	Jim Clark	5	Lotus 33	40	1 hr 04 min 14.0 sec	99.02 mph
2nd	Dan Gurney	7	Brabham BT11	40	1 hr 04 min 34.8 sec	
3rd	Mike Spence	6	Lotus 33	40	1 hr 05 min 03.8 sec	
4th	Jack Brabham	8	Brabham BT11	40	1 hr 05 min 24.0 sec	
5th	Graham Hill	3	B.R.M. P261	40	1 hr 05 min 25.6 sec	
6th	John Surtees	1	Ferrari 158	40	1 hr 05 min 29.2 sec	
7th	Jackie Stewart	4	B.R.M. P261	40	1 hr 05 min 35.6 sec	
8th	Jo Bonnier	12	Brabham BT7	39		
9th	Frank Gardner	18	Brabham BT11	39		
10th	Richard Attwood	16	Lotus 25	39		
11th	Jo Siffert	11	Brabham BT11	39		
12th	Bruce McLaren	9	Cooper T77	39		
13th	Jochen Rindt	10	Cooper T77	39		
14th	John Taylor	22	Cooper T60	38		
15th	Ian Raby	21	Brabham BT3	37		
16th	Ludovico Scarfiotti	15	B.R.M. P578	28		
dnf	Jo Schlesser	19	Lola T55	18	Dsq – outside assistance	
dnf	Mike Hailwood	17	Lotus 25	13	Accident	
dnf	Bob Anderson	20	Brabham BT11	10	Accident	
dnf	Masten Gregory	14	B.R.M. P578	1	Driveshaft failure	
Pole Position		5	Jim Clark		1 min 34.9 sec	
Fastest Lap (new record)		5 & 7	Jim Clark & Dan Gurney		1 min 35.6 sec (99.79 mph)	

Right
The start of the Ilford
Films Trophy race, with
from left to right, John
Rhodes (Mini-Cooper),
Jim Clark (on Pole),
Jack Sears (hidden),
Mike Salmon and Roy
Pierpoint (hidden).

To those who knew the cars and the drivers' form this was expected to be a fairly straight Ford versus Ford fight between the three 'big banger' Mustangs (driven by Sir Gawaine Baillie Bt., Roy Pierpoint and Mike Salmon) and the smaller but more nimble works Lotus-Cortinas of Jim Clark and Jack Sears.

The Blue Oval-backed division responsible for the two Team Lotus cars was run as a totally separate entity to the Formula 1 Team, the chief mechanic in charge of running two or even three cars at some events being Bob Dance. The team had two superb Ford Thames transporters built by Marshalls of Cambridge, one registered 428 VRO which was able to carry two race cars, and another (429 VRO) which carried a spare car and parts supply, as well as functioning as the team's mobile workshop.

Fully kitted out with all the equipment the mechanics could possibly need, and plenty of room for the spares, Dance recalls "*the crew couldn't have wished for more, and in fact, until the Formula One team got their new transporter in 1967 they were actually quite jealous of our set-up.*" At the start of the 1965 season Dance's diary entry for 15th February shows that the team had built up three new cars, consecutively registered JTW 496C, 497C and 498C. His meticulous records would refer to the three cars as E8, E9 and E10 respectively.

On the Wednesday prior to the first race of the season the team made the long slog to Snetterton to test all three cars, Dance noting that "*E8 seemed down on power and we only ran the car for 35 miles (about 13 laps).*" Unfortunately Clark was unable to attend but on

the cold, dry circuit Sears was clocked at 1m 49.8sec. which was well under the existing lap record. Later in the day Dance himself climbed into the passenger seat alongside Colin Chapman, his diary logging Chapman's time at 1m 48.9 sec. "*Maybe the extra weight on the passenger side helped keep the other two wheels on the ground*", was all Bob had to say of the experience.

Incredibly, in practice at Brands Hatch, Jim Clark proved to be more than a second faster than the Mustangs and in the race itself he confirmed his sheer ability behind the wheel by racing off into an easy lead. The Mustangs did their best to hold on to the Cortina as it three-wheeled its way round this corner of the Kent countryside but with the Flying Scotsman producing a masterful display of car control there was little or nothing they could do. Pierpoint managed to hold on to second place with Salmon third, Sears in the other works Cortina sandwiching the pair in fourth. Lying fifth Sir Gawaine's Mustang was clearly in trouble, and with braking now almost non-existent he was forced to shut off his engine as he passed the pits in an attempt to slow down sufficiently as he went into Paddock bend!

Clark's lead lasted just five of the scheduled 20 laps as on lap six he pitted complaining that a front wheel felt loose. Sally Stokes, remembers the occasion well, "*Jimmy was leading the race and doing fine when suddenly he came round the corner behind the pits, left the track and was reversing at great speed across the grass...towards us! When we asked him what he was thinking of making such a dramatic exit he said..."oh, if you can't win at least be spectacular and give them their money's worth,*" we just fell around laughing!"

Above left
At the start of 1965 the BRM tuned Ford based twin-cam engine in the Cortina was producing around 150bhp.

Above right
The saloon car team travelled in style, these are the two Ford transporters that were the envy of the Lotus Formula 1 crew.

The Ilford Trophy
For Saloon Cars
Results

Pos.	Driver	No.	Car	Laps	Time/Reason	Speed
1st	Roy Pierpoint	34	Ford Mustang	20	39 min 01.4 sec	81.50 mph
2nd	Mike Salmon	35	Ford Mustang	20	39 min 01.8 sec	79.36 mph
3rd	André Baldet	46	Lotus-Cortina	20	40 min 04.4 sec	79.24 mph
4th	John Rhodes	51	Austin Mini-Cooper S	20	40 min 08.0 sec	79.24 mph
5th	Gawaine Baillie	33	Ford Mustang	20	40 min 24.0 sec	
dsq	Chris Craft	64	Ford Anglia Super	20	Illegal track width & inlet manifold	
dsq	Mike Young	63	Ford Anglia Super	20	Illegal track width & inlet manifold	
6th	Harry Ratcliffe	53	Morris Mini-Cooper S	20	40 min 42.8 sec	
7th	Tony Lanfranchi	55	Morris Mini-Cooper S	20	40 min 47.0 sec	
8th	Boley Pittard	59	Austin Mini-Cooper S	20	40 min 48.0 sec	
9th	John Cannadine	60	Austin Mini-Cooper S	20	41 min 02.6 sec	
10th	John Nicholson	44	Lotus-Cortina	20	41 min 06.2 sec	
11th	Peter Pilsworth	66	Austin Mini-Cooper S	19		
12th	Warwick Banks	71	Austin Mini-Cooper S 970	19		
13th	David Wansborough	68	Austin Mini-Cooper S 970	19		
14th	Mike Campbell-Cole	76	Austin Mini-Cooper S 970	19		
15th	Rodney Bloor	69	Morris Mini-Cooper S 970	19		
16th	Tony Rutt	54	Morris Mini-Cooper S	19		
17th	Ted Savory	86	Morris Mini-Cooper S 970	19		
18th	Charles Stancomb	73	Austin Mini-Cooper S 970	19		
19th	Anita Taylor	75	Austin Mini-Cooper S 970	18		
dnf	Jack Sears	42	Lotus-Cortina	17	Puncture	
dnf	Ken Costello	52	Morris Mini-Cooper S	17		
dnf	Richard Cluley	58	Austin Mini-Cooper S	13		
dnf	Bill McGovern	61	Austin Mini-Cooper S	9	Accident	
dnf	Jim Clark	41	Lotus-Cortina	8	Lost wheel	
Pole Position		41	Jim Clark			
Fastest Lap (overall & class record)		41	Jim Clark		1 min 54.8 sec (99.79 mph)	
Class Winners			Pierpoint, Baldet, Rhodes, Banks			

Left
On the outside of the front row for both parts of the Race of Champions, eventual winner Mike Spence in 33R9 looks happy with his crew, Leo Wybrott, Willy Cowe and Jim Endruweit.

The wheel nuts quickly tightened, he set off in pursuit of the pack which had passed him. Unfortunately by the time he reached Dingle Dell the front left wheel had come adrift, parting company with the rest of the car and disappearing into the scenery, the hub fatally damaged by the strain of cornering on a loose wheel.

Seeing his chance for glory, Sears pulled out all the stops to pass Salmon's Mustang and steal second. With the leader Pierpoint now in his sights, by lap 18 he was looking for a way to take the lead when all hope for Team Lotus was dealt a sudden blow with another wheel problem. With just three laps left to go, a puncture became a blow-out 'Gentleman Jack' was forced to pull onto the grass.

This cruel reversal left Pierpoint and Salmon way out in front of André Baldet's Lotus-Cortina, with John Rhodes fourth in the works 1275 Mini-Cooper S and Sir Gawaine finished fifth ahead of the Superspeed Anglias of Chris Craft and Mike Young who finished sixth and seventh. (Following the race, however, both were excluded from the results due to incorrect track dimensions and something that was referred to as 'inlet manifolds irregularities.') Naturally several other contenders retired from the race itself, Paddock Bend claiming its usual hoard of victims with the Minis, of Montague, McGovern and Ross all coming to grief on the steep downhill section. The former two crashed on lap ten, both wrecking their cars quite badly.

Good And Bad For Team Lotus
With the pit crews free to repair the ravages of the first heat during the interval, it was fortunate that not much needed doing in the Lotus garage since, unlike the rest of the field, they were also competing for the Ilford Films Trophy. Gurney's Brabham needed to have a radiator bracket welded up, however, also an out-of-balance front wheel fixed and four new tyres. Although these days it would be unheard of for an F1 car to run two races on the same rubber, in the mid-60s it was by no means unusual.

That said, the new design of tyre from Goodyear had apparently worn at quite an alarming rate requiring a new set on both Brabhams, although Goodyear's own technicians insisted that this was by design rather than by accident, the theory being that that there was no sense in carrying more rubber (and therefore weight) than was necessary around the circuit. At the same time Bruce McLaren had a loose front upright bolt fixed on his Cooper T77, Bob Anderson changed brake pads and had the throttle linkage repaired, and yet more work was done on the ignition and fuel injection systems on the Ferrari of John Surtees. This was in addition to yet another eight new spark plugs, the third set of the day.

The grid for heat two was determined by the finishing order of the first heat with non finishers from the first heat rejoining the race at the rear of the grid. Behind them came the reserves, including Rodney Bloor and John Rhodes, and the aforementioned Paul Hawkins who was eager to get some track time in the ex-works Lotus Type 33.

The start was almost a re-run of the first heat except that this time it was Dan Gurney who found himself the meat in the Lotus sandwich. Once again Clark was first

Opposite page top
Early in the Ilford Trophy race Pierpoint leads Salmon and Sears at Bottom Bend.

Opposite page lower
After Chris Montague (No.57) had rolled his mini into the bank at Paddock Bend, Bill McGovern (No.61) followed suit, narrowly missing those assisting Montague.

Race of Champions
Results – Part II

Position	Driver	No.	Car	Laps	Time/Reason	Speed
1st	Mike Spence	6	Lotus 33	40	1 hr 06 min 38.2 sec	95.44 mph
2nd	Jo Bonnier	12	Brabham BT7	40	1 hr 06 min 45.0 sec	
3rd	Frank Gardner	18	Brabham BT11	40	1 hr 06 min 55.0 sec	
4th	Jackie Stewart	4	B.R.M. P261	40	1 hr 07 min 06.0 sec	
5th	Bruce McLaren	9	Cooper T77	40	1 hr 07 min 31.2 sec	
6th	Jo Siffert	11	Brabham BT11	40	1 hr 07 min 33.6 sec	
7th	Jochen Rindt	10	Cooper T77	39		
8th	John Taylor	22	Cooper T60	39		
9th	Ian Raby	21	Brabham BT3	38		
10th	Paul Hawkins	25	Lotus 33	36		
11th	John Rhodes	26	Cooper T71	30		
dnf	Jack Brabham	8	Brabham BT11	27	Oil leak	
dnf	Richard Attwood	16	Lotus 25	25	Water hose	
dnf	Rodney Bloor	23	Brabham BT14	16	Steering	
dnf	Dan Gurney	7	Brabham BT11	13	Ignition	
dnf	Graham Hill	3	B.R.M. P261	13	Overheating	
dnf	Jim Clark	5	Lotus 33	11	Accident	
dnf	Mike Hailwood	17	Lotus 25	7	Accident	
dnf	John Surtees	1	Ferrari 158	5	Fuel injection	
dnf	Bob Anderson	20	Brabham BT11	4	Throttle linkage	
Pole Position		5	Jim Clark		(1st in Part I)	
Fastest Lap (new record)		5	Jim Clark		1 min 35.4 sec (100.00 mph)	

Opposite Page.
Clockwise from top left. Bruce McLaren, Jo Siffert, Jo Bonnier & Richard Attwood. Bruce in the Cooper T77 and Bob Anderson in the DW Racing Brabham-Climax BT11 wait in the paddock. Jo Bonnier prepares to go out for practice in Rob Walker's older Brabham BT7. Jim Endruweit (damper in hand) and Bob Dance on the long walk from the Brands paddock to the pit lane.

"Jim Clark, driving his Lotus-Climax won the final major International of the Australian season at Lakeside, Brisbane, on March 7th. Following him home were Frank Gardner and Spencer Martin."

into Paddock, but the tall American was soon pressing the Lotus hard, with Spence, Hill, Stewart, Brabham, Bonnier, Surtees, Attwood, McLaren and Hailwood following close behind. In what was clearly going to be a real needle match with his good friend Clark, Gurney poured the pressure on mercilessly, keeping the nose of the Brabham tight up behind the gearbox of the Lotus, the two fastest men on the circuit revelling in their close, personal battle.

Of course Clark could have let Gurney pass, sat comfortably within a few seconds of the Brabham's exhaust for the rest of the heat and still won the overall race easily. But Jimmy was never one for driving like that, and remained determined to beat the only driver he saw as his real competition, fairly and squarely.

Behind the two gladiators, however, things were more complicated. Splitting its final drive, Bob Anderson's Brabham deposited a quantity of oil round the circuit causing Rindt to spin twice, once at Hawthorns and again at Bottom Bend. John Taylor and Richard Attwood had similar scares before recovering and carrying on. By lap four the lone Ferrari was sounding decidedly rough too and a lap later Surtees pulled into the pits, once again the mechanics were charged with changing the plugs until evidence of a more serious problem emerged to take the World Champion out of contention for good.

For his part Jack Brabham was having a better day than his team mate, moving up through the field to dispose of Hill and Stewart on successive laps. By lap 10 he had passed Mike Spence to sit in third place, settling in to keep a watching brief on the leaders up ahead and

waiting for the inevitable drama to unfold. Sure enough, within the next few laps, the pattern of the race changed decisively.

On lap 11 Clark was still being pressed hard by Gurney and, as yet again Dan pushed the nose of the Brabham inside Jimmy's Lotus at South Bend, it seemed to be just a matter of time before he would succeed in getting past. The following lap he tried again, this time attempting to find a way through on the outside at Paddock, Jimmy holding on by keeping tight at Druids hairpin before finding himself on the outside at Bottom Bend.

By now under huge pressure, Clark made a rare mistake, understeering wide on to the grass and fighting to keep the car pointing in the right direction as his two off-side wheels hit some ruts. The Lotus bounded across the infield before thudding into the earth bank that protected the back of the pits and, rebounding into the air, it crashed to the ground in several pieces. Winded and shaken, Jimmy stepped out with nothing more than a slightly tweaked knee. R10 fared less well however, and on returning to Cheshunt the complete chassis was consigned to the parts bin.

Back on the circuit, the Brabham duo was now lying in first and second place but once again the cars flattered only to deceive. Jack's had been trailing a plume of smoke for several laps, and looked as if it would soon have to retire. In the event, however, it was Gurney who came a cropper, dropping off the chart on lap 14 and crawling into the pits. His mechanics tried a change of plugs, but to no avail and the car was wheeled away with a fatally damaged engine.

Above
Jimmy speeds through the paddock on his way to take his place on Pole Position for the 'Race of Champions'

Race of Champions
Aggregate Results

Position	Driver	No.	Car	Laps	Time/Reason	Speed
1st	Mike Spence	6	Lotus 33	80	2 hr 11 min 42.0 sec	97.20 mph
2nd	Jackie Stewart	4	B.R.M. P261	80	2 hr 12 min 41.6 sec	
3rd	Jo Bonnier	12	Brabham BT7	79		
4th	Frank Gardner	18	Brabham BT11	79		
5th	Bruce McLaren	9	Cooper T77	79		
6th	Jo Siffert	11	Brabham BT11	79		
7th	Jochen Rindt	10	Cooper T77	78		
8th	John Taylor	22	Cooper T60	77		
9th	Ian Raby	21	Brabham BT3	75		
dnf	Jack Brabham	8	Brabham BT11	67		
dnf	Richard Attwood	16	Lotus 25	64		
dnf	Dan Gurney	7	Brabham BT11	53		
dnf	Graham Hill	3	B.R.M. P261	53		
dnf	Jim Clark	5	Lotus 33	51		
dnf	John Surtees	1	Ferrari 158	45		
dnf	Paul Hawkins	25	Lotus 333	36		
dnf	John Rhodes	26	Cooper T71	30		
Fastest Lap (overall – part II)		5	Jim Clark		1 min 35.4 sec (100.00 mph)	

Admitted y his team mate was now running well clear of Mike Spence, but with a disadvantage of more than 20 seconds from the first heat Jack knew he would have to pull out a huge lead if he was to win the race overall. For a few brief laps it looked like he might be able to pull it off too, but the plume of smoke coming from the back of his car spoke volumes and on lap 28 the Brabham finally had to duck into the pits, a hose clip on the oil cooler having worked loose and a lack of oil preventing the car from continuing.

With Graham Hill retiring with overheating problems, the now sadly depleted field continued to the flag with Spence holding on comfortably for his first major Formula 1 win. He certainly wasn't the fastest present, but he made a worthy number two to Jim Clark. Jo Bonnier finished second, ahead of Frank Gardner who had overhauled Jackie Stewart, while Bruce McLaren finished fifth ahead of Jo Siffert, Jochen Rindt, Ian Raby's Brabham and John Rhodes.

When the timekeepers had done their sums the overall order listed Spence, Stewart, Bonnier, Gardner, McLaren and Siffert in the top six places. The race had provided some excellent racing for the crowds in the early stages, and looking forward to the coming season Lotus quite clearly had the car to beat. Brabham too was looking good, Ferrari as ever something of an unknown quantity, BRM left to wonder at the ease with which their own cars were passed by the others, and Cooper – sadly with two quality drivers at its disposal – still no more competitive than it had been the previous season when their only half-decent results had been a brace of second place finishes by Bruce McLaren at Spa and Monza.

Above
True British style. Team owner Rob Walker was rarely seen without his flask of tea.

Right
1965 saw the emergence of a 'tyre war' between Goodyear, Dunlop and Firestone. Goodyear had this rather impressive set-up at every major UK race.

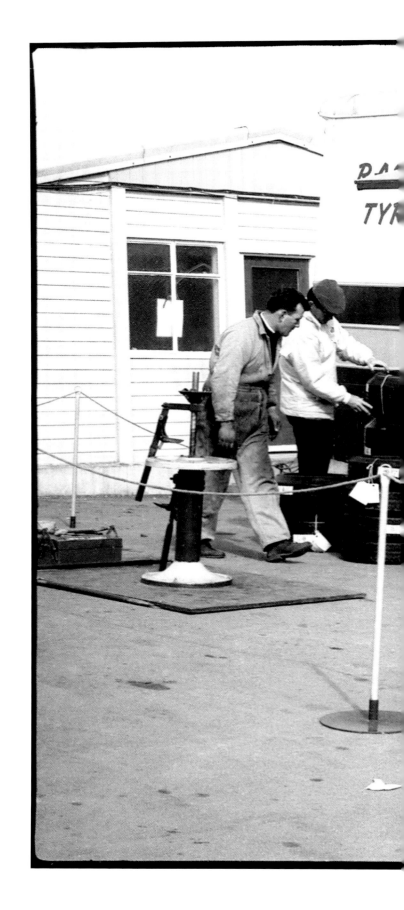

Chapter Two
Silverstone
20th March

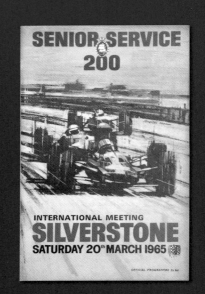

"MEETING ABANDONED AFTER JUST TWO RACES"

The BARC's Senior Service 200 International Race Meeting at Silverstone, the Formula 2 successor to the Aintree 200's of recent years, was drowned under a relentless downpour of rain and abandoned on the grounds of safety....

Above right
Practice for the Senior
Service 200 was a
damp affair and neith
Colin nor Jimmy look
too happy about the
situation. On race da
would only get worse

Timetable

Event: Senior Service '200' Meeting
Date: Saturday 20th March 1965
Location: Silverstone
Circuit Length: 2.927 miles

Time	Race	Laps	Distance
11:00 am	British Formula 3 Championship Race	10	29.0 miles
11:50 am	25-Lap Sports Car Race	18	52.2 miles
1:20 pm	British Saloon Car Championship Race	20	Cancelled
2:40 pm	Senior Service '200' for Formula 2 Cars	43	Cancelled
4:25 pm	15-Lap Grand Touring Car Race	15	Cancelled

Silverstone Grand Prix Circuit – Existing Lap Records

Formula 1	Jack Brabham	Brabham BT7	1m 33.6 sec.	112.56 mph.
Formula 2	Cliff Allison	Lotus 12	1m 43.4 sec.	101.91 mph.
Formula 3	John Fenning	Lotus 22	1m 44.2 sec.	101.12 mph.
Sportscars over 2000cc	Roy Salvadori	Cooper-Monaco	1m 37.6 sec.	107.96 mph.
Sportscars under 2000cc	Roger Nathan	Brabham BT8	1m 40.0 sec.	105.37 mph.
Saloon Cars over 2000cc	Jack Sears	Ford Galaxie	1m 49.6 sec.	96.14 mph.
Saloon Cars 1301cc to 2000cc	Jim Clark	Lotus-Cortina	1m 55.2 sec.	91.47 mph.

Senior Service '200'
For Formula 2 Cars
Entry List

No.	Entrant	Car	Engine	Driver
1	Brabham Racing Developments	Brabham BT16	Honda	Jack Brabham
2	Brabham Racing Developments	Brabham BT16	Cosworth SCA	Denis Hulme
3	Aurora Gear (Racing) Rotherham	Brabham BT16	Cosworth SCA	Trevor Taylor
4	Cosworth Engineering	Brabham BT10	Cosworth SCA	Mike Costin
5	Roy Winkelmann Racing	Brabham BT16	Cosworth SCA	Alan Rees
6	Roy Winkelmann Racing	Brabham BT16	Cosworth SCA	Jochen Rindt
7	Ford France	Brabham BT10	Cosworth SCA	Jo Schlesser
8	Ford France	Brabham BT6	Cosworth SCA	Guy Ligier
9	David Prophet Racing	Brabham BT10	Cosworth SCA	David Prophet
10	David Prophet Racing	Brabham BT10	Cosworth SCA	Bill Bradley
11	Normand	Brabham BT10	Cosworth SCA	Mike Beckwith
12	John Coombs	Brabham BT16	B.R.M./Cosworth SCA	Graham Hill
14*	The Cooper Car Company	Cooper T75	B.M.C. Cooper	Bruce McLaren (dna)
15*	Tyrrell Racing Organisation	Cooper T75	B.M.C. Cooper	Frank Gardner (dna)
16	Tyrrell Racing Organisation	Cooper T75	B.R.M.	Jackie Stewart
17	Bob Gerard Racing	Cooper T73	Ford TC	John Taylor
18	Frank Lythgoe Racing	Cooper T71	B.R.M./Cosworth SCA	Adam Wyllie
19	Ron Harris Team Lotus	Lotus 35	B.R.M./Cosworth SCA	Jim Clark
20	Ron Harris Team Lotus	Lotus 32	B.R.M./Cosworth SCA	Mike Spence
21	Ron Harris Team Lotus	Lotus 32	Cosworth SCA	Brian Hart
22	J.Maglia	Lotus 32	Cosworth SCA	Jacques Maglia
23*	Reg Parnell (Racing)	Lotus 35	B.R.M.	Peter Revson (dna)
24	Merlyn Racing	Merlyn Mk.9	Cosworth SCA	Chris Irwin
25*	Merlyn Racing	Merlyn Mk.9	Cosworth SCA	Roger Mac (dna)
26	Ian Raby (Racing) Ltd.	Merlyn Mk.9	Cosworth SCA	Chris Amon
27	John Willment Automobiles	Lola T55	Cosworth SCA	Tony Hegbourne
28	Midland Racing Partnership	Lola T60	Cosworth SCA	Richard Attwood
29	Midland Racing Partnership	Lola T55	Cosworth SCA	David Hobbs
30*	Team Alexis	Alexis Mk.6	Cosworth SCA	Paul Hawkins (dna)

New Season Promise

The BARC Senior Service 200 Race Meeting at Silverstone in March 1965 sadly fell prey to a relentless downpour of rain, starting at 2.30pm and forcing the stewards to abandon all racing on safety grounds.
In fact only one race in a busy programme ran for the scheduled distance, a 10 lap event for Formula 3 cars. The second race of five, for sports cars, started but was then terminated just 18 laps into an expected 25.

By this time bore the circuit bore more resemblance to a river than a race track. The heavy rain that had fallen during Friday's practice sessions had made conditions unpleasant. although nothing like those which would prevail on race day.

A glance at the entry list for what would have been the first major Formula 2 race of the season showed that all the major works F2 teams were in attendance together with an impressive list of past, present and future Formula 1 drivers and indeed World Champions. The big story in the paddock was the appearance of a works Honda engine fitted to Jack Brabham's sleek new BT16, a bespoke twin-cam, four-valve, fuel-injected power unit built in Tokyo to the existing 1000cc Formula 2 regulations. Thought by many to be a derivative of the engine used in the then-current S800 sportscar, it was actually a closer relation to Honda's Formula 1 engine and as such a forerunner of the twin-cam unit which was later to appear in a number of 1970s road cars.

Already competing in F1, and with three Grand Prix races under its belt in 1964, Honda was serious about its entry into Formula 2 and had sent over a team of three

mechanics to work alongside the Brabham crew to ensure that the first three power units delivered were properly installed and run according to strict Honda HQ guide lines. By the end of the season their efforts would start to pay off.

The rival works Lotus cars were represented by the Ron Harris Team Lotus squad, Jim Clark entering the fray with a new Type 35 while Mike Spence and Brian Hart were equipped with the elegant 1964 Type 32, a car which Clark had used in a highly modified 'Type 32B' form to win the Tasman Series earlier in the year.

The Cooper team, comprising Bruce McLaren, Frank Gardner and Jackie Stewart, was running a pair of BMC engines whilst trying out a new BRM unit in the back of Stewart's T75. The same engine was also listed on the provisional entry sheets as being used to power the Ron Harris Team Lotus cars and the Reg Parnell Lotus 35. (The latter was to be driven by the young American driver Peter Revson, although he was eventually a non-starter at this first meeting, as indeed were McLaren and Gardner.)

The only other car to appear with BRM power, and then only very briefly, was the John Coombs Brabham BT16 driven by Graham Hill. The team had the BRM engine in its transporter, but actually opted to use a Cosworth engine in practice. The rest of the field were also relying on the trusty SCA version of Cosworth-tuned and Cosworth-developed Ford engines

Lola meanwhile had hoped to debut three of its new T60 monocoque cars over the weekend, but the

Above
The Brabham team had a trio of Honda mechanics on hand to make sure the first official outing for the new Honda Formula Two engine went according to plan

Above
One for the record books. Wet Friday practice was the first competitive run for a works Brabham-Honda. With Jack at the wheel of the BT16 it wasn't the easiest of debut events for the team.

Left
Graham Hill in the John Coombs Brabham BT16 tried both BRM and Cosworth power during practice, opting for the tried & tested Cosworth unit for the race.

Senior Service '200'
Grid

				Pole Position	
Richard Attwood Lola-Cosworth 1 min 54.4 sec		Jim Clark Lotus-Cosworth 1 min 54.4 sec		Mike Costin Brabham-Cosworth 1 min 53.4 sec	
	Chris Irwin Merlyn-Cosworth 1 min 57.0 sec		Brian Hart Lotus-Cosworth 1 min 56.2 sec		
Jacques Maglia Lotus-Cosworth 1 min 58.4 sec		Jackie Stewart Cooper-B.R.M. 1 min 58.0 sec		Mike Beckwith Brabham-Cosworth 1 min 57.2 sec	
	Mike Spence Lotus-Cosworth 1 min 58.6 sec		Alan Rees Brabham-Cosworth 1 min 58.6 sec		
Jochen Rindt Brabham-Cosworth 1 min 59.2 sec		David Prophet Brabham-Cosworth 1 min 59.0 sec		Chris Amon Merlyn-Cosworth 1 min 58.8 sec	
	Jack Brabham Brabham-Honda 2 min 02.2 sec		John Taylor Cooper-Ford 1 min 59.8 sec		
David Hobbs Lola-Cosworth 2 min 03.6 sec		Jo Schlesser Brabham-Cosworth 2 min 03.2 sec		Denis Hulme Brabham-Cosworth 2 min 02.4 sec	
	Bill Bradley Brabham-Cosworth 2 min 05.8 sec		Adam Wyllie Cooper-Cosworth 2 min 04.2 sec		
Guy Ligier Brabham-Cosworth Reserve		Trevor Taylor Brabham-Cosworth Reserve		Graham Hill Brabham-Cosworth 2 min 07.0 sec	

"Jim Clark had a convincing victory in the Warwick Farm '100' at Sydney on February 14, his Lotus-Climax finished more than a minute ahead of Jack Brabham (Repco Brabham-Climax). Third, fourth and fifth went to Repco Brabham-Climax cars in the hands of Frank Matich, Bob Stilwell and Graham Hill."

inevitable delays on a new car build and development meant that only Richard Attwood's MRP car was ready in time and the other two drivers were forced back on the spaceframe T55.

The first practice session on Friday had seen all the Formula 2 cars out and those quickest in this session booking good placings on the grid. With the even heavier rain which came later in the day, times were much slower in the second session, so that Jim Clark saw his best (1m 54.4sec., 92.11mph) drop off to 1m 58.4sec.. Clearly there was going to be no chance of anyone who had missed out in the first session, managing to make up for it in the wetter second one.

The fastest half-dozen cars were those of Mike Costin (a fuel injected Brabham-Cosworth) on 1m 53.4sec., Jim Clark in the works Lotus exactly one second behind him, Attwood going well in the new Lola-Cosworth T60 (1m 56.2sec.), Brian Hart in a Lotus 32 (1m 56.2sec.), the Lola of David Hobbs (1m 56.2sec.) and Graham Hill's John Coombs Cooper which was briefly fitted with the new BRM power unit in the second session but quickly returned to 1964-spec Cosworth power.

The new style Goodyear tyres fitted to Jack Brabham's Honda-powered car were still, in his own words, "*unsorted*" and just didn't like the wet. Combined with the fuel injection problems he was suffering, his fastest time came in the much slower second session and was a miserable 2m 2.2sec.. That put him on only the sixth row of the grid although the Honda engine with its 140bhp and 10,000rpm rev limit clearly delighted everyone with its splendid noise!

Let The Fun Begin

By the start of the first (F3) race at 11:50 on Saturday the rain was falling heavily with spectators expecting a hairy race. They got one too, albeit not nearly as bad as the one which would follow it.

The big field of 30 cars got away cleanly enough, with Peter Gethin in the Charles Lucas-run Lotus 22 making a particularly neat job of his start to take the lead. By the end of the first lap he was a good distance in front of John Cardwell's Goodwin Racing Brabham BT15, Charles Crichton-Stuart's Stirling Moss Auto Racing Brabham BT10, and Warwick Banks in the Ken Tyrrell Cooper-BMC. Moments later, entering the second lap, Cardwell produced the first spin of the day, gyrating immediately after the start/finish line, right in front of the pits and brushing the pit wall. He managed to get away again and continued on his way, quickly working his way through the field to finish eighth.

His spin had put Crichton-Stuart into second place, but only for one lap, for he too spun in the ever worsening conditions and dropped back six places. With second place now going to Warwick Banks, the Cooper-BMC began to close up on Gethin who surrendered some of his advantage on the fourth lap after performing a neat 360 at Club. Repeating the manoeuvre just two laps later (and on the very same corner) he was soon passed by Banks who disappeared into the distance and eventually took the flag with a huge margin of more than 35 seconds.

Gethin meanwhile was chased but not caught by Clive Baker's Cooper-BMC and Crichton-Stuart, the three

Right
Jim Clark, complete with wet weather gear (Pac-a-Mac & baler twine) doesn't look too keen to go out for the first practice session.

"Jim Clark's 1964 Lotus-Cortina has just been prepared by Chris Williams (Sales) Ltd., at their Guildford workshops, for a season of Swedish ice racing by sports car champion Anders Josephson."

finishing the race very close together. Fifth place went to the German driver Kurt Ahrens in a Brabham-Ford BT10 with Gethin's team-mate Charles Lucas in sixth.

For 1965 the latter's team had chosen to compete using both Lotus and Brabham chassis, owner-driver Lucas and Jonathan Williams opting for the newer Brabham BT10 leaving the older Lotus 22 for Peter Gethin to use. Both Williams and Gethin would go on to drive in Formula 1, with Williams competing in just one race and Gethin famously winning the 1971 Italian Grand Prix just 0.01 of a second ahead of Ronnie Peterson

Gethin's two near-identical spins were perhaps the most significant of the day but by no means the only ones with the Brabham's of Williams, David Cole, the Australian Jim Sullivan and Tony Dean suffering likewise together with Dawson's Lotus and Terry Ogilvie-Hardy in an Alexis) in what one might call a rainstorm of quite Biblical proportions.

False Start Not New Start For The Sportscars
As such it was hardly a good day to judge the relative merits of the various V8-powered cars which were soon to sweep all before them in what was to become a new era of sports car racing. In fact, 13 of the new 'hairies' (as they were described at the time) were entered for the race, nine of which turned up, even though by the end of the day their drivers probably wished they had not bothered.

For the record, the four absentees were David Cunningham's Lola T70, John Coundley's Oldsmobile-powered McLaren-Elva M1A, Simon de Lautour's Lotus

30 and Julian Sutton's Attila-Chevrolet, the latter being ready for racing except for one hugely important part – the flywheel.

As expected the fastest in practice on the damp track was Jimmy Clark in J.C.Bamford's Ford V8-motivated Lotus 30. The car had originally been entered with the intention that Peter Sadler would drive it but in the event it fell to Clark to put it through its paces and, with a best of 1m 44.2sec., he emerged as the only competitor to exceed an average of 100mph during practice for any of the scheduled races.

Alongside Clark on the grid was John Surtees in the Lola T70 using a Traco-tuned Chevrolet V8 which posted a time 1m 45.8s. Bruce McLaren in his own red M1A with an Oldsmobile V8 and Firestone tyres recorded 1m 46.0sec. – although earlier in the week he had beaten the existing lap record by 0.2mph after posting a time of 1m 32.2sec. – whilst Roy Salvadori in a Cobra-Ford-engined Cooper completed the front row of the grid with a time of 1 min 49.6 sec.. That left the front row with four makes of car and three makes of engine, an encouraging sign of healthy variety.

The second row included two more of the big bangers, the Harold Young Lola T70-Ford of David Hobbs and the recently rebuilt Lotus 30 of driven by David Prophet. Alongside them was fastest of the smaller-engined 2-litre class, driver Tommy Hitchcock in his Coventry Climax-powered Brabham BT8 having equaled Prophet's sixth fastest practice time of 1m 53.2sec.. Rows three and four were filled by the new and very nicely presented Lotus Brabham-BMW of Chris Williams, Vic

10-Lap Formula 3 Race
Results

Pos.	Driver	No.	Car	Laps	Time/Reason	Speed
1st	Warwick Banks	41	Cooper T76	10	2 min 47.0 sec	80.82 mph
2nd	Peter Gethin	59	Lotus 22	10	22 min 22.0 sec	
3rd	Clive Baker	45	Cooper T76	10	22 min 23.0 sec	
4th	Charles Crichton-Stuart	64	Brabham BT10	10	22 min 25.8 sec	
5th	Kurt Ahrens	48	Brabham BT10	10	22 min 36.8 sec	
6th	Charles Lucas	58	Brabham BT10	10	22 min 56.6 sec	
7th	John Miles	66	Brabham BT6	10	23 min 25.4 sec	
8th	John Cardwell	53	Brabham BT15	10	23 min 46.8 sec	
9th	Roy Pike	49	Brabham BT16	10	24 min 11.6 sec	
10th	Derek Bell	83	Lotus 31	9		
11th	David Rees	54	Brabham BT9	9		
12th	Len Selby	47	Cooper T76	9		
13th	Natalie Goodwin	55	Brabham BT15	9		
14th	Steve Matchett	43	Cooper T76	9		
15th	Jean Denton	44	Cooper T72	8		
16th	Trevor Shatwell	46	Cooper T67	8		
Ret	Graham White	51	Brabham BT6	7		
Ret	Terry Ogilvie-Hardy	78	Alexis Mk.9	7	Crash	
Ret	Tony Dean	52	Brabham BT6	4	Engine	
Ret	Teddy Dawson	80	Lotus 31	4	Crash	
Ret	Jim Sullivan	62	Brabham BT15	3	Crash	
Ret	Jonathan Williams	56	Brabham BT10	2	Crash	
Ret	Allan Taylor	79	Alexis Mk.5	1	Steering	
Ret	Melvyn Long	71	Lotus 27	0	Crash	
Pole Position		64	Charles Crichton-Stuart		1 min 57.0 sec	
Fastest Lap		41	Warwick Banks		2 min 06.2 sec (83.50 mph)	

Wilson's Lotus 30, Graham Hill's Coombs McLaren-Elva M1A, Denis Hulme's Brabham-Coventry Climax (Sid Taylor's ex-Team Elite 2-litre) Brian Smith's Lotus 23 – by far the best of the 1150cc class – Tony Dean's ex-Julian Sutton Lotus 23B and J.W. Dean's Lotus 30 which at 2m 1.8sec. was the slowest of the American muscle-powered cars. All told the field totalled 33 cars, an excellent turnout for an event so early in the season.

If you wanted a full, graphic account of the race it was probably more pertinent that the non-spinners were the drivers that deserved to be recorded in a list of race incidents. Although it has to be said there were just a small number in this category.

Despite the quite dreadful conditions, Clark made his customary faultless start and, with Surtees very close behind, his Lotus 30 running on the softer Dunlop R7's compared to the Lola's R6s, was soon pulling an advantage of several seconds a lap.

First time through Beckett's, the running order was Clark, Surtees and McLaren, quickly followed by Hulme who had made an excellent take off from the third rank of the grid. By the end of lap one Hulme had overtaken McLaren, as had journalist Brian Smith who was going incredibly well in his tiny 1100cc Lotus. Roy Salvadori lay sixth, and then came Harry Stiller (Lotus 23), David Prophet (Lotus 30), the Lotus Brabham-BMW of Chris Williams, and Trevor Taylor in the cute little front-engined Aurora-BMC. The leading trio held station until their third trip through Becketts at which point Hulme spun on to the grass losing a lap before he could get his rain-soaked engine restarted.

Having overhauled Smith, McLaren was once more in third place until, incredibly, lap five saw Stiller's Lotus pass both of them. By the end of the lap, with the weather worsening, Roy Salvadori, Bruce McLaren and Graham Hill were all out. The latter had never really been in the running, both of the McLarens seemed to be shipping water into their engine bays and Salvadori felt quite reasonably that there was no point in continuing. Williams had similarly retired on his third lap, while Smith had wasted a possible class win by making a series of off-track excursions.

In the meantime, David Hobbs and Harry O'Brien were busy carving their way through the diminishing field. The former's smooth driving and deft car control compensating for his Lola's very poor third-gear getaway was making up three or four seconds a lap on the leaders, despite only having the one gear and a faulty rev-counter. O'Brien had also made a poor start, the only British car in the over 2,000cc class being way back in the grid thanks to the the poor practice times of this ex-BRP, ex-Pitt, Lotus Type 19.

The race, if it belonged to anyone, belonged to the larger engines and on lap five 5.3-litres of Chevrolet power enabled Surtees to take the lead from Clark's smaller-engined Lotus when he gyrated at Chapel Curve. Clark lost very little time over the manoeuvre, however, and was soon back on course and chasing the reigning World Champion very hard indeed.

Hobbs, who had somehow moved up to third place, surrendered it on the sixth lap when, coming out of Maggotts Curve, he spun his injured Lola putting it into

Above left
With plenty of time to kill and sporting some rather natty headwear, John Surtees wanders through the paddock

Above right
Friday practice was a dismal affair. Mike Spence doesn't look too happy. As you can see, there weren't many spectators present.

Above
John Surtees practices the Lola T70 in merely 'damp' conditions. Note the centralised and rather minimal rollover protection offered to the driver.

the ditch tail-first whilst clouting Vic Wilson's Lotus 30 which had arrived there a little earlier in the race.

He was followed shortly afterwards by another Lola, Bell's 1100cc car, meaning that Wilson's car was now in a very sorry state. As Hobbs struggled to extricate his Lola, still with only third gear available and burning out the clutch in the process, Surtees suddenly appeared out of the gloom heading right for him. Fortunately he managed to avoid hitting any of them, but as a result of this near-miss Hobbs and his helpers made no further salvage attempts.

Hobbs later recalled, "*I remember passing Graham Hill into Stowe and was very pleased to be passing a World Champion in the rain. Unfortunately I did spin it at Maggotts though, it just aquaplaned off the road.*"

Surtees soon repeated his action, this time at Club Corner, so that by the eleventh lap Clark held an even more decisive lead than he had before. By now it was raining even more than ever, but briefly the top ten held steady with Clark's Lotus positioned ahead of John Surtees (Lola 70), Harry O'Brien (Lotus 19), Trevor Taylor (Aurora-BMC), Jack Paterson (Lola-Climax), Harry Stiller (Lotus 23), Brian Smith (Lotus 23), Geoff Oliver (Lotus 23), Tommy Hitchcock (Brabham-Climax) and David Prophet in his Lotus 30. Denny Hulme had retired on his seventh lap, after yet another revolution, whilst similarly interesting experiences led to the retirement of Frank Gardner (Elva-BMW), Tony Dean (Lotus 23B), Keith St.John (Elva-BMW), Joe Payne (Elva-Climax), John Hine (Lotus 23) and Jeremy Delmar-Morgan in a Lotus 23. Dean had actually pulled out on the warm-up lap, as

had the Morley's Lotus 23, the 'other Dean' – J.W. – (John) stopping after making no headway whatever in his big Lotus 30 and, like a number of others, realising there was simply no point in going on.

That said, and in stark contrast to all the chaos, Jim Clark's driving was quite exemplary even though, amidst all the drama, much of his skill went unnoticed. Time and again the focus shifted to those drivers who were in trouble, like sixth-placed Smith who, losing his Lotus 23 yet again, somehow avoided the stationary pile at Maggots before stalling in the middle of the track

On that occasion nobody hit him, but Northern tiger Harry O'Brien was less fortunate. Comfortably holding third position on lap 15, he lost it big time and ploughed his Lotus 19 into the exit bank at Stowe Corner cutting his face and badly damaging the car. Shortly afterwards, as John Surtees enteretained yet another spin, officials began to confer and observing how narrowly the Lola had missed O'Brien's wreck they made the decision to stop the race then and there. After just over 40 minutes of hectic racing, the chequered flag was held out to the dozen or so stalwarts who were still bravely circulating in the murky conditions.

Jim Clark had somehow completed 18 of the scheduled 25 laps at an average speed of just over 75mph – and deserved great credit for having done so – whilst second place went to Surtees after a plucky fight which many a man would have far sooner abandoned. (As it happened he had actually passed behind the chequered flag, returning to the pits having minutes earlier made the same decision as the organisers and decided to stop.)

Above left
Early in the race Surtees, with a new nose section after a practice mishap, leads Delmar-Morgan's Lotus.

Above right
Roy Salvadori in the brutish Cooper-Cobra heads Harry Stiller's immaculate Lotus 23 in practice.

25-Lap Sports Car Race
Results

(Race stopped after 18 laps due to poor weather)

Pos.	Driver	No.	Car	Laps	Time/Reason	Speed
1st	Jim Clark	7	Lotus-Ford 30	18	42 min 06.4 sec	75.08 mph
2nd	John Surtees	1	Lola-Chevrolet T70	17		
3rd	Jack Paterson	32	Lola-Climax	17		
4th	Trevor Taylor	31	Aurora-BMC	16		
5th	Harry Stiller	38	Lotus-Ford 23	16		
6th	Geoffrey Oliver	44	Lotus-Ford 23	16		
7th	Tommy Hitchcock	27	Brabham-Climax BT8	15		
8th	Brian Smith	42	Lotus-Ford 23	15		
9th	David Prophet	10	Lotus-Ford 30	15		
10th	Jim Charnock	20	Lotus-Ford 23B	14		
dnf	Harry O'Brien	15	Lotus-Climax 19	14	Accident	
dnf	Frank Gardner	23	Elva-BMW		Withdrew	
dnf	Kieth St.John	24	Elva-BMW		Withdrew	
dnf	Joe Payne	35	Elva-Climax		Withdrew	
dnf	Jeremy Delmar-Morgan	45	Lotus-Ford 23		Withdrew	
dnf	Bob McArthur	43	Lotus-Ford 23		Withdrew	
dnf	Denis Hulme	26	Brabham-Climax BT8	6	Withdrew	
dnf	R.H. Bell	33	Lola-Climax	6	Accident	
dnf	David Hobbs	2	Lola-Ford T70	5	Accident	
dnf	Roy Salvadori	12	Cooper-Cobra	5	Withdrew	
dnf	Bruce McLaren	5	McLaren M1A	5	Withdrew	
dnf	Graham Hill	4	McLaren-Elva M1A	5	Withdrew	
dnf	Victor Wilson	9	Lotus-Ford 30	4	Accident	
dnf	Chris Williams	25	Lotus-Brabham BMW	3	Withdrew	
dnf	Tony Dean	28	Lotus-Ford 23B	0	Withdrew	
dnf	Jim Morley	39	Lotus-Ford 23	0	Withdrew	

Pole Position		7	Jim Clark		1 min 44.2 sec
Fastest Lap		7 & 1	Jim Clark & John Surtees		2 min 01.0 sec (87.08 mph)
Class Winners			Clark, Taylor		

"On stand 19 at the 1965 Racing Car Show, Lotus had two cars on display, the 1965 version of the Lotus-Cortina (Appendix J Group 2) saloon racing car, and the 1600cc racing version of the Lotus Elan (Group 3). On stand 20 there were three more Lotus competition cars, the Lotus 30, the Seven, and the brand new Lotus Type 35 F2 car."

Above
With the track drying Mike Salmon practices the dark blue Dawnay Racing/F. English Ltd. Ford Mustang.

Right
With nothing but Silverstone's legendary 'Brieze Blocks' between himself and the cars Peter bravely captured the duelling Minis of Ken Costello, Gerry Marshall and Warwick Banks at Copse corner in practice for the saloon car race. "Before the blocks were there, they had 5-gallon drums filled with sand marking the inside of the corners. The drums caused quite a lot of damage to the cars though. Prior to that they just had straw bales which weren't much good" Peter remembers.

Senior Service '200'
Results

Position	Driver	No.	Car	Laps	Time/Reason	Speed
Race cancelled due to waterlogged track						
Pole Position		4	Mike Costin		1 min 53.4 sec	

20-Lap Saloon Car Race
Results

Position	Driver	No.	Car	Laps	Time/Reason	Speed
Race cancelled due to waterlogged track						
Pole Position						

"Four Group 2 works Lotus-Cortinas have been entered for the Alpine Rally. Driver pairings are Henry Taylor/Brian Melia, David Seigle-Morris/Tony Nash, Vic Elford/David Stone and Bo Ljungfeldt/Nils Bjork."

Third overall was Jack Paterson, surely the driver of the day, who crossed the line within 12 seconds of the frustrated Surtees despite driving an elderly front-engined 1100cc Lola Coventry-Climax. Tenth after two laps, eighth after five and fifth after 10 laps, his was quite a drive. With O'Brien's retirement, Paterson moved up to fourth and shortly afterwards he overtook and drew away from Trevor Taylor, his intelligent and steady driving throughout the race deserving (and getting) the highest praise. Trevor Taylor too, applied himself to his task and brought the neat little transverse engined 1150cc Aurora home a very satisfactory fourth. That said, one of the happiest drivers, must have been John Scott-Davies whose ex-Chris Williams Lotus 23B had broken a doughnut on the start line and spared him the trauma of even taking part in the race.

The Aftermath

Shortly after two o'clock, with absolutely no improvement in the weather and no likelihood of the same, BARC secretary Graham Macbeth finally took the decision that "*not just one race but the whole meeting must be stopped.*"

That meant the 20 lap British Saloon Car Championship race, the Senior Service '200' International and the 15 lap race for Grand Touring Cars were deleted from the record books, making the weekend as a whole, in the words of Bob Dance, "*a bit of a waste of time.*"

Bob went on to explain the reason for the Cortina's problems at the Race of Champions. "*After the troubles at Brands we figured out that what we thought were front hub problems were actually caused by the new*

5½J wheels that Ford had supplied us with at the start of the season. Of course, at first we blamed the mechanic on Jimmy's car, Kiwi Allan McCall, for not tightening up the wheel nuts properly but we finally discovered the real cause. There was so much paint on the rear face of the factory supplied wheels where they faced up to the hub, as well as in the recesses where the wheel nuts tightened to the wheel, that no matter how hard you thought the nuts had been tightened they just kept working loose."

"*For Silverstone we replaced the front hubs on all three cars and of course we made sure there was no excess paint on the wheels. The front hubs were a standard Ford part supplied to us in limitless quantities so it wasn't a problem to swap them as much as we liked. In fact, over the course of the year's racing exploits Ford discovered that there was actually a problem with the material they were making the hubs from and changed their manufacturing process. I think the strain of Jimmy cornering on two wheels with the wider rims probably put more strain on the car than a lifetime of road use but for once we really did help with development of the roadcars.*"

For a while there was a faint hope of re-scheduling the Senior Service '200' meeting for later in the season, but despite trying their best the organisers were unable to find a date which didn't clash with any other major meetings. As for the organisers feeling that they had suffered bad luck in having so much rain on Saturday, that was eventually put into perspective when the following morning all the wet stuff turned to snow and the circuit was completely covered!

Above
Even in wet conditions Jimmy could place the car with inch perfect precision. In his usual efforts at making sure Peter could "get a good shot" he is just about to brush the wall.

Chapter Three
Oulton Park
3rd April

"TOUGH FORMULA 2 WIN FOR HULME"

The first Formula 2 race of the season was won by
Denis Hulme, driving a works Brabham-Cosworth.
He won the 40-lap Oulton Park race at an average speed
of 96.51mph, after a tough drive, holding off successive
challenges from both Jackie Stewart and Graham Hill....

Above right
Set in beautiful
parklands originally
belonging to Sir Philip
Gray-Egerton, early
morning mist at the
Oulton Park circuit in
Cheshire was a fairly
common occurence.

Timetable

Event: International Spring Meeting
Date: Saturday 3rd April 1965
Location: Oulton Park
Circuit Length: 2.761 miles

Time	Race	Laps	Distance	
2:00 pm	British Formula 3 Championship Race	19	52.46 miles	
3:10 pm	Spring Trophy Race for Formula 2 Cars	40	110.44 miles	
4:45 pm	British Saloon Championship Car Race	19	52.46 miles	

Oulton Park – Existing Lap Records

Formula 1	Jim Clark	Lotus 25	1m 39.2 sec.	100.20 mph.
Formula 2	Jim Clark	Lotus 32	1m 43.0 sec.	96.50 mph.
Formula 3	Jackie Stewart	Cooper T72	1m 47.6 sec.	92.38 mph.
Sportscars over 2000cc	Roy Salvadori	Cooper-Monaco	1m 43.8 sec.	95.76 mph.
GT Cars up to 2500cc	Jim Clark	Lotus Elan	1m 52.8 sec.	88.12 mph.
GT Cars 2500cc to 3000cc	Innes Ireland	Ferrari 250	1m 53.0 sec.	87.96 mph.
Saloon Cars over 2000cc	Dan Gurney	Ford Galaxie	1m 53.2 sec.	87.80 mph.
Saloon Cars 1301cc to 2000cc	Jim Clark	Lotus-Cortina	1m 57.0 sec.	84.95 mph.

"A single Lotus-Cortina will run in Willment colours this season. Apart from this car, the team will not be engaged in Saloon car racing. Negotiations have been going on with three works Formula 1 drivers to fill the cockpit."

Glorious Oulton

In a week which had seen the launch at Cheshunt of the new Len Terry-designed Lotus Type 38 Indy challenger, a gloriously sunny early April day at Oulton Park was to see New Zealander Denis Hulme driving the works Brabham-Cosworth to victory in a 40-lap Formula 2 race. The Mid-Cheshire Car Club Spring meeting attracted a crowd of approximately 30,000, Hulme having to fight hard for his win and only gaining command of the race on lap 18 when Graham Hill retired his leading John Coombs Brabham-BRM. With Hill out of the way, Hulme took a comfortable win from Jackie Stewart's sick-sounding Cooper-BRM, Alan Rees' Brabham-Cosworth, the Lola-Cosworth of Tony Maggs and Mike Beckwith's older model Brabham BT10.

The meeting was to have showcased a significant confrontation between four new Formula 2 engines, but as was so often the case, the 'old firm' of Cosworth won the day. BRM's new engine nevertheless showed its race-wining potential after demonstrating that it was good enough to lead the race in two different cars. It was good to see the twin-cam Honda fitted to Jack Brabham's Brabham BT16 too, although in truth it was never in with a chance. Neither was the BMC engine quite right either, the race organisers expecting to have at least one BMC engined car until a telegram arrived from the Cooper Car Company on Thursday confirming that the engine being prepared for Bruce McLaren's Cooper T75 was not ready.

The entry for Oulton was, even so, quite an impressive one, at least on paper, with 29 cars entered, of which twenty-one came to the starting line. Brabham Racing

Developments again entered two cars, one for Jack and the other for Denny Hulme, the former's car using the Honda engine while Hulme stuck with Cosworth power. (Hulme had been on the official entry list with a Honda unit but with one of the three engines supplied to the Brabham team having been returned to Japan for a rebuild, the decision was taken to stay with the highly developed but more reliable engine from Cosworth.)

As it happens, the Honda engine in Jack's chassis was still not giving full power and, until as late as Friday the three Japanese mechanics were working hard to try and trace the missing 1,000rpm at the top end. Their hunt was unsuccessful, so that Brabham found himself in the very unusual position of starting from the very rear of the grid. His problem was spotlighted by the speed taken in the 1/10th mile trap on the straight down to Knickerbrook: he was timed at 110mph, compared to the 129mph clocked by the fastest car, Brian Hart's Ron Harris SCA powered Lotus 35.

Both Brabhams were on Goodyear tyres, as was Tony Hegbourne's Willment Lola. The remainder were still running Dunlops, preferring to wait until the new Goodyears had some strong results to back them up. Equally untried was Tyrrell Racing Organisation's Type 75 Cooper-BRM for Jackie Stewart, a new car still requiring some attention in the handling department, the wet practice session at Silverstone having given the team little if any opportunity to learn anything useful about the new car. The BRM engine was clearly doing very well in terms of power however, and Stewart put up the second fastest time in practice with a strong 1min 41.2sec. and a touch over 126mph on the straight.

VI Spring Trophy
For Formula 2 Cars
Entry List

No.	Entrant	Car	Engine	Driver
1	Brabham Racing Developments	Brabham BT16	Honda	Jack Brabham
2	Brabham Racing Developments	Brabham BT16	Honda/Cosworth SCA	Denis Hulme
3	Tyrrell Racing Organisation	Cooper T75	B.R.M.	Jackie Stewart
4*	Tyrrell Racing Organisation	Cooper T75	B.M.C. Cooper	Frank Gardner (dna)
5	Ron Harris Team Lotus	Lotus 32	Cosworth SCA	Peter Revson
6	Ron Harris Team Lotus	Lotus 35	Cosworth SCA	Brian Hart
8	John Coombs	Brabham BT16	B.R.M.	Graham Hill
9*	The Cooper Car Company	Cooper T75	B.M.C. Cooper	Bruce McLaren (dna)
10*	Team Alexis	Alexis Mk.6	Cosworth SCA	Paul Hawkins (dna)
11	Aurora Gear (Racing) Rotherham	Brabham BT16	Cosworth SCA	Trevor Taylor
12	Ian Raby (Racing) Ltd.	Merlyn Mk.9	Cosworth SCA	Chris Amon
14	Normand	Brabham BT10	Cosworth SCA	Mike Beckwith
15	Merlyn Racing	Merlyn Mk.9	Cosworth SCA	Chris Irwin
16*	Merlyn Racing	Merlyn Mk.9	Cosworth SCA	Roger Mac (dna)
17	Bob Gerard Racing	Cooper T73	Ford TC	John Taylor
18*	E.Offenstadt	Lola T60	B.R.M.	Eric Offenstadt (dna)
19	Jacques Maglia	Lotus 32	Cosworth SCA	Jacques Maglia
20	Frank Lythgoe Racing	Cooper T72	Cosworth SCA	Alan Rollinson
21	Frank Lythgoe Racing	Brabham BT16	Cosworth SCA	Adam Wyllie
22	David Prophet Racing	Brabham BT10	Cosworth SCA	David Prophet
23	David Prophet Racing	Brabham BT10	Cosworth SCA	Bill Bradley
24	Roy Winkelmann Racing	Brabham BT16	Cosworth SCA	Alan Rees
25	Roy Winkelmann Racing	Brabham BT16	Cosworth SCA	Jochen Rindt
26*	Ecurie Alf Francis	Cooper T75	Alfa-Romeo	Jo Siffert (dna)
27*	Ecurie Alf Francis	Cooper T75	Alfa-Romeo	Bernard Plaisance (dna)
28	Midland Racing Partnership	Lola T60	Cosworth SCA	Richard Attwood
29	Midland Racing Partnership	Lola T60	Cosworth SCA	Tony Maggs
30	John Willment Automobiles	Lola T55	Cosworth SCA	Tony Hegbourne

Top left
Prior to the main race
Ron Harris (left) talks to
Colin Chapman.

Left
With Clark and Spence
away in Italy, Brian Hart
drove Ron's number
two entry.

Unfortunately a clash of dates with Sicily's non-championship Formula 1 Syracuse GP meant that regular drivers Clark and Spence were absent for the weekend so Ron Harris Team Lotus entered two cars for second string drivers Peter Revson and Brian Hart.

The former was using one of the previous year's Type 32s, whilst the latter was in one of the newer Type 35s. Both were fitted with Weber carburetted Cosworth engines rather than the new fuel-injected unit being developed by same Northamptonshire-based company. Practice performance was poor for both however, Hart finishing up on the third row of the grid with a time of 1min 43.6sec., two and a half seconds off pole, and Revson even further back on the fourth row and another 1.4 seconds behind the lead car.

John Coombs meanwhile had entered his 1964 Brabham for Graham Hill to drive, although this was now fitted with the BRM engine enabling the BRM works Formula 1 driver to achieve a 1 min 41.0sec. laptime making him joint-fastest with Richard Attwood who was driving very quickly in a new Lola T60 monocoque, fitted with the Cosworth engine. Attwood had set his time before Hill and this took pole position on the 4-3-4 grid. For the first time this year his team mate Tony Maggs was also driving one of the sleek new Lolas, his time of 1min 44.0sec. being good enough for tenth place. This meant the only older, 1964 Lola T55 in the field was that of John Willment's team, driven by Tony Hegbourne who started back in 13th place.

The works Merlyn team unfortunately still had only one car ready for its two contracted drivers and it went to

team leader Chris Irwin who had made the F3 Merlyn go so quickly the previous year. Roger Mac would have to wait until later in the season before another Mk.9 chassis was ready, although a similar car was already making an appearance in the hands of Chris Amon. In Ian Raby's car, Chris was well up the grid in 14th place, and actually three slots ahead of its works twin.

Thereafter the remainder of the field comprised the privately owned Brabhams of Mike Beckwith, Trevor Taylor, Adam Wyllie, David Prophet and Bill Bradley, the Roy Winkelmann Racing Brabham BT16s of Alan Rees and Jochen Rindt, and finally Jacques Maglia's Lotus 32 and the Cooper of Alan Rollinson. Several of the Brabhams were to prove very fast, and indeed three of them with Beckwith, Rindt and Rees at the wheel, made up the second row of the grid. Neither of the two Alf Francis Coopers listed in the programme to appear (with Alfa-Romeo engines) made it on the day.

Formula Three
With practice taking up much of the morning, proceedings got properly underway after lunch with a 19-lap Formula 3 race. This suffered from a large number of non-starters, mainly due to the carnage which had ensued at Silverstone a fortnight before. Seventeen cars made the start, however, with Charles Crichton-Stuart in the SMART Brabham BT10-Cosworth holding pole position with a lap of 1m 46.4sec. but making a poor start and being beaten into Old Hall corner by the other front row starters Piers Courage (Brabham BT10), Charles Lucas (Brabham BT10) and Peter Gethin in the Charles Lucas Lotus 22. In fact Californian Roy Pike in the newer model Brabham BT16

"In a poll organised by the Italian motoring magazine 'Motor', Jim Clark was chosen by 18 top motoring journalists from Europe and America as the driver most representative of the sport in 1964. Second place went to Dan Gurney, third to John Sutrees and fourth to Graham Hill."

got there ahead of too, as did Warwick Banks in the Tyrrell Cooper-BMC, even though both had started on the second row. Pike soon overhauled Courage too and began pulling out a lead he was never to lose, Banks similarly pressuring Gethin and Lucas with the latter looking very wild at times, sliding onto the grass on the exits from several corners and generally looking twitchy.

In fact the owner-driver soon dropped back from the leading group, making a pit stop to investigate an apparent lack of gears, while, as the more senior of his two drivers Gethin followed him on the next lap after becoming stuck in second gear. Gethin was at least able to continue in the race, although he was by this time several laps in arrears. For his part, and doubtless distracted by his gearbox problems, Lucas spun off on the sixth lap.

Banks had meanwhile also overtaken Courage to take second place, although he was now a good seven seconds behind the American who looked far more at ease than his followers. Courage soon lost third place too, this time to John Cardwell's Brabham BT15, while Crichton-Stuart had moved his own Brabham past John Fenning's struggling Merlyn to steal fifth. His progress up the field continuing, Crichton-Stuart was soon in third place, overtaking Cardwell who lost another place to Courage when his car began to experience ignition trouble. In fact Courage made his move just in time, and with his own machine faltering barely made it around the last lap.

For Pike then, it was a very comfortable win, setting a new F3 lap record with a time of 1m 46.2sec. at an average speed of 93.59mph and achieving a top speed down the short straight of 117.2mph. (Banks in second could muster only 114mph.) Surrounded by rivals in trouble, Malcolm Payne's Lotus 31 made it home in fifth place while Robert Lamplough in his ex-Formula Junior monocoque Lotus Type 27 was seventh. Fenning finally boiled his way into the pits with only a few laps of the race remaining.

Spring Trophy Race
As soon as the field for the big race of the day lined up on the dummy grid, mechanics began to swarm over the Brabham BT16s of both Graham Hill and Trevor Taylor. Hill's car had already received a gearbox change ahead of the race, and on the warm-up lap his throttle linkage had began playing up necessitating further work, right up until the very final seconds. Taylor's car also seemed to have a clutch problem, but this was quickly fixed. As the flag dropped Alan Rees stormed through from the second row. Shooting between Hulme and Stewart in a copybook start he glanced over his shoulder, moved over to the left in front of Hill and Attwood, and went into the lead on an inch-perfect line round Old Hall Corner. The remainder of the field streamed through behind him, Rees leading from Stewart, Attwood, Hulme, Beckwith and Rindt – and Hill who was still struggling to find some gears.

At the end of lap one the order among the leading seven remained the same, followed by Revson who had made up four places. Amon, Irwin, Maggs, Hart, Hegbourne, Prophet, Brabham, Maglia, Taylor, Wyllie and Rollinson followed together with Bill Bradley bringing up the rear after being push started on the grid. On lap two Rees

Formula 3 Racing Cars
Results

Position	Driver	No	Car	Laps	Time/Reason	Speed
1st	Roy Pike	51	Brabham BT16	19	34 min 06.0 sec	90.77 mph
2nd	Warwick Banks	31	Cooper T76	19	34 min 18.4 sec	
3rd	Charles Crichton-Stuart	33	Brabham BT10	19	34 min 33.4 sec	
4th	Piers Courage	38	Brabham BT10	19	34 min 37.4 sec	
5th	Malcolm Payne	41	Lotus 31	19	35 min 08.8 sec	
6th	David Rees	43	Brabham BT15	19	35 min 23.0 sec	
7th	Robert Lamplough	52	Lotus 27	19	35 min 56.0 sec	
8th	John Cardwell	44	Brabham BT15	18		
9th	Clive Baker	35	Cooper T76	18		
10th	Tony Dean	34	Brabham BT6	18		
11th	Brian Hough	50	Cooper T76	18		
12th	Steve Matchett	57	Cooper T76	18		
13th	Alan Taylor	47	Alexis Mk.5	17		
14th	Peter Gethin	37	Lotus 22	16	Gear selection problems	
Ret	John Fenning	32	Merlyn Mk.9	15	Engine overheating	
Ret	Charles Lucas	36	Brabham BT10	5	Crash	
Pole Position		33	Charles Crichton-Stuart		1 min 46.4 sec	
Fastest Lap (record)		51	Roy Pike		1 min 46.2 sec (93.59 mph)	

VI Spring Trophy
Grid

Pole Position

Richard Attwood	Graham Hill	Jackie Stewart	Denis Hulme
Lola-Cosworth	Brabham-B.R.M.	Cooper-B.R.M.	Brabham-Cosworth
1 min 41.0 sec	1 min 41.0 sec	1 min 41.2 sec	1 min 41.2 sec

Mike Beckwith	Jochen Rindt	Alan Rees
Brabham-Cosworth	Brabham-Cosworth	Brabham-Cosworth
1 min 42.2 sec	1 min 43.0 sec	1 min 43.0 sec

Brian Hart	David Prophet	Tony Maggs	Alan Rollinson
Lotus-Cosworth	Brabham-Cosworth	Lola-Cosworth	Cooper-Cosworth
1 min 43.6 sec	1 min 43.6 sec	1 min 44.0 sec	1 min 44.2 sec

Peter Revson	Tony Hegbourne	Chris Amon
Lotus-Cosworth	Lola-Cosworth	Merlyn-Cosworth
1 min 45.0 sec	1 min 45.0 sec	1 min 45.2 sec

Trevor Taylor	Jaques Maglia	Chris Irwin	Bill Bradley
Brabham-Cosworth	Lotus-Cosworth	Merlyn-Cosworth	Brabham-Cosworth
1 min 45.2 sec	1 min 45.5 sec	1 min 45.8 sec	1 min 48.0 sec

Jack Brabham	John Taylor	Adam Wylie
Brabham-Honda	Cooper-Ford	Brabham-Cosworth
1 min 48.2 sec	1 min 48.8 sec	1m 51.0 sec
	(dns)	

Left
To avoid possible damage to Jimmy's 1965 car, second string driver Peter Revson was given one of the previous years Type 32 cars for the Formula 2 Spring Trophy race.

surrendered the lead to Jackie Stewart while Rindt and Hill moved past Mike Beckwith whose gear-lever had broken off leaving him a very sharp stump with which to change gear (and, by the end of the race, a very badly cut hand).

The first to pit was Rollinson's Cooper with a detached oil hose, quickly repaired so that he was on his way. By lap four Attwood had replaced Rees in second place, but almost immediately his gear linkage started playing up forcing him to pull out on the far side of the circuit. (Stuck in gear, he eventually wrestled the car back to the pits but was too late to get back into the race.) Attwood's mishap would have put Rees back into second spot had he not been rapidly overwhelmed by the dicing duo of Hulme and Rindt who were followed on the next lap by Hill. This left a closely matched group at the front, comprising Stewart, Hulme, Rindt, Hill and Rees, then a large gap and then Mike Beckwith struggling valiantly with his broken gear lever. Even thus equipped he was able to stay well clear of the Lotus team cars of Hart and Revson, this pair being closely shadowed by Maggs and Hegbourne. Maglia and Amon were even further behind, both having to pit with misfiring troubles although both were able to rejoin the race at a later stage.

Chasing Stewart, Hulme at last managed to find some real speed and went on to break the lap record several times before taking the lead on lap seven. All the while his team leader languished back in unlucky 13th with a very flat sounding Honda engine, so flat indeed that it was even being pressed by Trevor Taylor's own, none too healthy sounding Brabham.

A similar dice was underway for third place between Hill and Rindt, the latter putting in a lap of 1m 41.4sec. – joint fastest for the race – although Hill was eventually able to get past him. Shortly afterwards Rindt too was forced to retire, another gear linkage problem denying him all but two gears. Looking suddenly to be in fine form, Hill quickly replaced his BRM team mate Stewart in second place and set about closing the one and a half second gap between himself and the race leader Hulme. This too he did rapidly, and by lap 14 he was in the lead although the Brabham works driver fought back hard, forcing Hill to put in his quickest lap of the day just before half distance (on lap 16), at 1m 41.4sec., a speed of 98.02mph.

His triumph was shortlived, however, his lead lasting barely four laps before the BRM engine died completely. Refusing to fire up again, the car was towed in after the race only instantly to be restored to life by the boffins from Lucas. Jack Brabham's race ended around the same time, when a spark plug was blown clean out of Honda's cylinder head, while a broken chassis member did for Rollinson's Cooper and both Amon and Taylor pitted with misfiring troubles.

Hulme then was back in the lead, and looking good too, with Stewart losing ground as his BRM engine fluffed badly and Rees in third place highly unlikely to catch either of them. Beckwith in fourth place was in turn gradually being caught by Maggs (who had squeezed past the Lotus of Brian Hart) just as Tony Hegbourne, after shadowing him for several laps, was able to force his Lola past the other Ron Harris Lotus driven by cosmetics heir Peter Revson.

Right
After qualifying the
Cooper-BRM an
excellent third, Jackie
Stewart went on to
finish the race second
behind Denny Hulme.

"Lotus-Cortinas driven by Jim Clark and Jack Sears finished first and second in the Sebring 3 hours production car race. Clark led throughout but Sears had to fight to recover from ground lost when refueling equipment failed at the pits, dropping him to fifth. He pulled back second place in the last five minutes."

An off-course excursion at Esso bend enabled Stewart to provide some excitement for the crowd by reappearing with his body and suspension covered in scenery. The grass and straw he had collected didn't seem to affect his performance, however, and the Cooper continued to stutter round in second place. Further back, and after a long struggle, Revson was able to ease his Lotus past Hegbourne's Lola, but very soon afterwards he pulled into the pits with no oil pressure in the Cosworth engine leaving the Willment driver in seventh place. This became sixth on the penultimate lap when Brian Hart's Lotus dumped itself into the grass and out of the race with a broken lower rear wishbone mounting. In fact it was a bad day all round for the Lotus Formula 3 team, and no better for Colin Chapman being there to see it, having decided not to go to Sicily that weekend.

Thereafter the only other positional change on the final laps occurred when, with just five laps to go, Maggs finally stole fourth from the luckless Beckwith although the latter fought back in the last two laps eventually losing out by just three seconds. Denny Hulme then was the winner of the first Formula 2 race of the year and, with Brabhams first, third and fifth, it looked very much as though the previous season was about to repeat itself.

The Saloons Move In

Because lead driver Jim Clark was away in Italy, it fell to Jack Sears in E8 and Sir John Whitmore Bt. using E9 as his race car and and the spare E10, in practice to spearhead the works effort in the Lotus Cortinas for round two of the British Saloon Car Championship.

With Bob Dance overseeing the whole Team Lotus Cortina programme the mechanics were assigned to cars rather than drivers so that, as at previous meetings, Bob Sparshott ran E8, Bob Cull was on E9 and Allan McCall worked on E10.

With top rival Mike Salmon in the third of the ex-Tour de France Mustangs effectively out of the action – experiencing dire engine trouble both in practice and in the race, he completed just two laps before retiring – only the Team Lotus cars and perhaps Frank Gardner in the Willment Cortina looked likely to upset the two Mustangs of Baillie and Roy Pierpoint who had won the first race of the season at Brands.

The start of the 19-lap race was ragged, with plenty of dust flying about and the loud clanging of metal on metal as five of the seven cars on the first two rows made contact. With Pierpoint, Whitmore, Sears, Gardner and John Fitzpatrick in a Mini-Cooper S all sustaining some damage, Jack Sears made it no further than Old Hall, the first corner, before a broken con-rod caused terminal engine failure. By the end of the first lap Pierpoint was leading followed by Whitmore, Gardner and Fitzpatrick, followed by André Baldet in another Lotus-Cortina and Sir Gawaine Baillie's Mustang.

The race was divided into four classes, essentially two for the Fords and another two for the Minis, and in the largest-capacity class Pierpoint was never seriously challenged and led throughout, although Baillie having somehow avoided the melée at the start, was able to improve his position as the race progressed and finished a close second. The demise of Sears meant that the

Above
Having taken part in his first Grand Prix (British) driving for Willment in '64, former boxer and lifeguard Australian Frank Gardner drove both F1 and saloon cars for them in 1965.

VI Spring Trophy
Results

Position	Driver	No.	Car	Laps	Time/Reason	Speed
1st	Denis Hulme	2	Brabham BT16	40	1 hr 08 min 39.6 sec	96.51 mph
2nd	Jackie Stewart	3	Cooper T75	40	1 hr 08 min 58.6 sec	
3rd	Alan Rees	24	Brabham BT16	40	1 hr 09 min 22.4 sec	
4th	Tony Maggs	29	Lola T60	40	1 hr 09 min 43.6 sec	
5th	Mike Beckwith	14	Brabham BT10	40	1 hr 09 min 47.0 sec	
6th	Tony Hegbourne	30	Lola T55	40	1 hr 10 min 23.6 sec	
nrf	Brian Hart	6	Lotus 35	39		
7th	David Prophet	22	Brabham BT10	39		
8th	Chris Irwin	15	Merlyn Mk.9	39		
9th	Bill Bradley	23	Brabham BT10	39		
10th	Jacques Maglia	19	Lotus 32	38		
11th	Adam Wyllie	21	Brabham BT16	37		
12th	Chris Amon	12	Merlyn Mk.9	34		
13th	Trevor Taylor	11	Brabham BT16	27		
nrf	Peter Revson	5	Lotus 32	34	Oil pressure	
dnf	Graham Hill	8	Brabham BT16	17	Engine	
dnf	Jack Brabham	1	Brabham BT16	16	Sparkplug problems	
dnf	Alan Rollinson	20	Cooper T72	14	Broken chassis	
dnf	Jochen Rindt	25	Brabham BT16	10	Gear linkage	
dnf	Richard Attwood	28	Lola T60	7	Gear linkage	
dns	John Taylor	17	Cooper T73	0		
Pole Position		28	Richard Attwood		1 min 41.0 sec	
Fastest Lap (record)		8 & 25	Hill & Rindt		1 min 41.4 sec (98.02 mph)	

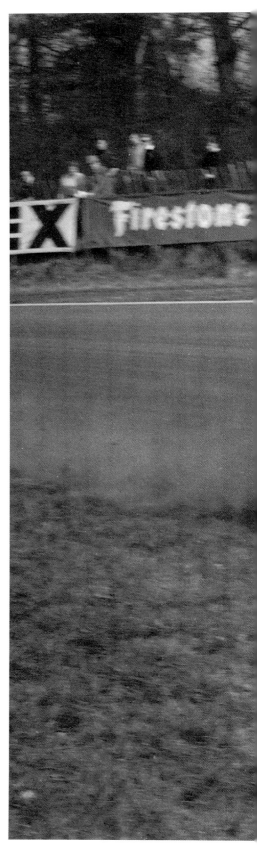

'Cortina Class' resolved itself into a more or less straight fight between Whitmore's works car and Gardner's Willment entry. The two battled it out making contact several times in the first half before Whitmore was forced to retire with yet another puncture, this time at the rear, possibly inflicted by his contact with Gardner. Thereafter Baldet's Cortina was a surefire class second until, in an effort to stave off John Rhodes in the works Mini-Cooper S, he managed to roll at Island Bend with just two and half laps to go.

Meanwhile in the 1000-1300cc category, the Broadspeed 1275cc Mini of John Fitzpatrick appeared to have things sewn up, lying fourth overall all the way from lap 11 to lap 16. His driving was extremely fast but very smooth, lacking the seemingly vicious 'tacking' movements for which many rival Mini racers had become notorious over the past year or so. Consequently it was enormously disappointing when the Broadspeed car slowed down three laps from home, handing the lead to John Rhodes in the works Cooper S. Even more disappointing was the fact that, as soon as Rhodes had overtaken him, Fitzpatrick rolled his car at Druids, writing it off and slightly injuring his face.

Worse still: as there was nothing wrong with the Broadspeed car before the accident, it was assumed that it occurred as a result of lack of concentration due to a sudden slackening of pace. Spectactors were thus left with the impression that Ralph Broad's team had lost a car not in the 'glory of battle' but simply through the complexities of team discipline. (In the end Fitzpatrick insisted it was his fault that he had crashed, but the crowd refused to blame him on the grounds

that his driving until the previous lap had been quite exemplary.) In the end it scarcely mattered: Rhodes works car won the class if only by default, Warwick Banks as reigning touring car champion of Europe took the small-car class in his factory-entered 970cc Mini.

When the final reckoning was made Pierpoint's battered Mustang came in ahead, followed by Baillie's similar but unmarked car, Gardner's Willment-entered Lotus-Cortina, Rhodes in the works Mini-Cooper S, Harry Ratcliffe's Vitafoam, and Jack Newman's privately entered Lotus-Cortina. As the Formula 2 cars had been, the saloon cars were timed over the measured tenth of a mile on the back straight, the fastest in each class being Pierpoint (at 118mph, just 11mph slower than the quickest F2 car and a touch faster than the F3 brigade), Gardner with 112.4mph, Steve Neal in the Arden Mini Cooper at 111.4mph and Phil de Banks in the Sutton Mini-Cooper S at 107.4mph.

Above
The start of the saloon car race had (right to left) Pierpoint on Pole, Gardner (row 2), Sears, Whitmore and Baillie.

Right
Jack Sears looked strong in practice but only made it as far as the first corner of the race before his engine expired in a big way.

Saloon Car Race
Results

Position	Driver	No	Car	Laps	Time/Reason	Speed
1st	Roy Pierpoint	89	Ford Mustang	19	37 min 37.6 sec	83.65 mph
2nd	Gawaine Baillie	88	Ford Mustang	19	37 min 38.0 sec	
3rd	Frank Gardner	85	Lotus-Cortina	19	37 min 59.8 sec	
4th	John Rhodes	69	Austin Mini-Cooper S	19	38 min 34.0 sec	
5th	Harry Ratcliffe	67	Morris Mini-Cooper S	19	39 min 10.4 sec	
6th	Jack Newman	82	Lotus-Cortina	19	39 min 23.0 sec	
7th	Phil Middlehurst	78	Morris Mini-Cooper S	19	39 min 24.4 sec	
8th	Steve Neal	75	Austin Mini-Cooper S	19		
9th	Robin Smith	81	Lotus-Cortina	18		
10th	Warwick Banks	64	Austin Mini-Cooper S 970	18		
11th	Tony Lanfranchi	73	Morris Mini-Cooper S	18		
12th	Mike Campbell-Cole	62	Austin Mini-Cooper S 970	18		
13th	Phil de Banks	65	Morris Mini-Cooper S 970	17		
dnf	John Fitzpatrick	77	Austin Mini-Cooper S	16	Accident	
dnf	André Baldet	80	Lotus-Cortina	16	Accident	
dnf	John Whitmore	84	Lotus-Cortina	10	Puncture	
dnf	Anita Taylor	61	Austin Mini-Cooper S 970	9		
dnf	Laurie Goodwin	72	Ford Anglia Super	6		
dnf	Chris McLaren	86	Jaguar MkII	6		
dnf	Ted Savory	63	Morris Mini-Cooper S 970	4		
dnf	Jack Sears	83	Lotus-Cortina	0	Engine	
Pole Position		89	Roy Pierpoint			
Fastest Lap (overall)		88	Gawaine Baillie		1 min 56.8 sec (85.10 mph)	
Class Winners			Pierpoint, Gardner, Rhodes, Banks			

Opposite
Clockwise from top left: Chris Parry of Firestone checks tyre pressures on the lead Mustang. Roy Pierpoint, looking relaxed in the driving seat took Pole Position and, once the first lap 'pushing and shoving' was over, led all the way to the flag. Sir Gawaine Baillie chased him all the way home but just couldn't find a way past.

Chapter Four
Snetterton
10th April

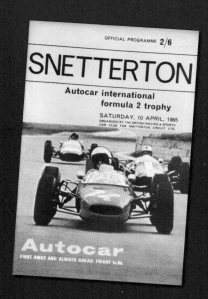

"CUT-THROAT DICING AT SNETTERTON"

The Autocar Trophy for Formula 2 cars at Snetterton, run in two 25 lap heats, was won by Graham Hill, driving John Coombs' Brabham BRM. In the first heat he had a race-long duel with Jim Clark in the works Lotus and only piped him on the finish line by half a wheel, both drivers being credited with the same time....

Above right
The saloon cars were stationed at the far end of the Snetterton paddock. Not the most hospitable of places in early April .

Timetable

Event: Autocar International Trophy Meeting
Date: Saturday 10th April 1965
Location: Snetterton
Circuit Length: 2.71 miles

Time	Race	Laps	Distance
2:00 pm	The Autocar F2 International Trophy (Part I)	25	67.75 miles
3:15 pm	British Saloon Car Championship Race	15	40.65 miles
4:10 pm	The Autocar F2 International Trophy (Part II)	25	67.75 miles

Snetterton Circuit – Existing Lap Records

Formula 1	Stirling Moss	Lotus-Climax	1m 33.6 sec.	104.23 mph.
Formula 2	Frank Gardner	Brabham-Cosworth	1m 38.2 sec.	99.35 mph.
Formula 3	Chris Irwin	Merlyn-Ford	1m 43.6 sec.	94.17 mph.
Sportscars over 2000cc	Innes Ireland	Lotus-Climax	1m 35.6 sec.	102.05 mph.
Sportscars under 2000cc	Jim Clark	Lotus-Ford	1m 38.4 sec.	99.15 mph.
Saloon Cars over 2000cc	Jack Brabham	Ford Galaxie	1m 46.4 sec.	91.69 mph.
Saloon Cars 1301cc to 2000cc	Jim Clark	Lotus-Cortina	1m 47.8 sec.	90.50 mph.

The Autocar Formula 2 International Trophy
Entry List

No.	Entrant	Car	Engine	Driver
1	Brabham Racing Developments	Brabham BT16	Honda	Jack Brabham
2	Brabham Racing Developments	Brabham BT16	Cosworth SCA	Denis Hulme
3	John Coombs	Brabham BT16	B.R.M.	Graham Hill
4*	Aurora Gear (Racing) Rotherham	Brabham BT16	Cosworth SCA	Trevor Taylor (dns)
5	Roy Winkelmann Racing	Brabham BT16	Cosworth SCA	Alan Rees
6	Roy Winkelmann Racing	Brabham BT16	Cosworth SCA	Jochen Rindt
7	Ford France	Brabham BT10	Cosworth SCA	Jo Schlesser
8	David Prophet Racing	Brabham BT10	Cosworth SCA	David Prophet
9	David Prophet Racing	Brabham BT10	Cosworth SCA	Bill Bradley
10	Normand	Brabham BT10	Cosworth SCA	Mike Beckwith
11	John Willment Automobiles	Lola T55	Cosworth SCA	Tony Hegbourne
12	Ron Harris Team Lotus	Lotus 35	Cosworth SCA	Jim Clark
14	Ron Harris Team Lotus	Lotus 35	B.R.M.	Mike Spence
14T*	Ron Harris Team Lotus	Lotus 35	Cosworth SCA	Brian Hart (dns)
15	J.Maglia	Lotus 32	Cosworth SCA	Jacques Maglia
16	Reg Parnell (Racing)	Lotus 35	B.R.M.	David Hobbs
17*	Sellers Racing Ltd.	Lotus 35	B.R.M.	Barrie Hart (dna)
18	Tyrrell Racing Organisation	Cooper T75	B.R.M.	Jackie Stewart
19	Bob Gerard Racing	Cooper T73	Ford TC	John Taylor
20	Merlyn Racing	Merlyn Mk.9	Cosworth SCA	Chris Irwin
21	Ian Raby (Racing) Ltd.	Merlyn Mk.9	Cosworth SCA	Ian Raby
22	Ecurie Ford France SA	Brabham BT6	Cosworth SCA	Guy Ligier
23	Scaradi Racing	Lotus 32	Cosworth Ford	Harry Stiller
24	Midland Racing Partnership	Lola T60	Cosworth SCA	Richard Attwood
25	Midland Racing Partnership	Lola T60	Cosworth B.R.M.	Tony Maggs

"Ian Walker has completed a new sleek road version of his special racing Elan, with reinforced chassis, 140 horsepower engine and twin headlamps."

Driving Between The Raindrops

With just a few days to recuperate after the thrills of Oulton Park, the Formula 2 circus moved to Snetterton for the Autocar International Trophy scheduled to be run in two 25-lap heats on Saturday 10th April. Once again rain threatened to stop play but fortunately, after an exceptionally wet early-morning, the clouds cleared and the circuit remained dry during the race itself. The deluge restarted soon after the end of the last race, but by that time several of the competitors were fighting their way out of the circuit in order to hurry to Le Mans for what remained of the practice weekend there.

Two of those who made it to France on time were Richard Attwood, down to drive a works Ford GT40, and race winner here, Graham Hill who by Sunday was busy at practice in the heavily-revised Rover BRM gas turbine car he would share with Jackie Stewart.

Back at the Norfolk circuit the main interest lay in the continuing battle between the engine manufacturers. The dispute between BRM, Cosworth and Honda was clearly still wide open, but by now it was apparent that the BMC powerplant was no longer in the running. The twin-cam engine which had first been due to race in mid-1964, still had to make an appearance at an actual race meeting nearly a year later. Clearly suffering some serious problems, to many observers the whole thing carried with it some uncomfortable echoes of the 'race' twin-cam MGA engine saga.

Joint fastest in practice were Jochen Rindt in the Winkelmann Brabham-Cosworth and Graham Hill in John Coombs' Brabham BRM. Both posted a time of

1m 34.0sec., although in doing so Rindt blew up his Cosworth engine forcing the team to fit an older, 1964-spec unit overnight. A third BRM-engined car, the Ken Tyrell Cooper driven as usual by Jackie Stewart, recorded the third best time of the day at 1m 34.4sec., the front row of the grid being completed by Mike Beckwith after pushing the ex-Jack Brabham Brabham Cosworth BT10 round the circuit in 1m 35.0sec.. This was a very respectable time, considering the previous year's fastest Formula 2 lap by Frank Gardner in a Brabham-Cosworth BT10 was three seconds slower at 1m 38.2sec.. Indeed, with several of the big banger sportscars – such as the Lola T70 of David Hobbs and Graham Hill's McLaren Elva-Oldsmobile M1A – lapping the course in under 1m 31sec. during unofficial practice sessions, the overall lap record was expected to fall during the course of the day.

Unusually Jim Clark was relegated to the second row of the grid, driving the Lotus 35 Cosworth that had been driven the previous weekend by Brian Hart. The collapsed rear wishbone which Hart had suffered at Oulton had of course been replaced, as had its opposite number as a safety precaution. At the same time a cross-piece had been added to the rear frame, joining the two wishbones together so that if anything came adrift from the chassis it would be held in place by the cross-piece. Thus equipped, Clark rounded the course in 1m 35.2sec. while team mate Mike Spence continued his attempts to sort out a brand new Lotus 35 chassis fitted with a BRM engine; in the event he only got in half a dozen laps or so but still managed a respectable 1m 37.4sec for eleventh on the grid (the outside of row 3 on the 'semi' 4-3-4 grid).

Above
Jim Clark and Ron Harris are shown how to modify what is obviously a very important piece of equipment.

"We've done it so that we can change wheels quicker than drivers can change their mind." Colin Chapman explaining why the Lotus GP cars were fitted with knock-on wheels in 1965."

Above

Jimmy looks thoughtful waiting in the car before the race. Note his trademark 'JC' branded gloves, Bell helmet, heavily taped goggles and mask to cover the lower part of his face. Jimmy is also wearing a spare pair of goggles behind his neck.

The Autocar Formula 2 International Trophy Grid

Pole Position

Mike Beckwith	Jackie Stewart	Graham Hill	Jochen Rindt
Brabham-Cosworth	Cooper-B.R.M.	Brabham-Cosworth	Brabham Cosworth
1 min 35.0 sec	1 min 34.4 sec	1 min 34.0 sec	1 min 34.0 sec

Jack Brabham	Alan Rees	Jim Clark
Brabham-Honda	Brabham-Cosworth	Lotus-Cosworth
1 min 35.4 sec	1 min 35.4 sec	1 min 35.2 sec

Mike Spence	Denis Hulme	Tony Maggs	Richard Attwood
Lotus-Cosworth	Brabham-Cosworth	Lola-Cosworth	Lola-Cosworth
1 min 37.4 sec	1 min 35.8 sec	1 min 35.6 sec	1 min 35.4 sec

Jacques Maglia	Chris Irwin
Lotus-Cosworth	Merlyn-Cosworth
1 min 37.6 sec	1 min 37.4 sec

David Prophet	David Hobbs	Jo Schlesser
Brabham-Cosworth	Lotus-B.R.M.	Brabham-Cosworth
1 min 38.6 sec	1 min 38.2 sec	1 min 38.2 sec

Bill Bradley	John Taylor
Brabham-Cosworth	Cooper-Ford
1 min 39.0 sec	1 min 38.8 sec

Tony Hegbourne	Ian Raby	Harry Stiller
Lola-Cosworth	Merlyn-Cosworth	Lola-Cosworth
1 min 41.2 sec	1 min 40.6	1 min 40.4 sec

Guy Ligier
Brabham-Cosworth
1 min 43.2 sec

Alan Rees could always be relied on to get his own Winkelmann Brabham-Cosworth into the fastest half dozen, and in fact he was only fractionally slower than Clark with 1m 35.4sec.. The real surprise of the day was Jack Brabham himself who at last got the Honda-engined Brabham motoring well enough to equal Alan's time. The 1,000rpm which has been missing since Silverstone had finally been traced by the Honda mechanics and the engine was finally revving its heart out, albeit with a peak still sightly below 10,000rpm. Richard Attwood in the monocoque T60 Lola-Cosworth also matched the time set by Rees, with Tony Maggs in a second MRP monocoque Lola (fitted for the first time with the BRM engine) just a fifth of a second slower. As for Hulme, the winner at Oulton Park in his Brabham-Cosworth, he got round in 1m 35.8sec. which was slightly slower than expected but still good enough to get him on the third row on the grid.

Thereafter there was a fairly big jump down to the next fastest, the Lotus of Mike Spence and Chris Irwin's Merlyn both managing 1m 37.4sec.. They were followed by Jacques Maglia (Lotus 32-Cosworth), Jo Schlesser (Brabham-Cosworth), David Hobbs in Tim Parnell's band-new Lotus 35 BRM, David Prophet (Brabham-Cosworth), John Taylor (Cooper-Cosworth), Bill Bradley (Erabham-Cosworth), Trevor Taylor (Brabham-Cosworth), Harry Stiller (Lotus-Cosworth), Ian Raby (Merlyn-Cosworth), Tony Hegbourne (Lola-Cosworth), and Guy Ligier (Brabham-Cosworth). Prophet had actually spun his car in practice knocking off a wheel but after a quick repair he took his place on the grid. Both Brian Hart who practiced the spare Ron Harris Lotus and Trevor Taylor were listed as non-starters.

Following a warm-up lap the cars took their places on the grid for part one of the two part race, but without the benefit of the dummy grid and with the field arranged in a slightly odd formation due to the intrusion of the pit safety barrier on the righthand side of the track. Jochen Rindt also had something of a last minute panic when his car was seen to be boiling over: his mechanics poured in two buckets water to rectify the problem but, unsurprisingly, the engine refused to restart and he was wheeled to one side as the remainder roared off to the first corner, Riches.

With Jackie Stewart jumping the start fractionally, he managed to wrest the lead from Beckwith, Brabham, Hill, Clark, Rees and Maggs. Unfortunately at Riches someone bumped Mike Spence, who collided with Denny Hulme so that both cars were sent spinning on to the grass. The cars were relatively undamaged, but after both drivers had vacated their seats David Prophet spun into Spence's car putting a big dent in the monocoque chassis. (After the race Spence was seen walking round the paddock, peering at the noses of other cars to see who pushed him off, although it seems he was unable to identify the culprit.)

This first drama over, Stewart managed to build an extraordinary long lead by the end of the first lap. Brabham was in hot pursuit, followed by Beckwith, Hill, Clark, Rees, Attwood, Irwin, Maglia, Hobbs and Schlesser although by lap two Hill had nipped past Beckwith and the following lap he managed to get past Brabham as well before setting off after Stewart. The following lap Jim Clark began duplicating the same manoeuvres, as observers began checking their

Above
As Jack Sears waits for the saloon car race it appears that Jim Endruweit and Sally Stokes have been trusted with looking after Jack's son David.

The Autocar Formula 2 International Trophy
Results – Part I

Pos.	Driver	No.	Car	Laps	Time/Reason	Speed
1st	Graham Hill	3	Brabham BT16	25	40 min 46.0 sec	99.71 mph
2nd	Jim Clark	12	Lotus 35	25	40 min 46.0 sec	
3rd	Jack Brabham	1	Brabham BT16	25	41 min 11.0 sec	
4th	Mike Beckwith	10	Brabham BT10	25	41 min 15.2 sec	
5th	Alan Rees	5	Brabham BT16	25	42 min 03.6 sec	
6th	Richard Attwood	24	Lola T60	25	42 min 08.4 sec	
7th	Jacques Maglia	15	Lotus 32	25	42 min 10.0 sec	
8th	Jo Schlesser	7	Brabham BT10	24		
9th	David Hobbs	16	Lotus 35	24		
10th	Chris Irwin	20	Merlyn Mk.9	24		
11th	Tony Maggs	25	Lola T55	24		
12th	John Taylor	19	Cooper T76	24		
13th	Tony Hegbourne	11	Lola T55	24		
14th	Harry Stiller	23	Lotus 32	24		
15th	Bill Bradley	9	Brabham BT10	23		
16th	Guy Ligier	22	Brabham BT6	23		
nc	David Prophet	8	Brabham BT10	21	not classified	
nc	Jochen Rindt	6	Brabham BT16	18	not classified	
dnf	Ian Raby	21	Merlyn Mk.9	12	Engine	
dnf	Jackie Stewart	18	Cooper T75	5	Ignition	
dnf	Denis Hulme	2	Brabham BT16	0	Crash	
dnf	Mike Spence	14	Lotus 32	0	Crash	
Pole Position		6	Jochen Rindt		1 min 34.0 sec	
Fastest Lap (record)		3 & 12	Hill & Clark		1 min 35.4 sec (102.26 mph)	

"Jim Clark became the first driver to lap Indy at over 160mph, but his time was later beaten by Foyt in the second works car at 161.958 mph."

stopwatches to ascertain whether or not Hill would be able to catch Stewart. Unfortunately the question soon became redundant, the Cooper beginning to stutter as it came past the pits heralding a repeat of the Oulton Park misfiring trouble. Having lead an F2 race for the first time that season, Stewart's car soon expired stranding the Scotsman out on the far side of the circuit.

Hill now had the lead but his position was far from comfortable with Clark rapidly catching him and for the rest of the 25 lap race harrassing him repeatedly by coming alongside and trying to take the inside line on several corners. Hill though seemed always to have the advantage on braking into the bends, and time and again was able to cut the Lotus off, so that the two eventually crossed the finishing line side. For a while it looked as though Clark might have done it, but the timekeepers eventually gave the win to Hill even though the two had recorded identical race times.

Not unnaturally this terrific duel had to a degree overshadowed the exploits of the rest of the field, especially Jack Brabham's drive in the Honda-powered car which had broken a throttle spring on lap four. At the time no-one but he realised what had happened, but it certainly gave him some anxious moments under braking. Despite this he managed to hold on to his third place position for his first good result of the season, and something to please his Japanese partners. Beckwith meanwhile stayed steady in fourth, with Rees finishing a comfortable fifth ahead of Attwood and Maglia (fighting hard but losing sixth to Attwood) while Irwin was robbed of eighth place when his engine expired on the final lap handing the place to Schlesser.

The Saloons Rumble On
Once again the interval between the two heats left the track free for the 15-lap saloon car race which made up round three of the British Championship. Here the tyre war was hotting up even more than in single seater racing, with new arrivals Firestone giving both Goodyear and Dunlop a very good run for their money although for the timebeing all the works Minis stuck with Dunlop 'Green Spot' R6s.

Even so, the race was a more-or-less carbon copy of the earlier races in the season. Mike Salmon in his Dunlop-shod Dawnay Racing/F. English-entered Mustang taking the lead from Roy Pierpoint who had started from pole in his own Firestone equipped Mustang. Thereafter he burbled his way round in the lead for all 15 laps, Alan Hutcheson briefly stealing second place in the big Goodyear Galaxie until the engine blew in a big way as he passed the pits at the start of lap five. That left the Mustangs of Pierpoint and Sir Gawaine Baillie in second and third places, and Hutcheson to reflect on his second Galaxie blow-up, the first having occurred in practice at Brands Hatch back in March.

Jim Clark, who this weekend was using Cortina 'E9' as his race car, held fourth place for a while before Frank Gardner in the Willment car shot past. Looking much more stable in the corners on his Goodyear tyres, Gardner had no problem holding off Clark for the rest of the race and finally opened up a gap of three seconds. Jack Sears had been forced to pit early when E10, the second works car, ran into the back of Clark requiring the bodywork to be straightened. Once this had been done he rejoined the race, spending the

Above
Jack Sears ready for the off.

Opposite
As the the flag dropped, Frank Gardner in the Willment Cortina burst through between Jimmy and Jack and managed to hold them off for the full 15 laps, finishing the race fourth behind the Mustangs.

Left
Jimmy tried everything
he could to catch
Gardner but the
Willment car clearly
handled better.
Something not well
appreciated by Colin
Chapman.

remaining laps picking up places to finish sixth which
was respectable enough under the circumstances
although he was almost a minute down on Clark's time.

As before the 1,300cc and 1,000cc classes comprised
the usual bunch of Minis although this time the pack
included a Fiat Abarth 1000 which John Anstead had
brought in from Italy. Initially three Minis – Tony
Lanfranchi in the Alexander car, John Handley in a
Broadspeed and John Rhodes in the works – ran virtually
side-by-side, but clearly that couldn't last long and it
came as no surprise when Handley was pushed off at
the hairpin as the three tried to go through together.
After this Lanfranchi spun at Sears, losing sight of
Rhodes who went on to win the class after finishing
seventh overall behind the Cortina of Jack Sears.

Rhodes' team-mate Paddy Hopkirk had the job of
'towing' Warwick Banks to a class win in the smaller
engined (970cc) works Mini-Cooper S in his 1275S car,
ensuring that none of Banks's rivals could get near.
Elsewhere Gerry Marshall's Newtune Mini took a well
deserved second place in the 1-litre class, keeping just
ahead of John Fitzpatrick in the other Broadspeed car.
Less fortunate was Richard Cluley, who escaped
unhurt after rolling his Mini into somewhat of a ball
at the hairpin.

Speaking more than 40 years later, Bob Dance
remembers the weekend well. "The Willment cars were
also Ford sponsored and had been getting quicker all
season. The Guv'nor was none too pleased about Frank
beating Jimmy, and he made it known to me. Very
unusually I had been pretty ill all weekend so didn't take

it very well. At the time I supposed that there must have
been a good reason for it, so I just had to figure it out
and get us back to the front of the grid."

At this meeting the two Team Lotus cars had been using
the new 'Yellow Spot' Dunlop R7 tyres rather
than the older 'Green Spot', an introduction which had
proved troublesome in F1. Although it seemed possible
that they were the reason behind the increase in lap
times, the team also felt that the new BRM-tuned Lotus
power units they were using were down on power
compared to the previous year's Cosworth units. Nor,
against such a background, was there much comfort
to be taken from the fact that, what with the damage
inflicted on the cars at Oulton, and then again here
at Snetterton, the team was doing its bit to help
local panel-beaters hone their skills.

That said, with the full backing of Ford, the help the
team received from the local dealer network was to
prove quite a boon. "Most weekends," recalls Dance
now, "we would base ourselves at whichever Ford
dealership was nearest to the circuit and, although
they didn't always have a fully-equipped workshop it
was good to be able to get inside, rather than under
the 'tarp' we otherwise had to stretch between the
two trucks. It was also very useful when we had body
damage. Back at Cheshunt after a race, we would run
the cars down to our local Ford Dealer in Cheshunt on
the Monday morning and by Tuesday they were back
in our workshop looking perfect. Of course they kept
plenty of the plain white bolt-on panels in stock and
just had to paint the green stripe on, so it wasn't too
difficult for them."

15-Lap Saloon Car Race
Results

Pos.	Driver	No.	Car	Laps	Time/Reason	Speed
1st	Mike Salmon	33	Ford Mustang	15	27 min 14.8 sec	89.52 mph
2nd	Roy Pierpoint	34	Ford Mustang	15	27 min 23.2 sec	
3rd	Gawaine Baillie	32	Ford Mustang	15	27 min 41.2 sec	
4th	Frank Gardner	44	Lotus-Cortina	15	27 min 47.0 sec	
5th	Jim Clark	41	Lotus-Cortina	15	27 min 50.0 sec	
6th	Jack Sears	42	Lotus-Cortina	15	28 min 48.6 sec	
7th	John Rhodes	51	Morris Mini-Cooper S	15	28 min 55.6 sec	
8th	John Nicholson	46	Lotus-Cortina	15	29 min 19.0 sec	
9th	Tony Lanfranchi	54	Morris Mini-Cooper S	14		
10th	Jacqui Bond-Smith	45	Lotus-Cortina	14		
11th	Paddy Hopkirk	52	Morris Mini-Cooper S	14		
12th	Chris Montague	60	Austin Mini-Cooper S	14		
13th	Warwick Banks	71	Austin Mini-Cooper S 970	14		
14th	Jim Sullivan	57	BMC Mini-Cooper S	14		
15th	Michaelle Burns-Grieg	59	Austin Mini-Cooper S	14		
16th	Gerry Marshall	72	Austin Mini-Cooper S 970	14		
17th	John Fitzpatrick	73	Austin Mini-Cooper S 970	14		
18th	Ken Costello	80	Morris Mini-Cooper S 970	14		
19th	Mike Campbell-Cole	75	Morris Mini-Cooper S 970	14		
20th	Anita Taylor	74	Austin Mini-Cooper S 970	14		
21st	John Anstead	81	Fiat Abarth 1000 TC	14		
dnf	John Handley	53	Morris Mini-Cooper S	12	Accident	
dnf	Richard Cluely	61	Austin Mini-Cooper S	8	Accident	
dnf	Alan Hutcheson	31	Ford Galaxie	5	Engine	
dnf	Harry Ratcliffe	55	Austin Mini-Cooper S			
dnf	Peter Harper	67	Austin Mini-Cooper S		Engine	

Pole Position		34	Roy Pierpoint		
Fastest Lap (overall)		33	Mike Salmon	1 min 46.8 sec	
Class Winners			Salmon, Gardner, Rhodes, Banks		

Back To The Single Seaters

The second part of the Autocar Trophy saw the cars lining up on the grid in the order in which they had finished the first heat meaning Hill, Clark, Brabham and Beckwith were on the front row. Once again Hill made a poor start, becoming engulfed by the pack as the field rushed into Riches and seeing Brabham steal the lead ahead of Beckwith and Clark. His throttle linkage having been fixed during the saloon-car race, Brabham managed to build up a clear lead by the end of the first lap, the Honda engine really showing its power although both Clark and Attwood were closing rapidly.

By lap three Attwood's Lola shot past both Clark and Brabham, taking the lead and holding it for a couple of laps before once more surrendering it to Brabham. Jackie Stewart, meanwhile, had disappeared on the first lap with yet another recurrence of his ignition trouble, while Hegbourne's T55 Lola was sounding very rough. (Lola may have been leading, but things weren't looking good for the marque generally, particularly when Tony Maggs was forced to pit on lap 5 with low fuel pressure from his Cosworth engine.)

With Hill gradually making up for his poor start, Clark soon caught sight of him in his mirrors as he pushed the Ron Harris Lotus past Attwood's Lola and set his sights on Brabham. A spate of retirements at this time saw Maglia retire from seventh with a detached balljoint in a front wishbone, Rindt dropping out with more engine trouble in his Brabham, and David Hobbs smoke his way into the pits with a broken oil pipe. "*Sadly my biggest memory of that race was walking down pit lane and Graham Hill said to me that it looked like someone had been sick on my helmet!*" recalled David forty-five years on. "*I had just a new colour scheme of blue and yellow done, which I used combinations of from then on. Graham thought he was very funny, I didn't!*"

For a while Brabham and Clark had been fighting for the lead, with Hill held up by Attwood going extremely well in the still relatively new Lola. By lap 17, however, Hill managed to pass and had soon caught Brabham who, again, was suffering throttle-linkage problems before his engine finally died out on the circuit. Now the scene was set for a terrific finish, Hill fighting hard to catch Clark and needing to beat him by any margin in heat two in order to gain an overall win.

With three laps to go the task looked impossible, but he suddenly gained tremendously and it was soon obvious that the Lotus was in trouble. Sure enough, on the penultimate lap, Hill took the lead with Attwood and Beckwith behind him and Clark back in fourth with the Lotus sounding dreadful. Winning the race four seconds ahead of Attwood and 24 ahead of Mike Beckwith, the day belonged to Hill with Clark finally finishing in only sixth place behind Rees and Hulme. Sadly Clark's oil pressure had begun to fail several laps from the end, the bearings eventually beginning to rattle before a con rod snapped on the final lap forcing him to switch off and coast in.

Certainly it was tough luck on both Brabham and Clark, but the BRM engine in the hands of Hill thoroughly deserved this first Formula 2 win – as indeed did its driver – although many could see that before long it may well have a worthy challenger in Jack Brabham's Honda.

Above right
Richard Cluely made a real mess of his Mini when he managed to roll at the hairpin.

Above left
The mighty Galaxie of Alan Hutcheson 'On Tow'. He retired on lap 5 with a blown engine and this is how his team took the car home.

Opposite
Unlike most of the other drivers, Jimmy always wore a scarf to protect his face.

The Autocar Formula 2 International Trophy
Results – Part II

Pos.	Driver	No.	Car	Laps	Time/Reason	Speed
1st	Graham Hill	3	Brabham BT16	25	40 min 08.2 sec	101.28 mph
2nd	Richard Attwood	24	Lola T60	25	40 min 12.8 sec	
3rd	Mike Beckwith	10	Brabham BT10	25	40 min 32.2 sec	
4th	Alan Rees	5	Brabham BT16	25	40 min 45.4 sec	
5th	Denis Hulme	2	Brabham BT16	25	40 min 55.6 sec	
6th	Jim Clark	12	Lotus 35	25	41 min 07.0 sec	
7th	Jo Schlesser	7	Brabham BT10	25	41 min 20.0 sec	
8th	John Taylor	19	Cooper T76	25	42 min 20.0 sec	
9th	Bill Bradley	9	Brabham BT10	24		
10th	Harry Stiller	23	Lotus 32	24		
11th	Ian Raby	21	Merlyn Mk.9	23		
12th	Jack Brabham	1	Brabham BT16	22		
13th	Tony Hegbourne	11	Lola T55	20		
dnf	David Hobbs	16	Lotus 35	15	Oil pipe	
dnf	Jochen Rindt	6	Brabham BT16	14	Engine	
dnf	Chris Irwin	20	Merlyn Mk.9	14	Track rod	
dnf	Jacques Maglia	15	Lotus 32	13	Front wishbone	
dnf	Tony Maggs	25	Lola T55	4	Fuel pressure	
dnf	Jackie Stewart	18	Cooper T75	0	Ignition	
dns	David Prophet	8	Brabham BT10	0	Crash damage	
dns	Guy Ligier	22	Brabham BT6	0	Oil pressure	
Pole Position		3	Graham Hill		1st in Part I	
Fastest Lap (record)		1	Jack Brabham		1 min 34.6 sec (103.13 mph)	

The Autocar International Trophy
Aggregate Results

Pos.	Driver	No.	Car	Laps	Time/Reason	Speed
1st	Graham Hill	3	Brabham BT16	50	1 hr 20 min 54.2 sec	100.49 mph
2nd	Mike Beckwith	10	Brabham BT10	50	1 hr 21 min 47.4 sec	
3rd	Jim Clark	12	Lotus 35	50	1 hr 21 min 53.0 sec	
4th	Richard Attwood	24	Lola T60	50	1 hr 22 min 21.2 sec	
5th	Alan Rees	5	Brabham BT16	50	1 hr 22 min 59.0 sec	
6th	Jo Schlesser	7	Brabham BT10	49		
7th	John Taylor	19	Cooper T76	49		
8th	Harry Stiller	23	Lotus 32	48		
9th	Jack Brabham	1	Brabham BT16	47		
10th	Bill Bradley	9	Brabham BT10	47		
11th	Tony Hegbourne	11	Lola T55	44		
nc	David Hobbs	16	Lotus 35	38		
nc	Chris Irwin	20	Merlyn Mk.9	38		
nc	Jacques Maglia	15	Lotus 32	38		
nc	Ian Raby	21	Merlyn Mk.9	35		
nc	Jochen Rindt	6	Brabham BT16	32		
nc	Tony Maggs	25	Lola T55	28		
nc	Denis Hulme	2	Brabham BT16	25		
nc	Guy Ligier	22	Brabham BT6	23		
nc	David Prophet	8	Brabham BT10	21		
nc	Jackie Stewart	18	Cooper T75	5		
Fastest Lap overall (part II)		1	Jack Brabham		1 min 34.6 sec (103.13 mph)	

Chapter Five
Goodwood
19th April

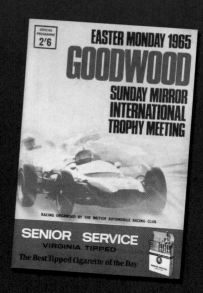

"THREE WINS FOR JIM CLARK AT GOODWOOD"

The Easter racing programme was badly affected by the weather, when snow and hailstorms swept the country. At the Goodwood International meeting fortunately only the Formula 3 race was affected by the weather. Jim Clark had a field day, winning the 100 mile Formula 1 race, the 21 lap sports car race and the shortened five lap saloon car race....

Above right
In a day of extreme weather conditions at Goodwood, this was one of the better moments.

Timetable

Event: International Trophy Meeting
Date: 19th April 1965
Location: Goodwood
Circuit Length: 2.40 miles

Time	Race	Laps	Distance
1:30 pm	Chichester Cup Race (Formula 3)	10	24.0 miles
2:00 pm	St. Mary's Trophy Race (Saloon Cars)	5	12.0 miles
2:55 pm	Sunday Mirror International Trophy Race	42	100.8 miles
4:25 pm	Sussex Trophy Race (Grand Touring Cars)	15	36.0 miles
5:10 pm	Lavant Cup Race (Sports Racing Cars)	21	50.0 miles

Goodwood, Long Circuit – Existing Lap Records

Formula 1	Graham Hill	B.R.M.	1m 21.0 sec.	106.67 mph.
Formula 2	n/a			
Formula 3	Jackie Stewart	Cooper-Austin	1m 32.2 sec.	93.71 mph.
Sportscars over 2000cc	Bruce McLaren	Cooper-Oldsmobile	1m 23.8 sec.	103.10 mph.
Sportscars under 2000cc	Denis Hulme	Brabham BT8-Climax	1m 35.8 sec.	100.70 mph.
Saloon Cars over 2000cc	Jack Sears	Ford Galaxie	1m 35.2 sec.	90.76 mph.
Saloon Cars 1301cc to 2000cc	Jim Clark	Lotus-Cortina	1m 35.8 sec.	90.19 mph.

Sunday Mirror International Trophy Race
Entry List

No.	Entrant	Car	Engine	C.C.	Driver
1*	SpA Ferrari SEFAC	Ferrari 158	Ferrari V8	1499	John Surtees (dna)
2*	SpA Ferrari SEFAC	Ferrari 158	Ferrari V8	1499	Lorenzo Bandini (dna)
3	Owen Racing Organisation	B.R.M. P261	B.R.M. V8	1498	Graham Hill
4	Owen Racing Organisation	B.R.M. P261	B.R.M. V8	1498	Jackie Stewart
5	Team Lotus	Lotus 33 (chassis R10)	Climax V8	1496	Jim Clark
6	Team Lotus	Lotus 33 (chassis R9)	Climax V8	1496	Mike Spence
7	Brabham Racing Organisation	Brabham BT11	Climax V8	1496	Dan Gurney
8	Brabham Racing Organisation	Brabham BT11	Climax V8	1496	Jack Brabham
9	The Cooper Car Company	Cooper T77	Climax V8	1496	Bruce McLaren
10	The Cooper Car Company	Cooper T77	Climax V8	1496	Jochen Rindt
11	R.R.C. Walker	Brabham BT7	B.R.M. V8	1498	Jo Bonnier
12	R.R.C. Walker	Brabham BT11	Climax V8	1496	Jo Siffert
14	D.W. Racing Enterprises	Brabham BT11	Climax V8	1496	Bob Anderson
15	D.W. Racing Enterprises	Lotus 33 (chassis R8)	Climax V8	1496	Paul Hawkins
16	Reg Parnell	Lotus 25 (chassis R3)	B.R.M. V8	1498	Richard Attwood
18	John Willment Automobiles	Brabham BT11	B.R.M. V8	1498	Frank Gardner
19	Gerard Racing	Cooper T60	Climax V8	1496	John Taylor
20	Gerard Racing	Cooper T71	Ford 4-cyl	1500	John Rhodes
21	Sports Motors Manchester	Brabham BT14	Ford 4-cyl	1500	Rodney Bloor
22	Robert Ashcroft Racing	Brabham BT14	Ford 4-cyl	1500	John Cardwell

"Jim Clark and Dan Gurney, prevented from taking part in the Monaco Grand Prix by a rule which does not permit an Indy driver to compete in a race within 24 hours of the '500', will be replaced by Pedro Rodriguez and Denis Hulme in the Lotus and Brabham teams, respectively. Clark had been hoping to compete in both races, and Ford were going to charter a jet plane to take him from Nice direct to Indianapolis."

Three Wins For Jimmy

Practice day at Goodwood on Easter Saturday was blessed with mixed weather so that neither times nor starting-grid positions gave a fair indication of the likely outcome of the race itself. The Formula One cars had two periods of practice, the first one dry and the second wet, meaning that several drivers were caught out after reserving their strongest effort for the afternoon session. That aside, the chief interest lay in Jim Clark's new four-valve Coventry-Climax V8 engine, his Lotus 33 chassis R10 also being fitted with new Dunlop R7 tyres for the first time. A 13-inch Formula One version of the new tyre seen testing at the Le Mans the previous weekend, the R7 had by this time been adopted by most of the top drivers although Jack Brabham and Dan Gurney remained with Goodyear.

Timekeeping at Goodwood in the mid-1960s was accurate only to the nearest fifth of a second. This was quite frankly inadequate once lap times got down to around 1m 20sec. and the results of the practice sessions produced numerous dead-heats. Stewart was given fastest time, at 1m 19.8sec., followed by Hill and Clark at 1m 20.6sec., and Spence and Anderson also evenly matched on 1m 20.8sec., all of them thereby comfortably beating the existing lap record of 1m 21sec. which had been set by Graham Hill.

Still in practice, in the big sports-car class there was an important indication of things to come with Bruce McLaren recording 1m 19.4sec. in his McLaren M1A Oldsmobile-V8 with 4.4-litre engine – and this on a very crowded track. Clark was in trouble, however, with a slipping clutch in the works Lotus 30 although with a

4.7-litre Ford V8 engine using Tecalemit-Jackson fuel-injection he still managed to clock a solid time of 1m 21.2sec.. Much was also expected from Surtees in the 5.3 litre Chevrolet-Lola T70, but sadly this broke a connecting-rod on its first lap.

On race day itself, as a large crowd came streaming into the Sussex circuit expecting a happy holiday meeting, there was a freak storm which left some areas literally inches deep in hailstones and for a while it looked as though yet another meeting would have to be abandoned. Fortunately brilliant sunshine and clear blue skies soon dried everything out, although the icy wind remained fierce.

The first event, scheduled to start at 1:30pm, was the 10-lap Chichester Cup race for Formula 3 cars. Jonathan Williams in the Charles Lucas Brabham-Ford made a cracking start from the second row, but as he did so, a second hailstorm arrived to cover everything at the far side of the circuit. By the time the first cars arrived at the chicane at the end of the first lap, BARC officials were rushing out to the pit wall where, to the surprise of the drivers, the chequered flag was waved to stop the race as they crossed the line.

The storm quickly passed, however, and in a bright interval the cars were lined up again and a second start made. This time things were looking better, a good race developing between Roy Pike's immaculate black-and-white Chequered Flag Brabham-Ford and Piers Courage in a similar car, wearing the rather gaudy blue and red Charles Lucas livery. Courage seemed to be much quicker on the faster bends, and set fastest lap of the

Chichester Cup Race
Results

Pos.	Driver	No.	Car	Laps	Time/Reason	Speed
1st	Roy Pike	149	Brabham BT16	10	16 min 17.2 sec	88.42 mph
2nd	Piers Courage	151	Brabham BT10	10	16 min 17.8 sec	
3rd	Jonathan Williams	152	Brabham BT10	10	16 min 26.4 sec	
4th	Melvyn Long	158	Lotus 27	10	16 min 34.2 sec	
5th	Charles Crichton-Stuart	139	Brabham BT10	10	16 min 34.8 sec	
6th	John Fenning	138	Merlyn Mk.9	10	16 min 49.8 sec	
7th	Charles Lucas	153	Brabham BT10	10	17 min 10.4 sec	
8th	Richard Peel	141	Merlyn Mk.9	10	17 min 16.6 sec	
9th	Denis O'Sullivan	150	Brabham BT10	10	17 min 24.4 sec	
10th	Malcolm Payne	159	Lotus 31	10	17 min 29.8 sec	
11th	Robert Lamplough	156	Lotus 27	10	17 min 44.8 sec	
12th	Derek Bell	157	Lotus 31	10	17 min 45.2 sec	
13th	John Cardwell	147	Brabham BT15	9		
14th	Andrew Fletcher	142	Cooper T72	8		
15th	David Rees	146	Brabham BT9	7		
ret	Harry Stiller	148	Brabham BT9	1	Mechanical	
ret	Clive Baker	137	Cooper T76	0	Accident	
ret	Peter Gethin	154	Lotus 22	0	Accident	
dns	Tony Denton	136	Cooper T72			
dns	Warwick Banks	132	Cooper T76			
dna	Rollow Fielding	133	Cooper T76			
dna	Jacque Bernusset	134	Cooper T76			
dna	Mike Knight	135	Cooper T76			
dna	Leslie Roberts	140	Brabham BT15			
dna	Kurt Ahrens	143	Brabham BT10			
dna	Roger Mac	144	Brabham BT16			
Pole Position		149	Roy Pike		1 min 28.8 sec	
Fastest Lap		151	Piers Courage		1 min 33.0 sec (92.9 mph)	

Left
Sunshine after the storm. Jimmy proudly displays the St. Mary's Trophy for the 5 lap 'TV' shortened race.

race, but Pike held him off for most of the time despite Courage briefly taking the lead on a couple of occasions. By the end of the 10 laps Pike had drawn out a small lead resulting in a Brabham 1-2-3 with Williams in the number two car and Charles Lucas himself in third. Melvyn Long driving a Lotus 27 was in fourth, the best of a rather poor showing for the marque, with Payne, Lamplough and Bell coming well down the results in tenth, eleventh and twelfth respectively. Peter Gethin, who had qualified the other Charles Lucas car, a Lotus 22 in an excellent 6th position, had also made a poor start, getting tangled up on the first corner with Clive Baker's Cooper which had started 12th. Both had retired on the spot.

Saloon Cars Delayed And Then Cut

With all the problems incurred during the Formula 3 fixture, and a further delay while wreckage was cleared from the track, the start of next race for saloon cars was already running late even before another flurry of hail and snow arrived to cover the track.

The grid was in place, but clearly racing would be impossible until conditions improved. When they did an announcement was made that the event would be cut from 10 to just five laps – not because of safety concerns, but rather to serve the great god Television who had paid to televise the Formula 1 race and needed the lost time to be made up. The fact that a large crowd had also paid – to see 10 laps of saloon-car racing – seemed unfortunately to cut little ice with the BARC.

With all this going on outside, Bob Dance recalls sheltering in the car with Jimmy Clark, "*chatting about this, that and the other, when suddenly they were trying to get the race started and I remember Jimmy saying, "if you don't get out soon you'll be coming racing with me." I didn't see that as a problem though: all the mechanics used to live for the chance to go round the circuit with any of the drivers.*"

Eventually the truncated, five-lap sprint got underway, effectively four races in one, the contestants being Ford Mustang in one of them, Lotus-Cortinas in another, and then Minis making up the last two depending on whether they were 1300cc or 1.0-litre cars. With two warm-up laps having allowed the drivers to get the feel for the new conditions, but putting the start time back by 20 minutes, the front row looked sensibly representative of the different classes, with Salmon's navy blue Mustang on pole, Clark in the middle (having briefly tried E10 during practice with a Cosworth engine fitted, he was now in E9) and the Broadspeed Mini of John Handley on the outside.

On such a very wet track, the Mustangs had difficulty finding any sort of traction and were soon put in their place with the Cortinas of Clark and Sears (in E8) shooting into the lead. With Salmon now lying third, and Handley briefly holding fourth before being overhauled by Rhodes in another Mini, Clark and Sears set the seal on a superb 1-2 for Lotus, despite E8 looking somewhat the worse for wear after being rolled in practice. Responsibility for this lay with Jack Sears, although Bob Dance remembers, "*the car landed back on its wheels and when finally he got it back to the pits he spent several minutes apologising profusely to Bob Sparshott who was looking after his car that weekend.*"

St. Mary's Trophy Race
Saloon Car Race
Results

Pos.	Driver	No.	Car	Laps	Time/Reason	Speed
1st	Jim Clark	106	Lotus-Cortina	5	9 min 01.0 sec	79.85 mph
2nd	Jack Sears	107	Lotus-Cortina	5	9 min 12.0 sec	
dsq	Mike Salmon	104	Ford Mustang	5	9 min 23.6 sec	
3rd	Roy Pierpoint	103	Ford Mustang	5	9 min 25.6 sec	
4th	Frank Gardner	105	Lotus-Cortina	5	9 min 26.6 sec	
5th	John Handley	121	Morris Mini-Cooper S	5	9 min 27.8 sec	
6th	Andrew Hedges	118	Austin Mini-Cooper S	5	9 min 32.6 sec	
7th	Gawaine Baillie	102	Ford Mustang	5	9 min 32.8 sec	
8th	Tony Lanfranchi	119	Morris Mini-Cooper S	5	9 min 33.8 sec	
9th	André Baldet	109	Lotus-Cortina	5	9 min 38.0 sec	
10th	John Cannadine	116	Austin Mini-Cooper S	5	9 min 43.6 sec	
11th	Tom Fletcher	108	Lotus-Cortina	5	9 min 47.6 sec	
12th	Mike Campbell-Cole	128	Austin Mini-Cooper S 970	5	9 min 57.0 sec	
13th	Tony Rutt	124	Morris Mini-Cooper S	5	9 min 58.8 sec	
14th	David Wansborough	114	Austin Mini-Cooper S	5	10 min 12.4 sec	
15th	Paul Layzell	117	Austin Mini-Cooper S	5	10 min 14.8 sec	
16th	John Rhodes	113	Austin Mini-Cooper	5	10 min 19.8 sec	1 min penalty
17th	Jacquie Bond-Smith	111	Lotus-Cortina	5	10 min 22.2 sec	
18th	John Anstead	131	Fiat Abarth 1000 TC	5	10 min 38.6 sec	
19th	Anita Taylor	127	Austin Mini-Cooper S 970	5	11 min 10.4 sec	
dnf	Peter Pilsworth	115	Austin Mini-Cooper S	2		
dnf	Graham Burrows	123	Morris Mini-Cooper S	2		
dnf	Alan Hutcheson	101	Ford Galaxie	1	Wipers	
dnf	John Terry	122	Austin Mini-Cooper S	0	Accident	
dnf	Warwick Banks	126	Austin Mini-Cooper S 970	0	Accident	
dns	Bruce McLaren	112	Isuzu Bellett	0	Engine	
Pole Position		104	Mike Salmon		1 min 45.0 sec	
Fastest Lap		106	Jim Clark		1 min 46.0 sec (81.51 mph)	
Class Winners			Salmon, Clark, Handley, Campbell-Cole			

Opposite
Jim Clark won what would turn out to be the last Formula One race on the sweeping Goodwood circuit. His joint lap record (with Stewart) at 107.46mph. would stand for all time.

Team Lotus have built a further Type 38 to replace the car lost at Trenton, when it was shunted by Roger McCluskey. Another 38 was written off before the qualifying trials when hit in the pits by another car.

Clearly well-placed to make the most of the wet conditions, John Rhodes in the works Mini Cooper S had also trounced the Mustangs but was later penalised one minute by the BARC which alleged he had jumped the start. Given that it was only going to be a 9-minute race anyway, such a penalty meant he needn't have bothered being there in the first place and the class win therefore went to John Handley's 1275cc Broadspeed run car. That said, Rhodes was seemingly enjoying himself out on the track, and he certainly gave the crowd an impressive display of car control in some very testing conditions.

A far less fortunate hand was dealt to Alan Hutcheson who had made a vain attempt to drive the big Galaxie without wipers before finally turning in. (If nothing else his experience makes one inclined to respect Jack Sears all the more; he had, after all, used just such a car to win several races the previous year and Hutcheson had yet to achieve a decent result this year.)

The day also ended badly for Mike Salmon when, in post-race scrutineering, his Mustang was excluded after being found to be running with a non-homologated rear axle ratio. That made Pierpoint the big-class winner – deservedly so as he was in the process of overhauling Salmon at the very moment the flag fell on the two Lotuses – while Don Moore's entry driven by Mike Campbell-Cole took the smaller engine class. (As a footnote to this: In July the RAC announced that Salmon's infringement was less serious than at first thought and that the driver would be re-instated in the results, and his points returned on payment of a monetary fine.)

No World Champion But A Fine Race

Sadly the main event of the day, the 42-lap International Trophy, had to be run without the reigning Formula 1 World Champion taking part, Enzo Ferrari's continuing refusal to take British non-championship races seriously meaning that John Surtees was present only as a spectator.

There were other problems too: as the cars went out on their warm-up lap the works Lotus 33 driven by Mike Spence experienced a malfunction in its metering system, flooding neat petrol into the eight cylinders of the flat-crank Coventry-Climax engine so that he was forced to join Frank Gardner's Willment Brabham-BRM V8 as a non-starter. Another Type 33, Paul Hawkins' bright-green Dickie Stoop car fared little better, retiring almost as soon as the race started with a massive oil leak brought on by a defective scavenge pump.

With those two out of the race, Hill drove his BRM into the lead ahead of Clark's Lotus with Gurney's third-row Brabham charging into third place and as the field of 16 cars swept round Madgewick Corner. For the first five laps the race settled down, with Hill, Clark and Gurney out in front followed closely by Stewart's BRM and Jack Brabham in fifth place but dropping back. Bruce McLaren in the Cooper was just managing to hold off Bonnier's older Brabham BT7, and scrapping behind them came Rindt (Cooper T77), Attwood in the Parnell Lotus 25 (R3), and Siffert and Anderson in a pair of Brabhams. Following at a distance came John Taylor (Cooper) and three Formula 2 cars fitted with Twin-cam Lotus-Ford engines, with Cardwell comfortably leading Rhodes and Bloor.

Above
The bad weather did nothing to deter Jimmy. He won all three races he entered, even the Lavant Cup in the much maligned Type 30.

Sunday Mirror International Trophy Race
Grid

			Pole Position

	Jim Clark	Graham Hill	Jackie Stewart
	Lotus-Climax	B.R.M.	B.R.M.
	1 min 20.6 sec	1 min 20.6 sec	1 min 19.8 sec

Bob Anderson	Mike Spence
Brabham-Climax	Lotus-Climax
1 min 20.8 sec	1 min 20.8 sec

Dan Gurney	Bruce McLaren	Jack Brabham
Brabham-Climax	Cooper-Climax	Brabham-Climax
1 min 21.4 sec	1 min 21.4 sec	1 min 21.0 sec

Jo Bonnier	Frank Gardner
Brabham-Climax	Brabham-B.R.M.
1 min 22.0 sec	1 min 22.0 sec

Jochen Rindt	Richard Attwood	Jo Siffert
Cooper-Climax	Lotus-Climax	Brabham-B.R.M.
1 min 24.2 sec	1 min 23.0 sec	1 min 22.4 sec

Rodney Bloor	John Taylor
Brabham-Ford	Cooper-Climax
1 min 29.2 sec	1 min 26.2 sec

Paul Hawkins	John Rhodes	John Cardwell
Lotus-Climax	Cooper-Ford	Brabham-Ford
1 min 43.2 sec	1 min 40.6 sec	1 min 40.4 sec

"Development of the new Lotus Three-7, announced at the Racing Car Show, has been temporarily suspended. The car has not been put into production because increased orders for the racing Elan S2 and Lotus-Cortina have left insufficient development capacity to complete the final testing and specification of the car in time for this season."

On lap six Clark managed to get by Hill and began to pull out a lead, the sound of the new 32-valve Climax engine, with its short exhaust pipes and megaphone ends, thrilling bystanders on its way to 10,000rpm. Thereafter the Scotsman never looked back, effectively unchallenged in the wind and sun, the tread pattern on his new R7 Dunlop tyres providing excellent drainage and proving equally good in the wet and dry.

His Lotus was clearly handling better than Hill's BRM too, and behind them Gurney – running Goodyear rain tyres in anticipation of another downpour – was using a lot of opposite lock as he fought to catch up. Stewart in the second works BRM looked secure in fourth, but an unhappy-looking Jack Brabham was definitely dropping further and further back as the race progressed.

With such a strong performance from the leaders the tail-enders were soon lapped, one of them (Cardwell) foolishly lifting off and slowing in the middle of Madgewick when he saw Gurney coming up to overtake. The move upset the Californian's calculations considerably, and caused him to shake an angry fist as he went by. Bob Anderson for his part got the better of Rindt, Siffert and Attwood, but then overdid it by piling through the chicane wooden fence and continuing on his way with a length of wood jammed into his front suspension. Stopping to remove it, he was promptly disqualified for taking a short cut, Rindt being later disqualified for doing much the same thing.

Just after half-distance Hill's BRM ran into troubles of its own, showing signs of losing power with something going awry inside and the plugs suffering as a result.

Gurney got past, and then Stewart too before attention switched to Siffert. Very much in the Goodwood groove, he was closing on his team mate Bonnier but then he too fell victim to the chicane, catching a front wheel on the wall on one side before being bounced head-on into the opposite one. His Brabham-BRM bent nearly double, he was lucky to escape with only very minor injuries

All the while the immaculate and faultless Clark was racing on to victory, now followed by Gurney, Stewart and Hill until lap 38 that was, when Stewart came to rest out with another engine failure just before Gurney too dropped out with his oil pressure all but gone. Hill, unbelievably, was now back in second place despite a very sick-sounding BRM, with Brabham third having lapped everyone else in the field – even fourth-placed Bruce McLaren in the works Cooper.

Having chalked up a highly significant win for the new Coventry Climax engine – it was the unit's very first race – Clark was himself brought to rest on his slowing down lap by a flat front tyre, and had to be collected and taken back to receive the winner's laurels.

Another Four-in-One
The fourth event of the day was the Sussex Trophy for GT cars, another four races in one, with the race itself dominated by Roger Mac in the Chequered Flag Shelby American Cobra until a spin at the chicane let Peter Lumsden into the lead with his lightweight E-type Jaguar. Mac caught him again soon afterwards, Lumsden taking his own spin at Fordwater, and went on to win despite, rather sensibly, deciding to run with both hood and sidescreens in place. Third and fourth

Sunday Mirror International Trophy Race
Results

Pos.	Driver	No.	Car	Laps	Time/Reason	Speed
1st	Jim Clark	5	Lotus 33	42	57 min 33.8 sec	105.07 mph
2nd	Graham Hill	3	B.R.M. P261	42	57 min 58.0 sec	
3rd	Jack Brabham	8	Brabham BT11	42	58 min 24.6 sec	
4th	Bruce McLaren	9	Cooper T77	41		
5th	Jo Bonnier	11	Brabham BT7	41		
6th	Richard Attwood	16	Lotus 25	41		
7th	John Taylor	19	Cooper T60	40		
8th	John Rhodes	20	Cooper T71	39		
9th	Dan Gurney	7	Brabham BT11	37		
10th	Jackie Stewart	4	B.R.M. P261	37		
11th	John Cardwell	22	Brabham BT14	37		
12th	Rodney Bloor	21	Brabham BT14	37		
dsq	Jochen Rindt	10	Cooper T77	30	Missed chicane	
ret	Jo Siffert	12	Brabham BT11	28	Crash	
dsq	Bob Anderson	14	Brabham BTT11	24	Missed chicane	
ret	Paul Hawkns	15	Lotus 33	1	Oil leak	
ns	Mike Spence	6	Lotus 33	0	Metering Unit	
ns	Frank Gardner	18	Brabham BT11	0		
Pole Position		4	Jackie Stewart		1 min 19.8 sec	
Fastest Lap (record)		5 & 4	Clark & Stewart		1 min 20.4 sec	107.46 mph

Left
Waiting on the grid
Jimmy looks concerned.
It was unusual to see
him racing an open car
without a peak on his
helmet, especially in
such difficult conditions.

Above
Looking somewhat
happier, Jimmy collects
the Sunday Mirror
Trophy for a fine
performance.

were the Ferrari GTO pair of Peter Sutcliffe and Mike Salmon, followed closely by the Jaguar E-Types of Lumsden and Wansborough.

Having qualified tenth on the grid, finishing seventh and on the same lap as the leaders was the very quick class winning Elan 26R of Lotus Components employee Ray Parsons. Although not a full 'works' car, with Colin Chapman's blessing the Elan was entered under the Team Lotus banner to help Ray obtain race entries and was usually amongst the fastest of the Elans entered.

Further back the Porsche 914 of Mike de Udy had been going well until he too spun and hit the bank at Woodcote, bending the back of the car badly. Roy Salvadori in another Cobra had fared little better, having been entered by Ford Advanced Vehicles of Slough only to have a radiator hose burst on the line thus preventing him joining the race until the fourth lap. In a bit of a last-minute swap 'Gentleman Jack' Sears drove the Willment Cobra Coupé, which Bob Bondurant had tried in practice but declined to drive, Jack in turn having declined the offer of the Willment Elva-BMW which he had used in practice.

With the bad weather that had been causing trouble all day just about holding off, the final race of the day, the Lavant Cup, was a three class affair for sports cars and

once again Jim Clark in a works Lotus ran away with the event. Driving the much maligned Type 30 with Ford V8 power, he was chased home with seemingly little chance of victory by Bruce McLaren in his Oldsmobile-powered car. Clark finished 20 seconds ahead of McLaren, with the Lola-Ford of David Hobbs a further minute down. "*The problem was we had a Ford engine which was a smaller capacity engine than the Chevy (289cu in. to 327cu in.) and we were simply lacking in power. This applied the whole year really and we just wished we had been able to use the Chevy in the first place.*" was how David saw the sitaution.

Surtees in the other Lola was also out of contention when the Ford V8 that the works team brought in as a replacement for his broken Chevrolet unit refused to run properly and he didn't even make the start. Salvadori in the Ford Advanced Vehicles entered Cooper-Cobra didn't fare much better, he only got as far as the start line before the gearbox on his car expired.

With Clark taking the fastest lap in this race as well as in the other two races he had won, the weekend turned into a Team Lotus benefit meeting. Unbeknown to the crowds as they left, sadly this would be the last ever Formula 1 race at Goodwood and Jimmy's equal fastest lap time in the main event would stand as the all time Goodwood lap record.

Above
A rather cold and damp looking Jackie Stewart asks Jack Sears for his opinion on the weather.

Sussex Trophy
Grand Touring Car Race
Results

Position	Driver	No.	Car	Laps	Time/Reason	Speed
1st	Roger Mac	65	Shelby Cobra	15	22 min 34.2 sec	95.70 mph
2nd	Jack Sears	61	Shelby Cobra Coupé	15	22 min 40.0 sec	
3rd	Peter Sutcliffe	67	Ferrari 250 GTO	15	23 min 04.8 sec	
4th	Mike Salmon	68	Ferrari 250 GTO	15	23 min 12.0 sec	
5th	Peter Lumsden	71	Jaguar E-type	15	23 min 13.4 sec	
6th	David Wansborough	70	Jaguar E-type	15	23 min 16.2 sec	
7th	Ray Parsons	76	Lotus Elan	15	23 min 30.2 sec	
8th	Adrian Chambers	77	Lotus Elan	15	23 min 50.0 sec	
9th	Tony Hegbourne	83	Alfa-Romeo Giulia TZ	15	23 min 54.4 sec	
10th	Boley Pittard	82	Alfa-Romeo Giulia TZ	15	24 min 06.4 sec	
11th	John Lepp	81	Lotus Elan	14		
12th	Neil Dangerfield	63	Shelby Cobra	14		
13th	John Mackay	84	Lotus Eleven GT	14		
14th	J.B.Moore	89	Austin Healey Sprite	14		
15th	John Wingfield	75	TVR Grantura	14		
nc	Harry Digby	64	Shelby Cobra	12		
nc	Roy Salvadori	62	Shelby Cobra	11	Started late	
nc	A.Gough	85	Lotus Eleven GT	10		
nc	John Dickinson	86	Lotus Eleven GT	10		
dnf	Mike de Udy	72	Porsche 904 GTS	10	Accident	
dnf	Mike Beckwith	78	Lotus Elan	1		

Pole Position		68	Mike Salmon	
Fastest Lap		71	Peter Lumsden	1 min 28.2 sec (97.96 mph)
Class Winners			Mac, Wingfield, Parsons, Mackay	

Left
Third trophy of the day for Clark was the Lavant Cup. Once he had beaten Pole sitter Bruce McLaren off the line Jimmy led all the way to the flag.

Lavant Cup
Sports Racing Cars
Results

Position	Driver	No.	Car	Laps	Time/Reason	Speed
1st	Jim Clark	33	Lotus 30	21	29 min 14.0 sec	103.44 mph
2nd	Bruce McLaren	35	McLaren M1A	21	29 min 34.0 sec	
3rd	David Hobbs	32	Lola T70	21	30 min 38.0 sec	
4th	Hugh Dibley	38	Lola T70	20		
5th	Denis Hulme	41	Brabham BT8	20		
6th	Tommy Hitchcock	42	Brabham BT8	20		
7th	John Hine	52	Lotus 23	19		
8th	Robin Widdows	59	Lotus 23	18		
9th	Jeremy Bouckley	48	Merlyn	17		
10th	Robert Lamplough	56	Lotus 23	17		
11th	Jim Morley	54	Lotus 23	16		
dnf	Roger Nathan	38	Brabham BT8			
dnf	John Coundley	36	McLaren-Elva M1A			
dnf	Tony Lanfranchi	37	Atilla-Chevrolet Mk.3			
dnf	Roy Salvadori	40	Cooper-Cobra	0	Gearbox	
dns	John Surtees	31	Lola T70	0	Engine in practice	
Pole Position		35	Bruce McLaren		1 min 19.4 sec	
Fastest Lap		33	Jim Clark		1 min 20.8 sec (106.93 mph)	
Class Winners			Clark, Hulme, Hine			

"Jim Clark recently gained his pilots (air) licence.
Graham Hill is thinking of taking to the air as well."

Opposite & above
Jimmy, Geoff Murdoch (Competitions Manager for ESSO) and Jim Endruweit discuss Peter Darley's idea for an impromptu photo shoot with a cardboard tiger that he had noticed tied to a fence. Photographer Max LeGrand helped with holding the tiger and when Jimmy eventually agreed to be part of the shoot they managed to get some hilarious shots that hung on the walls of the ESSO hospitality wagon for a couple of years.

Chapter Six
Oulton Park
1st May

OFFICIAL PROGRAMME 2/6

R.A.C. INTERNATIONAL
TOURIST TROPHY RACE
WITH THE SENIOR SERVICE TROPHY

OULTON PARK CHESHIRE
Saturday 1 May 1965

Autocar
FIRST AWAY AND ALWAYS AHEAD - FRIDAY 1s.6d.

"DENNY HULME'S BRABHAM WINS DISPUTED T.T."

David Hobbs ran away with the second part of the T.T. race and was catching Hulme on overall time, but the timekeepers seemed to lose track of the overall positions and at one point advised Hobbs' pit that he was in the lead with the result that they slowed him down. When they realised that he still had not caught the Brabham they signalled him to speed up, but it was too late to catch Hulme. A protest was made but rejected by the stewards....

Above right
For 1965 ESSO were contracted to supply all fuel and lubricants to Team Lotus. Even though they had other teams to service, with only two races on the schedule the supply crew had a pretty easy weekend.

Timetable

Event: R.A.C. International Tourist Trophy Race
Date: Saturday 1st May 1965
Location: Oulton Park
Circuit Length: 2.761 miles

Time	Race	Laps	Distance	
12:00 pm	Tourist Trophy (Part I)	69 (2 hours)	190.51 miles	
3:30 pm	Tourist Trophy (Part II)	70 (2 hours)	193.27 miles	

Oulton Park – Existing Lap Records

Formula 1	Jim Clark	Lotus 25-Climax	1m 39.2 sec.	100.20 mph.
Formula 2	G.Hill & J.Rindt	Brabham BT16	1m 41.4 sec.	98.02 mph.
Formula 3	Roy Pike	Brabham-Cosworth	1m 46.2 sec.	93.59 mph.
Sportscars over 2000cc	Roy Salvadori	Cooper-Monaco	1m 43.8 sec.	95.76 mph.
Saloon Cars over 2000cc	Dan Gurney	Ford Galaxie	1m 53.2 sec.	87.80 mph.
Saloon Cars 1301cc to 2000cc	Jim Clark	Lotus-Cortina	1m 57.0 sec.	84.95 mph.
GT Cars up to 2500cc	Jim Clark	Lotus Elan	1m 52.8 sec.	88.12 mph.
GT Cars 2500cc to 3000cc	Innes Ireland	Ferrari 250	1m 53.0 sec.	87.96 mph.

Tourist Trophy Race
Entry List

No.	Entrant	Car	Engine	C.C.	Driver
1	Team Surtees Ltd.	Lola T70	Oldsmobile V8	5300	John Surtees
2	Harold Young Ltd.	Lola T70	Ford V8	4762	David Hobbs
3	H.P.K. Dibley	Lola T70	Chevrolet V8	5960	Hugh Dibley
4	Team Lotus	Lotus 30	Ford V8	5300	Jim Clark
5*	J.C.B. Research Ltd.	Lotus 30	Ford V8	4727	Trevor Taylor (dna)
6	David Prophet Racing	Lotus 30	Ford V8	4727	David Prophet
7	Team Chamaco-Collect	Lotus 30	Ford V8	4727	Victor Wilson
8	Chris Williams Ltd.	Lotus-Brabham	B.M.W. 4-cyl	1991	Chris Williams
9	Bruce McLaren Motor Racing Ltd.	McLaren M1A	Oldsmobile V8	4500	Bruce McLaren
10	Bruce McLaren Motor Racing Ltd.	Elva Mk.8	B.M.W. 4-cyl	1991	Chris Amon
11	John Coundley Racing	McLaren-Elva M1A	Oldsmobile V8	4450	John Coundley
12*	Maranello Concessionaries	Ferrari 365 P2	Ferrari V12	4400	Graham Hill (dna)
14	David Piper (Auto Racing) Ltd.	Ferrari 250 LM	Ferrari V12	3286	David Piper
15*	Roger Nathan Racing	Brabham BT8	Oldsmobile V8	4500	Roger Nathan (dns)
16	Sidney Taylor Racing	Brabham BT8	Coventry-Climax	2160	Denis Hulme
17	Celerity Inc.	Brabham BT8	Coventry-Climax	1942	Tommy Hitchcock
18*	Mill Garages (Sunderland) Ltd.	Attila Mk.7	Chevrolet V8	5700	Julian Sutton (dna)
19	Weybridge Engineering Co. Ltd.	Attila Mk.3	Ford V8	4727	Tony Lanfranchi
20*	Ford Advanced Vehicles Ltd.	Cooper-Cobra	Ford V8	4728	Roy Salvadori (dna)
21	Alan Mann Racing Ltd.	Shelby Cobra	Ford V8	4727	Sir John Whitmore
22	Alan Mann Racing Ltd.	Shelby Cobra Coupé	Ford V8	4727	Jack Sears
23	John Willment Automobiles	Shelby Cobra Coupé	Ford V8	4727	Frank Gardner
24	Chequered Flag Ltd.	Shelby Cobra	Ford V8	4727	Roger Mac
25	Radford Racing	Shelby Cobra	Ford V8	4727	Allen Grant
26	Radford Racing	Shelby Cobra	Ford V8	4727	Neil Dangerfield
27	Dawnay Racing	Ferrari 250 GTO	Ferrari V12	2953	Mike Salmon
28	P.Sutcliffe	Ferrari 250 GTO	Ferrari V12	2953	Peter Sutcliffe
30	D.Protheroe Ltd.	Jaguar E-type	Jaguar 6-cyl	3785	David Wansbrough
31	Red Rose Motors	Jaguar E-type	Jaguar 6-cyl	3785	Richard Bond

Left
With only one car to run and two races the TT weekend wasn't as pressurised as usual. Colin jokes with Jimmy and tempts Sally Stokes with something that looks like bread. Sally doesn't look impressed.

Early Promise Left Unfulfilled

As befits such an historic and longstanding fixture, the RAC International Tourist Trophy Race started out full of promise but sadly lost much of its interest for 1965 when five of the big sports racers withdrew from the event. From this point of view things deteriorated still further in the first heat when the big banger class demonstrated appalling unreliability: and finally the race wound up as a complete farce when – at the finish of the second heat – no one seemed quite sure whether it was Denis Hulme or David Hobbs who was the outright winner. Certainly, as a race of hitherto international status and with a considerable history, most of those who witnessed the days events felt it had betrayed its fine reputation.

The race itself was split into two parts, each of two hours' duration, the clear expectation being that the big sports-racing cars would win comfortably. Unfortunately they quickly ran into trouble and Hulme, in Sid Taylor's 2.2-litre Brabham-Climax – having covered a total of 138 laps at an average speed of 94.07mph – was finally declared the winner of the race. He was closely followed by David Hobbs in a Lola-Ford V8, who covered 137 laps over the two parts, and behind him David Piper (Ferrari 275 LM, 133 laps), Sir John Whitmore (Shelby Cobra, 130 laps), Peter Sutcliffe (Ferrari GTO, 130 laps) and American Allen Grant in another Shelby Cobra with a tally of 128 laps.

On paper then the entry had looked promising, although it has to be said that there was a distinct lack of foreign opposition in the largely domestic field. The entry list was split into two classes with some 28 listed under 'Sports Cars And Prototypes With Engine Capacity Over 1600cc' (see page 108 for more details) and the remaining cars in the GT section for engines over 2 litres, with this first part of the race also making up a qualifying round of the British GT Championship. With Shelby Cobras enjoying an almost overwhelming dominance in this section, Carroll Shelby was obviously content to rely on the privateers rather than feeling the need to field any 'works' entries.

These included a pair of cars entered by Alan Mann, a coupé for Jack Sears and an open version for Sir John Whitmore. (The coupé was the car previously used by Shelby at Sebring while the open car was a 1964 model used by Tommy Atkins and driven by Roy Salvadori in its first season.) Willment entered another coupé, a red and white example for Frank Gardner, which had been bodied by themselves, while Chequered Flag fielded their usual white and black car driven by Roger Mac. Radford Racing brought along another two cars for Grant and Chris McLaren, whilst Mike Salmon and Peter Sutcliffe entered a pair of Ferrari GTOs. The field being completed by the Jaguar E-types of David Wansborough and Richard Bond. Wansborough was further to enliven the proceedings later in the day by depositing his car into the lake at Cascades although it seemed none the worse for wear by the time he made it onto the grid at noon on Saturday.

The Race

Race day turned out to be as fine and warm as the practice sessions on Friday and the picturesque Oulton Park circuit was looking its best as the 37,000 strong crowd poured into the stands. Such a strong turnout

Tourist Trophy Race
Chassis list – Class 1

Taken in order of racing numbers the following notes for the cars in the sports/racing car section of the 1965 Tourist Trophy at Oulton Park were taken in period:

No 1. Lola 70 chassis # 1, John Surtees. Fitted with a Traco-modified Chevrolet 5.4-litre V8 engine as used at Silverstone and Goodwood. During unofficial practice on Thursday Surtees recorded a very quick lap of around 1min 35.0sec. Despite some minor braking problems Surtees was fastest in both official sessions on Friday with 1min 38.0sec. and 1min 36.6sec..

No 2. Lola 70 chassis #3, David Hobbs. Fitted with high performance Ford 4.7-litre V8 engine built by Lola at Slough. Power output was quoted at 385bhp at 7,000rpm. Hobbs was third fastest in first practice despite broken valve springs. With new springs fitted he was second fastest in the afternoon practice at 1min 39.6sec..

No 3. Lola 70 chassis #4, Hugh Dibley. 5.9-litre Chevrolet V8 engine. This was the first Lola chassis built by Abbey Panels, chassis' # 1, 2 and 3 having been built at the Lola works. In unofficial practice on Thursday the car suffered damage to the rear of the monocoque and was taken back to London for stiffening steel panels to be incorporated. With the car arriving back too late for practice, Dibley qualified in David Hobbs' car and started the race in own car at the rear of the grid.

No 4. Lotus 30/S2/1, Jim Clark. Fitted with a 5.3 litre Ford V8 engine. This engine wasn't the latest 5.3-litre from Shelby, but had modifications to shorten the stroke of the original 4.7-litre unit by welding the crankshaft. Clark lapped at 1min 42.2sec. in the morning session, then broke a connecting rod and the car was taken away to have a standard 4.7-litre unit fitted. Clark drove Victor Wilson's Lotus 30 in the afternoon session lapping in 1min 47.2sec..

No 5. Lotus 30/S2/4, Trevor Taylor. This car entered by JCB Research was badly damaged when Peter Sadler suffered gear selection problems during unofficial practice and crashed. It could not be readied in time for the race.

No 6. Lotus 30/L/11, David Prophet. Fitted with 4.7-litre Ford V8 engine using Tecalemit-Jackson fuel injection and ZF gearbox. Prophet lapped in 1min 47.2sec. in morning and 1min 45.6sec. in afternoon session.

No 7. Lotus 30, Victor Wilson. Fitted with 4.7-litre Ford V8 engine. With the car not ready for the morning session Wilson finally lapped in a time of 1min 51.8sec. in the afternoon, Clark used the car to record 1min 47.2sec..

No 8. Lotus-Brabham BMW, Chris Williams. This highly individual car which appeared for first time this season fitted with a 2-litre BMW engine. Williams lapped in 1min 50.2sec. in the morning and 1min 45.0sec. in the afternoon.

No 9. McLaren M1A-Oldsmobile, Bruce McLaren. Fitted with Traco-tuned 375 bhp Oldsmobile 4.5-litre V8 and Ferguson automatic transmission, the works car was using Firestone tyres. After doing 1min 39.4sec. in the morning session an oil seal in the experimental automatic boxed failed. This was changed but on the first lap in the afternoon the engine broke, so the car was taken away for a spare to be fitted.

No 10. Elva-B.M.W., Chris Amon. Entered by Bruce McLaren Motor Racing, this car was fitted with a 2-litre B.M.W. engine. Unhappy with the handling whilst using Firestone tyres in the morning session, Amon lapped in 1min 49.6sec.. In the afternoon he reverted to Dunlop tyres and set a time of 1min 44.4sec..

No 11. McLaren-Elva M1A-Oldsmobile, John Coundley. An early Elva built production version of the McLaren M1A with 4.5-litre Traco Oldsmobile engine and Hewland gearbox. Lapped in 1min 50.6sec. in the morning and 1min 45.2sec. in the afternoon session.

Tourist Trophy Race
Chassis list – Class 1

No 12. Ferrari 365P2, Graham Hill. Intended to be an all new car with 4.4-litre single ohc engine, this car was not ready in time. The entry was withdrawn, although it was rumoured that Hill was offered another car by the organisers, the former World Champion would not race.

No 14. Ferrari 250LM, David Piper. David's usual green car with 3.3-litre engine. Not ready for morning session but timed at 1min 46.0sec. in the afternoon session.

No 15. Brabham BT8-Olsmobile, Roger Nathan.1964 Brabham-Climax car fitted with British tuned Oldsmobile 4.5-litre V8 engine, giving a claimed 425bhp. Recorded a time of 1min 46.6sec. in the morning session despite gear change problems. This was later traced to a cracked bell housing which was welded up. Nathan did a time of 1min 46.2sec. in the afternoon session but on race morning the clutch seized due to parts of the bell housing welding dropping into it. The car could not be readied in time for the first heat.

No 16. Brabham-Climax, Denis Hulme. Sid Taylor's immaculately prepared 2.2-litre Climax-engined Brabham BT8. Very fast in both practice sessions, recording 1min 42.2sec. in the morning and 1min 42.0sec. in the second practice session of the day.

No 17. Brabham BT8-Climax, Tommy Hitchcock. Fitted with 1,942cc four cylinder Coventry-Climax engine, Tommy's best lap in practice was an excellent 1min 43.0sec., set in the second session.

No 18. Attila-Chevrolet, Julian Sutton. Entry withdrawn.

No 19. Attila-Ford, Tony Lanfranchi, 4.7-litre V8 engine. Running on Goodyear tyres, Lanfranchi lapped at 1min 50.0sec. in the morning and 1min 46.6sec. in the afternoon.

No 20. Cooper-Cobra, Roy Salvadori. Entry withdrawn.

The Lotus Group of Companies
Delamare Road Cheshunt Hertfordshire
Telephone Waltham Cross 26181
Telegrams Lotuscars London

TO WHOM IT MAY CONCERN.   1st May, 1965.

This to confirm that the bearer of this letter, Peter Darley, of 3, Old Bath Road, Cheltenham, Glos., is engaged to take photographs of Team Lotus cars during the 1965 season. Any assistance given to him will be appreciated.

Rosemary Seers,
Press Officer,
Lotus Group

"The latest leather steering wheel cover comes from Tarantella, makers of Jim Clark driving gloves. Available in two colours (black or tan) and in two sizes, it laces on to the wheel and costs 27s 6d."

Above
It doesn't look like the Type 30 would have had too much trouble passing the surprise 'ride height test' imposed by the stewards at the TT.

Tourist Trophy Race
Grid

Pole Position

John Surtees Lola T70 1 min 36.6 sec	Bruce McLaren McLaren M1A 1 min 39.4 sec	David Hobbs Lola T70 1 min 39.6 sec
	Denis Hulme Brabham BT8 1 min 42.0 sec	Jim Clark Lotus 30 1 min 42.2 sec
Tommy Hitchcock Brabham BT8 1 min 43.0 sec	Chris Amon Elva Mk8 1 min 44.4 sec	Chris Williams Lotus-Brabham 1 min 45.0 sec
	John Coundley McLaren-Elva M1A 1 min 45.2 sec	David Prophet Lotus 30 1 min 45.6 sec
David Piper Ferrari 250 LM 1 min 46.0 sec	Roger Nathan Brabham BT8 1 min 46.2 sec	Jack Sears Shelby Cobra Coupé 1 min 46.6 sec
	Tony Lanfranchi Attila Mk3 1 min 46.6 sec	Roger Mac Shelby Cobra 1 min 47.4 sec
Mike Salmon Ferrari 250 GTO 1 min 48.8 sec	John Whitmore Shelby Cobra 1 min 48.2 sec	Peter Sutcliffe Ferrari 250 1 min 48.8 sec
	Frank Gardner Shelby Cobra Coupé 1 min 49.2 sec	Victor Wilson Lotus 30 1 min 51.8 sec
David Wansborough Jaguar E-type 1 min 52.0 sec	Allan Grant Shelby Cobra 1 min 52.0 sec	Neil Dangerfield Shelby Cobra 1 min 53.2 sec
	Hugh Dibley Lola T70 No Time	Richard Bond Jaguar E-type 1 min 53.0 sec

Above
By the time of the T.T. in May, the Lola T70 of John Surtees had extra ducting to the front brakes along with a rather more substantial looking roll-hoop.

Left
At the T.T. Jimmy was still using his crash helmet without a peak.

"Jim Clark's Indy Lotus had its exhaust pipes painted with bright yellow spray on Sperex VHT, for which the Edgware Racing Stables are the sole European distributors. The coating is also used on the McLaren Elva sports cars, amongst others."

suggests that the TT was more than able to hold its own against the 84th FA Cup Final which was being held on the same day at Wembley and which eventually saw Leeds United go down 2-1 to Liverpool.

After a surprise, last minute ground-clearance check by the scrutineers, the cars began filtering out on to the track for the first two hour heat with around 20 minutes to go. Most cars passed at the first attempt, but those which didn't were wheeled away and given a surreptitious lift by the mechanics to raise the cars on their springs before they could pass with ease. Faced with the aforementioned depleted entry, the scrutineers didn't argue with this solution to the problem – thus making the whole exercise look a bit pointless.

Part of the event's popularity, as a press report noted later, was that "*the sound of 24 sports and GT cars on the grid was something worth going a long way to hear…There was more sheer horsepower on display than the circuit had ever seen before [as] the deep hollow growl of the Cobras mingled with the scream of the Ferraris and the bark of the Climaxes caused the ground to vibrate in sympathy. As Graham Macbeth dropped the flag, the roar rose to a crescendo and the field roared off into Old Hall Corner.*"

John Surtees quickly took the lead from Bruce McLaren, with Jim Clark, David Hobbs and Denny Hulme following and behind them Tommy Hitchcock, David Piper, Chris Amon, Tony Lanfranchi and Mike Salmon in the leading GT car. Having already recieved a 2-lap penalty for a push start, Jack Sears brought up the rear in the Cobra Coupé, and having suffered brake failure on the warm-up

lap come in at the end of the first lap for the brakes to be checked.

The first sign of the sports cars' fragility came when Surtees surrendered the lead to McLaren and then stopped at the pits on the next lap to investigate what the team later reported as 'handling problems.' In fact his crew couldn't find anything wrong, so he returned to the fray only to come in again after 13 laps whereupon the crew began to dismantle the steering rack in the hope that they could discover and fix a problem which Surtees had traced to the steering. This of course put him out of the race, leaving McLaren and Clark dicing for the lead with Hobbs holding third place ahead of Hulme. The fight for fifth place between Amon and Piper was equally as hard, the little Elva proving to be much quicker through the corners although the Ferrari had it on the straights.

Having started from the back of the grid, Hugh Dibley was meanwhile moving like a rocket, his big, 6-litre Lola slicing through slower traffic with extraordinary ease so that after 15 minutes he was up to fifth, immediately behind Hulme. Sadly just few minutes later he too was limping into the pits, the car's rear end damaged by a wishbone breaking away from the chassis. The car could almost certainly have been repaired, but with Surtees already in the pits undergoing work and fully occupying the available mechanics Dibley's car was pushed to one side with the crew presumably mindful that it may later need to be raided for spare parts.

The next disaster among the big-bangers was Bruce McLaren's, the New Zealander losing the lead to Jim

"Jim Clark has joined forces with Motor Racing's Editor, Alan Brinton, to edit the 'Ford Book of Competition Motoring', to be published by Stanley Paul in September."

Clark when he he was forced to visit the pits with a recurrence of a transmission oil-seal failure that he had suffered in practice. His mechanics immediately began the long job of replacing the automatic's seal yet again, but rather than letting the team push the car out into the paddock the scrutineers insisted that if was to remain in the race, all the work had to be done in the pits. Besides displeasing the mechanics this ruling resulted in little more than the pit lane being liberally coated in copious amounts of transmission oil.

Clark and Hobbs were by this time running well clear of Hulme's Brabham and most of those who had prophesied a 2-litre victory were beginning to think it would soon come to pass. The American V8s seemed to be dropping like flies, and then after just 40 minutes Lanfranchi's Attila took a dive when the car coasted to a halt on the straight with a collapsed rear suspension. He took the blow philosophically – remarking that, "*it was too hot in there anyway*" – with Prophet's Lotus 30 the next into the pits where a fire in the engine bay was fortunately extinguished without further incident.

In the GT category Sir John Whitmore had meanwhile wrestled the lead from Mike Salmon's Ferrari with Gardner also managing to ease past in his Willment coupé. Also making up ground rapidly was Jack Sears, at least until he was given a 2-lap penalty after being push-started out of the pits. After 45 minutes' racing the lead changed again as Clark brought his Lotus in for a wheel change, a refuel and a brakepad check. While he was able to rejoin the race pretty rapidly he was soon back in the pits again after suffering 'a bit of a moment' when his rear suspension rearranged itself

as a consequence of a mechanic having forgotten to tighten one of the bolts. Clark, fortunately, had managed to gather it all together get back onto the track.

Surtees too made a further attempt to get back into the race at the half-way stage, but he stopped again shortly afterwards, retiring for good when the team could find no visible damage even though the front suspension seemed somehow to have gone badly out of alignment. With these big cars topping 150mph down the short straight driving a car with poor handling or steering was clearly a bad idea and indeed Mac had a dicey moment of his own when a rear wheel parted company with his Cobra. Fortunately it happened on the straight, and he managed to stop safely.

Back in the thick of it Hobbs was now comfortably clear of Hulme with Piper and Amon still battling fiercely behind them for third. In fifth place, and as such the lead GT driver, Whitmore was closely followed by Gardner and Salmon at least until the latter had a brake caliper fail on his GTO, forcing him into the escape road at Cascades. He too managed not to hit anything and immediately afterwards returned to the pits for repairs.

After 70 minutes Hobbs sadly surrendered the lead when the need for 15 gallons of fuel cost him nearly two minutes. It also lost him a full lap to Hulme, although he managed to hold on to second place when he returned to the fray. Clark finally rejoined the race shortly afterwards, following his own a 12 minute pit stop, proceeding as rapidly as ever and eventually posting the day's joint-fastest lap with John Surtees: 1m 39.4sec. at a speed of precisely 100mph. After

Above
Jack Sears and John Surtees discuss Jack's older, more 'pudding bowl' style of head protection.

Tourist Trophy Race
Results – Part I

Pos.	Driver	No.	Car	Laps	Time/Reason	Speed
1st	Denis Hulme	16	Brabham BT8	69	2 hr 01 min 17.8 sec	94.24 mph
2nd	David Hobbs	2	Lola T70	67	2 hr 00 min 17.6 sec	
3rd	John Coundley	11	McLaren-Elva M1A	67	2 hr 01 min 05.2 sec	
4th	David Piper	14	Ferrari 250 LM	67	2 hr 01 min 10.4 sec	
5th	Tommy Hitchcock	17	Brabham BT8	66		
6th	Peter Sutcliffe	28	Ferrari 250 GTO	65		
7th	Frank Gardner	23	Shelby Cobra Coupé	65		
8th	Sir John Whitmore	21	Shelby Cobra	65		
9th	Allen Grant	25	Shelby Cobra	64		
10th	Richard Bond	31	Jaguar E-type	63		
11th	Neil Dangerfield	26	Shelby Cobra	63		
12th	David Prophet	6	Lotus 30	62		
13th	David Wansborough	30	Jaguar E-type	62		
14th	Victor Wilson	7	Lotus 30	62		
15th	Jack Sears	22	Shelby Cobra Coupé	61		
16th	Jim Clark	4	Lotus 30	61		
dnf	Chris Amon	10	Elva Mk.8	54	Overhaeting	
dnf	Chris Williams	8	Lotus-Brabham	53	Gearbox	
dnf	Mike Salmon	27	Ferrari 250 GTO	38	Brakes	
dnf	Roger Mac	24	Shelby Cobra	29	Lost Wheel	
dnf	Tony Lanfranchi	19	Attila Mk.3	19	Driveshaft	
dnf	Bruce McLaren	9	McLaren M1A	14	Gearbox	
dnf	John Surtees	1	Lola T70	13	Steering	
dnf	Hugh Dibley	3	Lola T70	12	Suspension	
Pole Position		1	John Surtees		1 min 36.6 sec (102.89 mph)	
Fastest Lap		1 & 4	Surtees & Clark		1 min 39.4 sec (100.00 mph)	
Class Winners			Hulme, Sutcliffe			

Hobbs long stop in the pits, his Lola began suffering from overheating problems, and was soon back in again to take on additional water. This was to cost him a further two minutes, thereby enabling Hulme to pull out an even more substantial lead with the Climax engine in his Brabham sounding as crisp as ever.

Someway further back John Coundley had meanwhile been quietly working his way up the field and immediately before the two hours were up managed to push past Piper's Ferrari to take third place. Amon, Piper's 'shadow', had by this time disappeared into the pits with overheating problems, the considered opinion on the day being the problem was largely due to his proximity over an extended period to the Ferrari's rear end. His radiator had been topped up, but the Elva refused to fire up again leaving the mechanics with little choice but to strip the engine in an attempt to find the cause – and hope they could get him back out on the track for the second part of the race.

At 2pm the chequered flag was held out and, as luck would have it, Hobbs took it despite having slowed once again with his battery on fire. Denny Hulme had passed the line moments before the flag appeared, but the implications of this were not realised at the time. The effect was to present Hulme with a free lap after the two hours had elapsed, a lap which was to prove vital to David Hobbs in the second part of the race.

Unsurprisingly given everything which had happened, the one and a half hour interval between the two heats was characterised by some pretty feverish work in the pits with engines being dismantled and hastily put

together again, and even some gear boxes being changed. Jim Clark's rear suspension was checked yet again, Bruce McLaren's crew put the automatic box back together, and Chris Amon's BMW engine was fitted with a new head gasket, while Chris Williams' crew installed a new gearbox in his Lotus-Brabham BMW. For only a very lucky few the 90 minutes were less frantic, just the routine chores of filling up with fuel or changing wheels and brake pads.

As the field lined up for the second heat there were, as a result, still a number of cars which were not yet ready so that Amon, Williams and Gardner actually joined the race only after it had started. Thereafter the second heat looked like it might be a repeat of the first with – of course – the big bangers out in front. Accordingly, at the drop of the flag, Coundley took the lead followed by Piper, Hobbs, Hulme, Clark, Whitmore, Hitchcock and McLaren. Hobbs soon got his Lola past Piper's Ferrari but struggled to get past Coundley who (he felt) needlessly held him up for several laps.

The crowd were treated to what appeared to be a splendid dice for the lead, however, and the Lola's problems also allowed Clark and McLaren to work their way up through the field and to close up on the leading duo. Hobbs eventually managed to pass Coundley and was soon followed by Clark and McLaren, the three running in close company for several laps with the Lola and McLaren looking far more stable than the Lotus which was kicking up clouds of dust as Clark slid wide on several corners. Eventually Clark and McLaren both pushed their way past Hobbs whereupon – as they were so far behind from the first heat – there was little point

Above
Peter Darley was asked to set up this picture for a Firestone promotion. Left to right. Jack Sears (Cobra Coupé), Jimmy with Victor Wilson's borrowed Type 30 (his works car was having a replacement engine fitted) and John Surtess alongside the Lola T70. The 'OP' of Dunlop on the sign behind had to be touched out on the final print.

Opposite
'Gentleman Jack' looking very dapper alongside the Alan Mann Shelby Daytona Coupé that, as a works car, had finished 2nd at Daytona in February.

in Hobbs trying to hold on to them thereby risking the chance of more overheating problems.

Unfortunately the race among these front runners very soon broke up completely when McLaren headed for his pit with what turned out to be incurable engine problems and shortly afterwards Coundley came clanking in with a broken drive shaft, his mechanics leaping onto McLaren's now-retired similar car and cannibalising it for a new shaft.

After half an hour's racing Hobbs spun at Lodge Corner although he managed to get going again without losing too much time which was good as – clearly – he needed to put as much road as possible between his car and Denny Hulme's. Now out front on his own, Clark's Lotus began jumping out of gear so that he too went for a spin, this time at Esso. Briefly he kept the lead, but then retired with gearbox failure leaving Hobbs with a good lead on Hulme, and behind them David Piper, Jack Sears (once again the leading GT car), Mike Salmon, John Whitmore and Peter Sutcliffe.

The interest therefore now lay in whether or not Hobbs could regain the two-lap lead with which Hulme had been credited in the first heat. His task looked possible but difficult, even though he was now lapping some five seconds quicker than Hulme. In the pits fierce calculations were being made, the timekeepers far from certainty about the true position and feeding the commentator contradictory information about both the overall leadership and the GT class positions. Initially they give the GT class lead to Sutcliffe but then several re-checks established that Whitmore was in the lead.

As 5.30pm came the chequered flag was held out, and once again it fell between Hulme and Hobbs. Hulme was immediately declared the winner but with little certainty and eventually it took several checks on the lap charts before the declaration was made official. The Hobbs team not unnaturally put in a protest, but after a consultation with the regulations the Stewards rejected their appeal on the basis that (even though the race was of four-hours duration) the number of laps completed was the real deciding factor. This farcical finish spoiled the race completely for everyone – by no means least all for David Hobbs and his team who, hoping to make up for the traumas of the other Lola T70s, badly wished to give the stylish car its first ever win.

All these years later David Hobbs still feels he won the 1965 Tourist Trophy fair and square. "*The biggest disappointment for me that year was the TT. I must admit I had forgotten all about our car troubles but the crux of the matter is that it turned into a distance race, not a timed race. If you take my average speed over the two 2-hour races I won. Simple. That dropping of the flag business was unbelievable, both times right behind Denny and right in front of me. As Denny always used to say about bad luck or other unusual circumstances, [in his strong Kiwi accent] "you wouldn't read about it mate" Well he was dead right that time!*"

"*After they announced the result, Eric Broadley of Lola Cars and all our crew went to see the stewards to protest, and in the end all they said to Eric was "you are right, we messed it up but it's too late now." Eric was in tears as this would have been the first big win for his wonderful Lola T70. I wasn't too happy myself.*"

Tourist Trophy Race
Results – Part II

Pos.	Driver	No.	Car	Laps	Time/Reason	Speed
1st	David Hobbs	2	Lola T70	70	2 hr 00 min 53.4 sec	95.92 mph
2nd	Denis Hulme	16	Brabham BT8	69	2 hr 01 min 43.6 sec	
3rd	Jack Sears	22	Shelby Cobra Coupé	66		
4th	Mike Salmon	27	Ferrari 250 GTO	66		
5th	David Piper	14	Ferrari 250 LM	66		
6th	Sir John Whitmore	21	Shelby Cobra	66		
7th	Peter Sutcliffe	28	Ferrari 250 GTO	65		
8th	Allen Grant	25	Shelby Cobra	64		
9th	John Sparrow	26	Shelby Cobra	63		
10th	David Prophet	6	Lotus 30	60		
11th	Frank Gardner	23	Shelby Cobra Coupé	54		
12th	Richard Bond	31	Jaguar E-type	44		
dnf	Jim Clark	4	Lotus 30	41	Gearbox	
dnf	John Coundley	11	McLaren-Elva M1A	34	Driveshaft	
dnf	Chris Williams	8	Lotus-Brabham	28	Head Gasket	
dnf	Bruce McLaren	9	McLaren M1A	16	Engine	
dnf	Chris Amon	10	Elva Mk.8	6	Engine	
dnf	Victor Wilson	7	Lotus 30	6	Clutch	
dnf	Tommy Hitchcock	17	Brabham BT8	6	Transmission	
Pole Position		16	Denis Hulme		(First in part I)	
Fastest Lap		9	Bruce McLaren		1 min 39.0 sec (100.40 mph)	
Class Winners			Hobbs, Sears			

Right
After receiving a 2-lap penalty and suffering brake failure in the first part of the race, Jack Sears in the Cobra Coupé finished an excellent third in part two. However, John Whitmore in the other Alan Mann car took the GT class win by 3 laps.

Tourist Trophy Race
Aggregate Results

Pos.	Driver	No.	Car	Laps	Time/Reason	Speed
1st	Denis Hulme	16	Brabham BT8	138	4 hr 03 min 01.4 sec	94.069 mph
2nd	David Hobbs	2	Lola T70	137	4 hr 01 min 01.0 sec	
3rd	David Piper	14	Ferrari 250 LM	133	4 hr 03 min 36.3 sec	
4th	Sir John Whitmore	21	Shelby Cobra	130	4 hr 01 min 16.8 sec	
5th	Peter Sutcliffe	28	Ferrari 250 GTO	130		
6th	Allen Grant	25	Shelby Cobra	128		
7th	Jack Sears	22	Shelby Cobra Coupé	127		
8th	John Sparrow	26	Shelby Cobra	126		
9th	David Prophet	6	Lotus 30	122		
10th	Frank Gardner	23	Shelby Cobra Coupé	119		
11th	David Wansborough	30	Jaguar E-type	117		
12th	Mike Salmon	27	Ferrari 250 GTO	114		
13th	Richard Bond	31	Jaguar E-type	107		
14th	Jim Clark	4	Lotus 30	102		
15th	John Coundley	11	McLaren-Elva M1A	101		
dnf	Chris Williams	8	Lotus-Brabham	81	Gearbox/engine	
dnf	Tommy Hitchcock	17	Brabham BT8	72	Engine	
dnf	Victor Wilson	7	Lotus 30	68	Clutch	
dnf	Chris Amon	10	Elva Mk.8	60	Overheating	
dnf	Bruce McLaren	9	McLaren M1A	30	Oil leak	
dnf	Roger Mac	24	Shelby Cobra	29	Wheel	
dnf	Tony Lanfranchi	19	Attila Mk.3	19	Driveshaft	
dnf	Hugh Dibley	3	Lola T70	13	Suspension	
dnf	John Surtees	1	Lola T70	13	Steering	
Fastest Lap overall (part II)		9	Bruce McLaren		1 min 39.0 sec (100.40mph)	
Class Winners			Hulme, Whitmore			

"Drivers World Championship placings after the first round of the 1965 Championship held in January in South Africa were: 1st. Clark 9 points; 2nd. Surtees 6 points; 3rd. G.Hill 4 points; 4th. Spence 3 points; 5th. McLaren 2 points; 6th. Stewart 1 point. The next race would not be until the Monaco GP at the end of May."

Clockwise from top left.
Sir John Whitmore chats to TV presenter Raymond Baxter in the pit lane. The Radford Racing Cobra of Neil Dangerfield finished eighth overall. Team Lotus mechanic Arthur Birchall hangs the pit board out to Jimmy.

Chapter Seven
Silverstone
15th May

"STEWART TROUNCES THE STARS AT SILVERSTONE"

Driving the number two works B.R.M., Jackie Stewart won the International Trophy for Formula 1 cars at Silverstone on Saturday, covering the 52 laps of the Silverstone Grand Prix circuit at an average speed of 111.66mph. This was only Stewart's fourth Formula 1 race since he joined the B.R.M. team just before the South African GP and it is little more than a year ago since he first drove a single-seater....

Above right
Jackie Stewart tell his friends he just got a copy of a great photo (in his right hand) taken by Peter Darley at Goodwood (see p98).

Timetable

Event: International Trophy Meeting
Date: 15th May 1965
Location: Silverstone
Circuit Length: 2.927 miles

Time	Race	Laps	Distance	
10:15 am	International Formula 3 Race	25	73.18 miles	
11:30 am	International Sports Car Race	25	73.18 miles	
12:45 pm	International 'Senior Service' Touring Car Race	12	35.15 miles	
2:30 pm	XVII International Trophy	52	152.36 miles	
4:45 pm	International Historic Racing Cars	12	35.15 miles	

Silverstone Grand Prix Circuit – Existing Lap Records

Formula 1	Jack Brabham	Brabham BT7	1m 33.6 sec.	112.56 mph.
Formula 2	Cliff Allison	Lotus 12	1m 43.4 sec.	101.91 mph.
Formula 3	John Fenning	Lotus 22	1m 44.2 sec.	101.12 mph.
Sportscars over 2000cc	Roy Salvadori	Cooper-Monaco	1m 37.6 sec.	107.96 mph.
Sportscars under 2000cc	Roger Nathan	Brabham BT8	1m 40.0 sec.	105.37 mph.
Saloon Cars over 2000cc	Jack Sears	Ford Galaxie	1m 49.6 sec.	96.14 mph.
Saloon Cars 1301cc to 2000cc	Jim Clark	Lotus-Cortina	1m 55.2 sec.	91.47 mph.

Above
A rare occasion. Ferrari
finally chose to send
their cars to the UK for
a non-championship
race. This one one of
Lorenzo Bandini's few
race appearances in
England. He finished 7th.

Jackie Stewart Arrives

After a week of sunshine, sending the temperature soaring into the eighties day after day, the BRDC's annual May Festival of Speed – in which the 17th International Daily Express Trophy Race formed the feature event – was blessed with fine, sunny weather in marked contrast to the disastrous Senior Service '200' Formula 2 meeting run (or not) earlier in the year.

The BRDC rather optimistically claimed a crowd of 85,000 although the ease with which it was possible to enter and leave the circuit (not to mention the bare patches in the stands) would seem to indicate that a considerable more conservative estimate of 40,000 would have been nearer the mark. Of those, anyone who had suffered at the aforementioned Senior Service meeting must have been praying that the weekend's five-race programme would not experience a similar washout.

Indianapolis sadly had a prior claim on Jim Clark and Dan Gurney, but otherwise a full Formula One entry was listed with Ferrari sending a flat-12 and a brace of V8s despite their well-advertised reluctance to attend non-championship races. Surtees tried all three of them, Bandini practicing one of each, the reigning World Champion eventually settling for an 8-cylinder car whilst Bandini opted to stick with the 12.

Choosing not to use a 32-valve car in Clark's absence, Team Lotus had Mike Spence driving chassis R9, a flat-crank V8 Type 33 and a conventional V8 Type 33 (R6) for stand-in driver Pedro Rodriguez. The BRMs of Hill and Stewart were equipped with new gearboxes, whilst the

works Coopers of Rindt and McLaren included one – Rindt's – with a new fuel pump which had been fitted to combat surge and ensure the car could access the full contents of the tank. Chris Amon had an older 1963 5-speed Centro-Sud Type 57 BRM for the weekend, whilst Robert Bussinello in the other Centro-Sud car was running a new 6-speed gearbox.

In the supporting races Piers Courage was to win the F3 race in his Brabham, Roy Pierpoint (in a Ford Mustang) the saloon car race, the Hon. Patrick Lindsay in a Maserati 250F the historic fixture, and Bruce McLaren the sports car race with his own McLaren-Oldsmobile. All four saw new lap records set with McLaren in the latter race putting up a new outright circuit record of 1m 31.6sec. – incredibly, almost one and a half seconds faster than the F1 cars.

First With Formula 3

The programme opened with the Formula 3 race which was sadly rather depleted with no fewer than 12 cars listed as dns. These included Roger Mac in the second Chequered Flag car, Charlie Crichton-Stewart in the SMART Brabham, Charles Lucas in the fourth of his own team's entries, and John Miles in the Willment Lotus 35.

Of the survivors, the fastest in practice was John Fenning who put in an excellent performance in the Merlyn Mk.9 although it was Piers Courage in one of the two Charles Lucas Brabham BT10s and Roy Pike (in the only Chequered Flag car of the weekend) who leapt to the fore and began a race-long dice for the lead. Pike got ahead on lap two but Courage clearly had the upper hand and soon got back in front. Although over the first

Above left
Pedro Rodriguez made his third Formula One appearance for Team Lotus when he deputised for Jimmy at the International Trophy meeting.

Above right
Rosemary Seers was Team Lotus Press Officer and helped Peter Darley gain access to race meetings (see p109).

XVII International Trophy
For Formula 1 Cars
Entry List

No.	Entrant	Car	Engine	C.C.	Driver
1	S.E.F.A.C. – Ferrari	Ferrari 158/63	Ferrari V8	1497	John Surtees
2	S.E.F.A.C. – Ferrari	Ferrari 158/63	Ferrari V8	1497	Lorenzo Bandini
3	Owen Racing Organisation	B.R.M. P261	B.R.M. V8	1498	Graham Hill
4	Owen Racing Organisation	B.R.M. P261	B.R.M. V8	1498	Jackie Stewart
5	Team Lotus	Lotus 33 (chassis R9)	Climax V8	1496	Mike Spence
6	Team Lotus	Lotus 33 (chassis R6)	Climax V8	1496	Pedro Rodriguez
7	Brabham Racing Organisation	Brabham BT11	Climax V8	1496	Jack Brabham
8	Brabham Racing Organisation	Brabham BT11	Climax V8	1496	Denis Hulme
9	The Cooper Car Company	Cooper T77	Climax V8	1496	Bruce McLaren
10	The Cooper Car Company	Cooper T77	Climax V8	1496	Jochen Rindt
11	R.R.C. Walker	Brabham BT7	B.R.M. V8	1498	Jo Bonnier
12	D.W. Racing Enterprises Ltd.	Brabham BT11	Climax V8	1496	Bob Anderson
14	D.W. Racing Enterprises Ltd.	Lotus 33 (chassis R8)	Climax V8	1498	Paul Hawkins
15	Gerard Racing	Cooper T60	Climax V8	1496	John Taylor
16	Gerard Racing	Cooper T71	Ford 4-cyl	1498	John Rhodes
17	Reg Parnell	Lotus 25 (chassis R7)	B.R.M. V8	1498	Mike Hailwood
18	Reg Parnell	Lotus 25 (chassis R3)	B.R.M. V8	1498	Richard Attwood
19	John Willment Automobiles	Brabham BT11	B.R.M. V8	1498	Frank Gardner
20	Ian Raby (Racing) Ltd.	Brabham BT3	B.R.M. V8	1498	Ian Raby
21*	Sports Motors Manchester	Brabham BT14	Ford 4-cyl	1498	Rodney Bloor (dna)
22	Scuderio Centro-Sud	B.R.M. P578	B.R.M. V8	1496	Robert Bussinello
23	Scuderio Centro-Sud	B.R.M. P578	B.R.M. V8	1498	Chris Amon

"Jim Clark now holds the unofficial Brands Hatch Club circuit lap record for 3 ton trucks! During a recent 'shakedown' session with John Whitmore and Jackie Stewart, Jim drove a new Ford D300, carrying a one-ton load, flat out in top all the way round for a best time of 1m 29.8sec.. Whitmore's best was 1m 30.0sec., and Stewart, who had never driven a truck before, only slightly slower with 1m 30.2sec.."

6 laps he was seldom more than a few feet ahead of Pike, the brewery heir eventually managed to pull out a small gap finally crossing the line four seconds ahead of Pike, followed by the Ford-engined trio of Fenning (Merlyn), Blokdyk (Alexis) and – in fifth place more than a minute behind – Hitchcock in a Brabham.

Prior to this Jonathan Williams in the other Charles Lucas Brabham had managed to hold onto third place for four laps, until its fuel pump packed up, whilst the top BMC powered car to make it home was Len Selby's Cooper T67. Warwick Banks had a somewhat faster BMC-engined car in the Ken Tyrrell Cooper T76 and was well up in the field on lap 19 when his engine expired. None kept pace with Courage, however, who eventually put up the fastest lap of the race – and a new Formula 3 lap record – of 1m 41.6sec. at 103.71mph.

Sports Cars vs Formula 1
The big sports cars had their turn next, the main interest in practice for the 25 lapper having been to see who would be quickest round the high speed Silverstone Grand Prix circuit, the Formula 1 cars or the sports racing cars? In the end it was the sports cars just about did it, Surtees taking his works supported Team Surtees Lola-Chevrolet T70 round in a time of 1m 31.0sec. (115.79mph), against Graham Hill's pole time of 1m 31.4sec. (115.29mph) in the Formula 1 BRM P261.

Being 1.2 seconds faster in practice than Bruce McLaren's 4.5-litre McLaren-Oldsmobile M1A – now back to running a regular gearbox rather than the automatic – Surtees had expected to win the race quite comfortably. McLaren had other ideas, however, and

from second on the grid he fairly rocketed off the line to stay ahead of Surtees for the first half-dozen laps. In what was to be an epic battle for the lead, Surtees finally managed to outbrake his rival going into Stowe and slipped inside to take the lead on lap 7. Thereafter he led for the next nine laps, the two of them setting a terrific pace and pulling out a huge lead over Coundley's McLaren-Elva. Surtees, however, couldn't get away from Bruce, the two of them running nose to tail, their Firestones carving a path through the slower traffic until they were both very nearly caught out when Julian Sutton's Attila-Chevrolet shed a wheel as they prepared to lap it.

As for Coundley, he was soon out, retiring after becoming entangled in a collision at Becketts, shortly followed by the Lola of David Hobbs which, after a quantity of engine trouble in practice, dropped out with clutch trouble. David remembers the Silverstone weekend well "*The race at Silverstone where I retired with clutch trouble was another big disappointment. My team mate at Lola John Surtees who was driving for Ferrari in Formula 1 had been building me up to possibly drive an F2 or sports car for Ferrari. I was on the front row and somehow managed to select third instead of first for the start, with disasterous consequences. I was swamped by the field and of course terminally damaged the clutch. The Ferrari team manager Forgheri who watching on the pit wall had only one comment, "don't call us - we'll call you!"*"

Meanwhile, on lap 14, McLaren took the lead back (after pulling an almost identical manoeuvre to that of Surtees at Stowe) and began to build a small lead over the Lola.

Above
With the demise of John Surtees and David Hobbs in the other two Lola T70s, Hugh Dibly finished second to Bruce McLaren in the sports car race. He was nearly a minute down.

Opposite top
Bob Waterman and Arthur Birchall cruise through the paddock in the Type 30.

Opposite lower
Jack Sears said the 30 was the fastest car he had ever driven. After several test sessions at Snetterton Colin was impressed and asked Jack to drive in Jimmy's place at Silverstone.

International Formula 3 Race
Results

Position	Driver	No.	Car	Laps	Time/Reason	Speed
1st	Piers Courage	11	Brabham BT10	25	42 min 49.8 sec	102.51mph
2nd	Roy Pike	6	Brabham BT16	25	43 min 02.8 sec	
3rd	John Fenning	30	Merlyn Mk.9	25	43 min 19.6 sec	
4th	Trevor Blokdyk	1	Alexis Mk.5	25	43 min 32.8 sec	
5th	Tommy Hitchcock III	15	Brabham BT16	25	43 min 51.0 sec	
6th	Malcolm Payne	28	Lotus 31	25	44 min 02.0 sec	
7th	Tony Lanfranchi	23	Lotus 31	25	44 min 16.8 sec	
8th	Harry Stiller	3	Lotus 27	25	44 min 16.8 sec	
9th	Melvyn Long	27	Lotus 27	25	44 min 18.0 sec	
10th	David Rees	9	Brabham BT9	25	44 min 26.6 sec	
11th	David Cole	32	Brabham BT15	24		
12th	Ken Bass	37	Merlyn Mk.9	24		
13th	Len Selby	19	Cooper T76	23		
14th	Len Gibbs	21	Lotus 31	23		
15th	Jim Sullivan	4	Brabham BT16	23		
16th	Mike Herbertson	34	Cooper T76	22		
dnf	Warwick Banks	17	Cooper T76	17	engine	
dnf	Derek Bell	25	Lotus 31	13	electrics	
dnf	Jonathan Williams	33	Brabham BT10	11	fuel pump	
dnf	Peter Gethin	14	Lotus 22	6	valve	
dnf	Thomas Bibb	35	Cooper T72	1	engine	
Pole Position		30	John Fenning		1 min 41.2 sec (104.45 mph)	
Fastest Lap (record)		11	Piers Courage		1 min 41.6 sec (103.72 mph)	

International Sports Car Race
Results

Position	Driver	No.	Car	Laps	Time/Reason	Speed
1st	Bruce McLaren	21	McLaren M1A	25	38 min 39.4 sec	113.58 mph
2nd	Hugh Dibley	33	Lola T70	25	39 min 33.8 sec	
3rd	Jack Sears	29	Lotus 30	25	39 min 52.6 sec	
4th	Denis Hulme	17	Brabham-Climax BT18	24		
5th	Richard Attwood	32	Ford GT40	24		
dnf	John Surtees	34	Lola T70	22	Overheating	
dnf	Julian Sutton	39	Attila Mk.7		Lost Wheel	
dnf	John Coundley	22	McLaren-Elva M1A		Accident	
dnf	David Hobbs	31	Lola T70		Clutch	
Pole Position		34	John Surtees		1 min 31.0 sec (115.79 mph)	
Fastest Lap (record)		21	Bruce McLaren		1 min 31.6 sec (115.03 mph)	

"After Clark, Whitmore and Stewart had set thier 'serious' truck times at Brands, they all had a go the 'wrong way' round, and all recorded a time of 1m 30.6sec.. For their 'piece de resistance', Clark and Whitmore attempted a handbrake turn, and only just failed! The whole affair had been arranged by the Ford Motor Company for inclusion in 'Challenge' their new quarterly, all colour truck magazine."

By lap 20 it was clear that Surtees had other problems too, and a couple of circuits later he pulled off with an obvious power deficit. (As was subsequently revealed, the Lola had begun to overheat after taking some grass into its intakes when avoiding Sutton's errant wheel.) The advantage was thus Dibley's, who moved up to second after maintaining a steady but uninspiring third place, while third now went to the works Lotus 30 of Jack Sears which had pulled ahead of Hulme's 2-litre Brabham-Climax. Fifth went to Richard Attwood, deputising for Graham Hill in the Ford GT40 in what was actually the UK debut of what was to become a crucially significant machine in the history of sports-car racing.

Fords Make It Salooner The Better

A 12-lap Touring-Car race passed the time before lunch, at the same time demonstrating that now, more than ever to secure a win in a British saloon-car race you really needed to have a Ford. Originally it was a Galaxie, then the Cortina, but now in 1965 a Mustang seemed to be the machine of choice, the pair driven by Pierpoint and Baillie posting the fastest practice time of 1m 51.2sec. while Mike Spence and Jack Sears in works Lotus-Cortinas recorded times of 1m 53.7sec. and 1m 53.2sec. respectively.

On this occasion Spence was using chassis E9 (with Bob Cull as chief mechanic) while Sears was launching a brand new car which appeared in the 'Dance Diaries' as E11. This had been built up to replace E8, which Jack had rolled at Goodwood after which the team felt it really needed an all-new shell. Just to confuse the many Lotus-Cortina enthusiasts, the car still carried the same registration plate JTW 496C.

From the start of the race Pierpoint took the lead ahead of Sears, Spence and Gardner in the Willment Lotus-Cortina, with Baillie fifth after making a poor start and very soon sounding like he had exhaust problems. Even so it only took a couple of laps for him to out-accelerate the works Cortinas and by lap 4 the Firestone shod Mustangs had settled into their customary one-two formation. Thereafter, on such a fast circuit, it was by no means certain that, even the great driving of Jim Clark would have been able to keep up with this display of American Muscle.

With the 12 hectic laps soon completed, it was Pierpoint who headed Baillie home, beating him by 5.8 seconds with Sears another 15.4 seconds in arrears. Spence was next up, then Frank Gardner in the Willment Lotus-Cortina, and Tom Fletcher in the very well driven John Coundley-entered Cortina. Behind them the battles in the 1000cc and 1300cc classes were as tremendous. As ever, the Mini brigade were indulging in their usual sideways antics and by the end of the race new lap records being set for all four classes, large and small.

Warwick Banks and Mike Campbell-Cole disputed the smaller category particularly splendidly, never being more than a doorhandle apart, while John Anstead's little Fiat Abarth went very quickly to take a well-deserved third place. Tony Lanfranchi in the Alexander-tuned entry looked very ragged indeed holding off John Fitzpatrick's Broadspeed Cooper S in the 1300cc class, and when the latter finally got past he managed to hang on to his lead until the very last corner when, somehow, Lanfranchi managed to hurl his car past as they crossed the line.

Above
Jack Sears and Jim Endruweit were good friends and spent much time together during race weekends.

Senior Service
Touring Car Race
Results

Pos.	Driver	No.	Car	Laps	Time/Reason	Speed
1st	Roy Pierpoint	42	Ford Mustang	12	22 min 33.0 sec	93.46 mph
2nd	Gawaine Baillie	40	Ford Mustang	12	22 min 38.8 sec	
3rd	Jack Sears	30	Lotus-Cortina	12	22 min 54.2 sec	
4th	Mike Spence	31	Lotus-Cortina	12	23 min 01.6 sec	
5th	Frank Gardner	33	Lotus-Cortina	12	23 min 08.8 sec	
6th	Tom Fletcher	36	Lotus-Cortina	12	23 min 18.6 sec	
7th	André Baldet	32	Lotus-Cortina	12	23 min 34.2 sec	
8th	Tony Lanfranchi	17	Morris Mini-Cooper S	12	23 min 37.4 sec	
9th	John Fitzpatrick	22	Austin Mini-Cooper S	12	23 min 37.4 sec	
10th	John Lewis	19	Austin Mini-Cooper S	12	23 min 51.6 sec	
11th	Mike Young	45	Ford Anglia Super	12	23 min 51.8 sec	
12th	John Handley	18	Morris Mini-Cooper S	12	23 min 52.0 sec	
13th	Warwick Banks	1	Austin Mini-Cooper S 970	11		
14th	Mike Campbell-Cole	3	Austin Mini-Cooper S 970	11		
15th	John Anstead	2	Fiat-Abarth 1000 TC	11		
	Gerry Marshall	4	Austin Mini-Cooper S 970			
	Anita Taylor	5	Austin Mini-Cooper S 970			
	Phil de Banks	7	Morris Mini-Cooper S 970			
	Chris Craft	10	Ford Anglia Super			
	Paddy Hopkirk	14	Austin Mini-Cooper S			
	John Nicholson	34	Lotus-Cortina			
	Bill Vaughan	50	Lotus-Cortina			
dnf	John Rhodes	15	Morris Mini-Cooper S			
dnf	Harry Ratcliffe	20	Morris Mini-Cooper S			
dnf	Jacquie Bond-Smith	43	Ford Galaxie			
Pole Position		42	Roy Pierpoint		1 min 51.2 sec (94.81 mph)	
Fastest lap		42	Roy Pierpoint		1 min 50.4 sec (95.21 mph)	
Class Winners			Pierpoint, Sears, Lanfranchi, Banks			

Left
Bruce McLaren in the
Cooper T77 finished the
International Trophy
sixth but one lap down.

Far left
Jackie Stewart started
second on the grid and
was always in with a
chance of a win. When
Brabham had engine
trouble he held off
Surtees to take his first
Formula One victory,
and that in only his
fourth F1 race.

The International Trophy

After the lunch interval, during which several go-karts had demonstrated their unsuitability for such a long fast circuit by expiring all over the place, the Formula 1 cars came out for their warm-up ahead of the 52-lap feature. In pole position Graham Hill's BRM was much as before except that the six speed gearbox with quick change gears had been restored to use. Putting this to good use he had lapped in 1m 31.4sec. with team-mate Jackie Stewart in an identical car following him round in 1m 31.6sec. to join him on the front row. Alongside was John Surtees in a V8 Ferrari (1m 32.1sec.) and Lorenzo Bandini in the flat-12 Ferrari which he had pushed round in 1m 32.3sec..

In the absence of Clark and Gurney, Mike Spence was leading the Team Lotus attack, lapping R9 in 1m 32.3sec. to take the inside slot on row 2 whilst alongside him was the Brabham duo of Jack himself (1m 32.4sec.) and his new team-mate Denis Hulme (who was moving up from F2) who was deputising for Dan Gurney. With his team-mate Jo Siffert still out of action, Jo Bonnier managed a creditable 1m 33.8sec. in the Rob Walker Brabham-Climax as did Bruce McLaren in the works Cooper-Climax T77.

Jochen Rindt in the second works Cooper lapped in 1min 31.1sec., while Richard Attwood in the Parnell Lotus 25-BRM – Clark's 1962 US GP-winning chassis R3 – was almost as quick at 1m 32.3sec.. Pedro Rodriguez was in the second works Lotus 33 (R6, the previous season's triple GP-winner) with a normal V8 Climax engine. He lapped at 1m 34.4sec., only slightly quicker than Bob Anderson's Brabham-Climax. The field

XVII InternationalTrophy
Grid

Pole Position

Lorenzo Bandini	John Surtees	Jackie Stewart	Graham Hill
Ferrari	Ferrari	B.R.M.	B.R.M.
1 min 32.3 sec	1 min 32.1 sec	1 min 31.6 sec	1 min 31.4 sec

Denny Hulme	Jack Brabham	Mike Spence
Brabham-Climax	Brabham-Climax	Lotus-Climax
1 min 33.8 sec	1 min 32.4 sec	1 min 32.3 sec

Jochen Rindt	Frank Gardner	Bruce McLaren	Jo Bonnier
Cooper-Climax	Brabham-B.R.M.	Cooper-Climax	Brabham-Climax
1 min 34.1 sec	1 min 33.9 sec	1 min 33.8 sec	1 min 33.8 sec

Bob Anderson	Pedro Rodriguez	Richard Attwood
Brabham-Climax	Lotus-Climax	Lotus-B.R.M.
1 min 34.5 sec	1 min 34.4 sec	1 min 34.3 sec

Ian Raby	John Taylor	Paul Hawkins	Mike Hailwood
Brabham-B.R.M.	Cooper-Climax	Lotus-Climax	Lotus-B.R.M.
1 min 36.0 sec	1 min 35.5 sec	1 min 34.9 sec	1 min 34.7 sec

John Rhodes	Robert Bussinello	Chris Amon
Cooper-Ford	B.R.M.	B.R.M.
1 min 38.5 sec	1 min 36.8 sec	1m 36.6 sec

XVII International Trophy
Results

Pos.	Driver	No.	Car	Laps	Time/Reason	Speed
1st	Jackie Stewart	4	B.R.M P261	52	1 hr 21 min 47.0 sec	111.66 mph
2nd	John Surtees	1	Ferrari 158/63	52	1 hr 21 min 50.0 sec	
3rd	Mike Spence	5	Lotus 33	52	1 hr 22 min 43.4 sec	
4th	Pedro Rodriguez	6	Lotus 33	52	1 hr 23 min 20.6 sec	
5th	Jo Bonnier	11	Brabham BT7	51		
6th	Bruce McLaren	9	Cooper T77	51		
7th	Lorenzo Bandini	2	Ferrari 158/63	51		
8th	Richard Attwood	18	Lotus 25	51		
9th	Mike Hailwood	17	Lotus 25	51		
10th	Paul Hawkins	16	Lotus 33	51		
11th	John Taylor	15	Cooper T60	50		
12th	Ian Raby	20	Brabham BT3	50		
13th	Robert Bussinello	22	B.R.M. P578	49		
14th	Bob Anderson	12	Brabham BT11	44	Not classified	
dnf	Jack Brabham	7	Brabham BT11	35	Gearbox	
dnf	Frank Gardner	19	Brabham BT11	25	Clutch	
dnf	Jochen Rindt	10	Cooper T77	23	Connecting rod	
dnf	Graham Hill	3	B.R.M. P261	16	Camshaft	
dnf	John Rhodes	16	Cooper T71	14	Overheating	
dnf	Denis Hulme	8	Brabham BT11	6	Oil leak	
dnf	Chris Amon	23	B.R.M. P578	6	Engine	
Pole Position		3	Graham Hill		1 min 31.4 sec (115.28 mph)	
Fastest lap (new record)		1	John Surtees		1 min 33.0 sec (113.30 mph)	

was completed by Mike Hailwood in R7, the other BRM powered Parnell car, Paul Hawkins in the DW Racing Lotus-Climax Type 33 (R8), John Taylor in a Cooper-Climax, Ian Raby's Brabham-BRM, Chris Amon and Roberto Bussinello in the two Centro-Sud BRMs, and lastly, John Rhodes in a Cooper-Ford.

As the field screamed off the line and into Copse corner for the first lap, Surtees snatched the lead by going round the outside only to have Graham Hill immediately out-accelerate him on the run through the left-hander at Maggots and up to Becketts. Jackie Stewart was only fifth-placed, having made a poor start to put him behind both Brabham and Bandini although he quickly took the Italian. By the end of the first lap the race order was Hill, Surtees and Brabham, followed by Stewart, Bandini, Rindt, Spence, Bonnier, Hulme, Attwood, Hailwood, Rodriguez, McLaren, Gardner, Taylor, Hawkins, Anderson, Raby, Amon, Bussinello and Rhodes.

On lap two, however, Brabham moved ahead of Surtees and set off after the leader while his team-mate Hulme called at the pits with an oil leak. (After a long stop he finally got on his way but only made it as far as the 6th lap before pulling off for good.) Jo Bonnier sadly spun away his eighth place, dropping to the back of the field, while Rhodes – despite his Cooper apparently boiling away furiously – was soon locked in combat with Businello before lap 14 saw him off and out.

In fact in the early laps there were number of signficiant positional changes, with those better drivers who had made poor starts soon moving up into their accustomed positions Jackie Stewart got past John Surtees into

third place; Mike Spence jumped up to fifth; Bruce McLaren moved up to eighth; while Frank Gardner continued to show many more experienced Formula 1 drivers the way round, his Willment Brabham holding ninth place and looking like he could go even higher.

At the front Jack Brabham was by now pressing Graham Hill very hard indeed, and on lap eight he got past the BRM number one all the while mindful that Stewart was only a few lengths behind in the team's second car with the reigning World Champion's Ferrari in similarly close attendance. Thereafter there was quite a gap ahead of Spence in fifth place but behind him Gardner was making excellent progress having overhauled the likes of Bandini, Rindt, McLaren and Rodriguez. For a while the first three of these had been really mixing it, changing places more or less constantly, the unlucky Amon having early retired at Copse with an oil leak in his BRM.

Further drama occurred on Lap 17 when Hill coasted into the pits with smashed valve gear on one bank of cylinders. This left Stewart in second place behind Brabham, at least until Surtees chose his moment to attack so that within a couple of laps he was past the young Scotsman. It was only Stewart's fourth Formula 1 race, and he held on magnificently, but neither he nor the more experienced Surtees were able to do much about closing the nine second gap which had opened up behind Jack Brabham.

The heat of their battle unfairly if understandably drew attention from a number of other good drives, notably by Paul Hawkins, who had passed Mike Hailwood for 11th place, and Frank Gardner who was still holding his fifth

Above
Mike Spence took Jimmys seat in the Cortina but couldn't match Jack Sears on lap times. Here in practice he was ahead of Jack on the road, but come the race Jack led Mike home in a Team Lotus 3-4.

"Lotus Cortinas are to be provided with more power (they are hoping for another 20 horses) to combat the threat in saloon car racing from the BMW 1800ti and the Alfa-Romeo Giulia."

place. Unfortunately his drive came to an end on lap 26 when the clutch gave out, Jochen Rindt also being forced to retire when a con-rod let him down at Copse.

Later, on lap 35, a tell-tale puff of smoke could be see coming from the tail of the leading Brabham around the same time that Stewart managed to nip inside Surtees at Copse to take second place. Thereafter the crowd was keen to see if Stewart could reduce that nine second gap, and he did so in pretty short order, reducing it to just six seconds in a single lap. By now it was obvious to all that Jack was in serious trouble, and within no time Stewart was past him and into the lead. To his credit Jack carried on for a short while but finally ground to a halt with his gearbox well and truly on fire.

Brabham's bad fortune was of course Stewart's very good luck: all he had to do now to secure his first Formula 1 win was hold off Surtees, two seconds behind and with very few laps left to play with. Very reasonably most in the crowd expected the more experienced driver to find a way past the young pretender, but Jackie kept the lead around the 1.5 to 2 second mark and was looking every bit as polished as the World Champion. Indeed when the pair lapped Bonnier, McLaren and Bandini, he actually picked up half a second on the Ferrari, although if Bandini had been fully aware of what was going on he might well have tried some 'team tactics' at this point.

Stewart nevertheless survived the pressure extremely well and although the commentator became almost hysterical over the World Champion's efforts to catch Stewart on the last lap, Jackie calmly led Surtees across the line by three seconds, having averaged 111.66mph for the 52 lap race. By way of compensation, during the last few, frantic laps, Surtees was credited with a new lap record of 1m 33.0sec. (113.30mph). Otherwise it was very much Stewart's day, however, and rightly so. For a driver who had competed in his first Formula 1 race less than six months ago in South Africa Jackie Stewart's drive proved beyond all doubt that he was the stuff of which future World Champions are made.

Historics Close The Day

The long day slowly drew to a close, concluding with an excellent Historic Racing-Car event which saw a varied collection of machines coming out on to the grid. The stars of the show were without doubt the three 250F Maseratis, driven in turn by the Hon. Patrick Lindsay, Richard Attwood and Warwick Banks. All three looked immaculate in Italian red and brought back fond memories of Fangio, Moss, Behra and Co. driving them in their heyday. Unsurprisingly the three quickly escaped a straggling field, in which Keith Schellenberg's 8-litre Bentley never really got going, Dan Margulies' Connaught made only spasmodic Gonzalez-like wheel twirling appearances, and J.R. Brown 's Cooper-Bristol needed six laps to catch Brewer's ERA.

Away from this lot Banks, Lindsay and Attwood put on a particularly good show, passing and repassing continually. Lindsay eventually managed to break away from the other two, winning at 96.42mph and putting in the fastest lap of the day at 1m 47.6sec., some three seconds faster than he had managed in practice.) Attwood just pipped Banks by a second. J.R.Brown was fourth, more than a minute and a half behind the leader.

Above
Spence did however take a good third in the main race of the day, behind Stewart in the B.R.M. and the Ferrari of John Surtees.

Chapter Eight
Crystal Palace
7th June

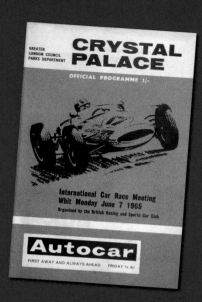

"INDY 500 VICTOR CLARK WINS AT CRYSTAL PALACE"

Returning from his £70,000 victory at Indianapolis Jim Clark drove nearly as hard at Crystal Palace on Whit Monday to pick up a modest £150. Driving a Cosworth powered Ron Harris Team Lotus Type 35 he won both heats of the Formula 2 London Trophy. Graham Hill, driving John Coombs' Brabham-BRM finished second with Richard Attwood's Lola-Cosworth in third place....

Above right
Fresh from his victory at Indianapolis Jim Clark was once again accepting the laurels at Crystal Palace.

Timetable

Event: International Car Race Meeting
Date: Monday 7th June 1965
Location: Crystal Palace
Circuit Length: 1.39 miles

Time	Race	Laps	Distance
1:30 pm	Grand Touring Cars	15	20.85 miles
2:10 pm	The Norbury Trophy for Saloon Cars over 1300cc	15	20.85 miles
3:00 pm	The London Trophy for Formula 2 cars (Part I)	25	34.75 miles
3:45 pm	The Elva Trophy for Sports Cars	20	27.80 miles
4:30 pm	The London Trophy for Formula 2 cars (Part II)	25	34.75 miles
5:15 pm	The Anerley Trophy for Saloon Cars under 1300cc	15	20.85 miles

Crystal Palace – Existing Lap Records

Formula 1	n/a			
Formula 2	Jochen Rindt	Brabham-Cosworth	58.2 sec.	86.26 mph.
Sportscars under 2000cc	Jim Clark	Lotus-Ford	58.6 sec.	85.37 mph.
Sportscars under 1150cc	John Hine	Lotus-Ford	61.0 sec.	82.03 mph.
Saloon Cars over 2000cc	Jack Sears	Ford Galaxie	63.8 sec.	78.43 mph.
Saloon Cars 1301cc to 2000cc	Jim Clark	Lotus-Cortina	65.2 sec.	76.75 mph.

The London Trophy
Entry List

No.	Entrant	Car	Engine	Driver
1	Brabham Racing Developments	Brabham BT16	Honda/Cosworth SCA	Jack Brabham
2	Brabham Racing Developments	Brabham BT16	Cosworth SCA	Denis Hulme
3	John Coombs	Brabham BT16	B.R.M.	Graham Hill
4	Roy Winkelmann Racing	Brabham BT16	Cosworth SCA	Alan Rees
5	Roy Winkelmann Racing	Brabham BT16	Cosworth SCA	Jochen Rindt
6	Aurora Gear (Racing) Rotherham	Brabham BT16	Cosworth SCA	Trevor Taylor
7	Normand	Brabham BT16	Cosworth SCA	Mike Beckwith
8	David Prophet Racing	Brabham BT10	Cosworth SCA	David Prophet
9	David Prophet Racing	Brabham BT10	Cosworth SCA	Bill Bradley
10	Frank Lythgoe Racing	Brabham BT16	Cosworth SCA	Adam Wyllie
11	Midland Racing Partnership	Lola T60/T55	B.R.M./Cosworth SCA	Chris Amon
12	Midland Racing Partnership	Lola T60	Cosworth SCA	Richard Attwood
14*	Race Proved by Willment	Lola T55	Cosworth SCA	Frank Gardner (dna)
15	Ron Harris Team Lotus	Lotus 35	Cosworth SCA	Jim Clark
16	Ron Harris Team Lotus	Lotus 35	B.R.M./Cosworth SCA	Mike Spence
17*	Reg Parnell (Racing)	Lotus 35	B.R.M.	David Hobbs (dnq)
18	Tyrrell Racing Organisation	Cooper T75	B.R.M.	Jackie Stewart
19	Tyrrell Racing Organisation	Cooper T75	B.R.M.	John Surtees
20	Frank Lythgoe Racing	Brabham BT16	Cosworth SCA	Alan Rollinson
21	Ron Harris Team Lotus	Lotus 35	B.R.M.	Peter Revson
22*	Ian Raby (Racing) Ltd.	Merlyn Mk.9	Cosworth SCA	Ian Raby (dnq)
23*	E. Offenstadt	Cooper T75	B.R.M.	Eric Offenstadt (dnq)
24*	Colchester Racing Develpments	Merlyn Mk.9	Cosworth SCA	Chris Irwin (dnq)
25*	Colchester Racing Develpments	Merlyn Mk.9	Cosworth SCA	Roger Mac (dna)
26*	Ecurie Alf Francis	Cooper T75	Alfa-Romeo	Jo Siffert (dnq)
27*	Ecurie Alf Francis	Cooper T75	Alfa-Romeo	Bernard Plaisance (dnq)
28*	B. Collomb	Lotus 35	Cosworth SCA	Bernard Collomb (dnq)

Jim Clark Dominates At The Palace

Estimated at more than 45,000, a huge crowd squeezed into South London's Crystal Palace circuit on Whit Monday for the first race car meeting run under the auspices of the new GLC (Greater London Council), namely the annual BRSCC International. With a full entry list and some top class racing promised for the main event – the London Trophy for Formula 2 cars – the sun shone brightly for most of the day and some first-class racing had the excepionally large crowd on its toes for much of the time.

The one-day Bank Holiday event comprised a particularly hectic schedule, with five practice sessions for the six races to be run in the morning followed by a short lunch break which included a parade lap by Jim Clark and Colin Chapman (in the back of a huge and impressive Ford Fairlane convertible) to celebrate their history-making victory at the Indianapolis 500 the previous weekend.

The opening race of the day was one for GT cars up to 1600cc, the front row of the grid being occupied by Ray Parsons and Jackie Oliver in a pair of works supported Lotus Elans, with Boley Pittard in Ian Walker's gorgeous little Alfa-Romeo GTZ sandwiched between them. The three had practice times a clear two seconds faster than the rest of the field, and well inside lap record for their class.

As the flag dropped, the three drew away in the expected close company but then, three-quarters of the way around the first lap (just as they were coming up Ramp Bend by the railway station) Parsons lost a wheel and pulled off onto the grass.

From there on Pittard led from Oliver until the latter managed to force his way past after seven laps and then slowly drew increase his lead to win rather easily, at an average speed of 78.89mph. Behind Pittard, third and fourth places went to Eric Liddle and Malcolm Wayne (both in Lotus Elans) while the under-1150cc class was led by John MacKay, John Dickinson (Team Garnett) and Graham Capel in a trio of Lotus Eleven GTs. These were closely followed by Dickie Attwood in a Triumph Spitfire, the four finishing in that order with Attwood and MacKay sharing the fastest lap with a time of 1m 06.0sec.. Further interest came from John Sprinzel driving a rather unusual 1,579cc Isuzu Bellett, but this seemed to lack both power and handling and he finished well down the field.

Race two on the agenda, the Norbury Trophy for the larger capacity saloon cars, promised plenty of excitement given the tight confines of the picturesque parkland track where the run-off area was either the shrubbery or some rather stout railway sleepers, set four high just feet from the edge of the track. Splitting the saloon car entry into two separate races was an understandable move given the nature and length of the track, but it made for two rather sparsely populated races. The front row of the grid for this race consisted of Jimmy Clark and Frank Gardner in Lotus-Cortinas alongside Roy Pierpoint in the Weybridge Engineering Ford Mustang, with Hutcheson's huge Galaxie on the second row in sixth position sitting on the outside of Jack Sears in the other works Cortina.

The weekend had seen a move around of personnel within the Cortina camp at Team Lotus. With the

Left
The start of the Norbury Trophy with, from left to right, Pierpoint (Mustang), Hutcheson, Clark and Gardner.

Below
Even on the confines of the Crystal Palace circuit Jimmy performed in his usual spectacular style.

The Norbury Trophy
Results

Pos.	Driver	No.	Car	Laps	Time	Speed
1st	Roy Fierpoint	103	Ford Mustang	15	16 min 18.2 sec	76.72 mph
2nd	Jim Clark	110	Lotus-Cortina	15	16 min 20.4 sec	76.56 mph
3rd	Jack Sears	111	Lotus-Cortina	15		
4th	Frank Gardner	112	Lotus-Cortina	15		
5th	Gawaine Baillie	104	Ford Mustang	15		
6th	Jack Brabham	105	Ford Mustang	15		
7th	Bill Shaw	118	Lotus-Cortina	14		
8th	Andre Baldet	113	Lotus-Cortina	14		
dnf	Alan Hutcheson	101	Ford Galaxie	12	Accident	
	Alan Mann	102	Ford Galaxie			
	Rosemary Smith	115	Lotus-Cortina			
	Bill Vaughan	116	Lotus-Cortina			
	R.Burton	117	Lotus-Cortina			
	W Shaw	118	Lotus-Cortina			
dns	John Nicholson	114	Lotus-Cortina			
dns	Tom Fletcher	119	Lotus-Cortina			

Pole Position		112	Frank Gardner	
Fastest Lap		103 & 110	Pierpoint & Clark	1 min 04.2 sec (77.93 mph)
Class Winners			Pierpoint, Clark	

departure of Bob Cull, Bob Dance took over the running of E9 for Jim Clark and Sid Carr moved over to work on Jack's car E11. In an attempt to find a few more horsepower, both cars were now fitted with new specification BRM rods and pistons while the spare car (E10) still had the standard engine set up and was destined, as usually, to remain in the transporter for the whole weekend. (At most events the spare car would be given a handful of laps during practice, if only to make sure it was ready in case of any dramas.)

Sitting in middle of the front row Clark outdragged Pierpoint and the pole-placed Gardner but the Mustang's superior power along the top straight meant Pierpoint was able to get to North Tower first and retake the lead. Thereafter the Scotsman was really pushing his car to the limit trying to stay with the red Mustang, but the extra torque of the big V8 really told on the deceptively fast track and he was soon falling back a fraction with each passing lap.

The first lap was further enlivened by Alan Hutcheson spinning the 'two-tone' 7-litre Galaxie right in the middle of North Tower bend to form a mobile chicane for those behind who had to work hard to find a space to slip through. Somehow they all managed but it spread the meagre field out and made for a rather dull race. Sears was left chasing the leaders, Pierpoint and Clark, followed by Gardner who was performing a series of acrobatics in the red Willment Cortina. Jack Brabham for Alan Brown Racing and Sir Gawaine Baillie, both in Mustangs, were meanwhile dicing furiously between themselves a little way behind Gardner, with André Baldet and Bill Shaw in Cortinas, following at a distance.

The F2 Cars Take To The Track

Next on the menu was the first part of the London Trophy for Formula 2 cars, an impressive field of cars turning out for this race with a number of drivers flying in from all over the world.

Jimmy Clark flew in late from the USA and so had a very hectic practice on race morning, but nevertheless managed to secure a place in the middle of the front row with a time of 56.2 seconds in the Ron Harris Lotus 35-Cosworth. On pole was Graham Hill, who recorded a time of 55.8 seconds in the John Coombs BRM-engined Brabham BT16. On the outside of the front row sat Jackie Stewart in Ken Tyrrell's Cooper-BRM with John Surtees making a guest appearance in Tyrrell's other Cooper-BRM and on the fifth row with 57 seconds dead. With only a limited number of cars allowed to compete, several of the slower cars were bumped from the field altogether, including the Merlyn of Chris Irwin and the Tim Parnell Lotus-BRM of David Hobbs.

Hobbs in was disappointed but not completely unsurprised to not make it into the race "To be honest, *Tim was not the greatest team owner. Everything was done on the cheap and his mechanics were not great either. There were some days when we couldn't even get the car race ready and would miss half the practice session, or be late onto the grid,"* this must have been one of them.

In the race, Jimmy Clark made another of his good starts, leading Jackie Stewart into the first bend with Graham Hill dropping back after a relatively slow getaway. Clark soon built up a good lead, with Stewart

Above left
Having started near the back of the grid in heat one, young American driver and Revlon heir Peter Revson fought his way up to finish seventh, only to be disqualified from the second heat for a push start.

Above right
Quasi 'works' Elan driver Ray Parsons was one of a crop of excellent Australians.

The London Trophy
Grid

Pole Position

Jackie Stewart	Jim Clark	Graham Hill
Cooper-BRM	Lotus-Cosworth	Brabham-BRM
56.4 sec	56.2 sec	55.8 sec

Denis Hulme	Mike Beckwith
Brabham-Cosworth	Brabham-Cosworth
56.4 sec	56.4 sec

Jack Brabham	Richard Attwood	Mike Spence
Brabham-Cosworth	Lola-Cosworth	Lotus-Cosworth
56.8 sec	56.8 sec	56.6 sec

Alan Rees	Jochen Rindt
Brabham-Cosworth	Brabham-Cosworth
57.0 sec	57.0 sec

David Prophet	Alan Rollinson	John Surtees
Brabham-Cosworth	Brabham-Cosworth	Cooper-BRM
57.8 sec	57.2 sec	57.1 sec

Trevor Taylor	Peter Revson
Brabham-Cosworth	Lotus-BRM
58.0 sec	57.8 sec

Bill Bradley	Adam Wyllie	Chris Amon
Brabham-Cosworth	Brabham-Cosworth	Lola-Cosworth
59.0 sec	58.6	

The London Trophy
Results – Part I

Pos.	Driver	No.	Car	Laps	Time	Speed
1st	Jim Clark	15	Lotus 35	25	23 min 32.6 sec	89.19 mph
2nd	Graham Hill	3	Brabham BT16	25	23 min 42.2 sec	
3rd	Richard Attwood	12	Lola T60	25	23 min 59.0 sec	
4th	Jochen Rindt	5	Brabham BT16	25	24 min 00.2 sec	
5th	Mike Beckwith	7	Brabham BT16	25	24 min 12.0 sec	
6th	Alan Rees	4	Brabham BT16	25	24 min 12.6 sec	
7th	Peter Revson	21	Lotus 35	25		
8th	Mike Spence	16	Lotus 35	25		
9th	Jack Brabham	1	Brabham BT16	25	(1 min penalty)	
10th	David Prophet	8	Brabham BT10	24		
11th	Adam Wyllie	10	Brabham BT16	24		
12th	Chris Amon	11	Lola T55	24		
13th	Trevor Taylor	6	Brabham BT16	24		
14th	Alan Rollinson	20	Brabham BT16	24		
15th	Bill Bradley	9	Brabham BT10	23		
ret	John Surtees	19	Cooper T75	21	Connecting rod	
ret	Jackie Stewart	18	Cooper T75	16	Half shaft	
ret	Denis Hulme	2	Brabham BT16	14	Valve gear	
dnq	David Hobbs	17	Lotus 35			
dnq	Ian Raby	22	Merlyn Mk.9			
dnq	Eric Offenstadt	23	Cooper T75			
dnq	Chris Irwin	24	Merlyn Mk.9			
dnq	Jo Siffert	26	Cooper T75			
dnq	Bernard Plaisance	27	Cooper T75			
dnq	Bernard Collomb	28	Lotus 35			
Pole Position		3	Graham Hill		55.8 sec	
Fastest Lap		15 & 18	Clark & Stewart		55.8 sec (89.68 mph)	

"Jim Clark is forsaking Ford and General Motors on November 7th. He due to drive a 1903 Cadillac in the London-to-Brighton Veteran Car Run, one of four enteries from the Montagu Motor Museum out of a total field of 250 cars."

just managing to hold off Jack Brabham for second place. Brabham in the works Brabham-Cosworth – once again preferring to use the Ford engine rather than the Honda unit – had made a terrific start from the fourth row of the grid, in fact it was so good that the stewards later docked him a minute for a jumped start.

Hill was rapidly catching this pair, and when they all got mixed up there was a good deal of pushing and shoving with Brabham coming through in fourth place and waving his fist furiously at Hill as he passed. Stewart dropped out with a lack of gears, while Denny Hulme went out with engine trouble on his Brabham-Cosworth. John Surtees had meanwhile worked his way up to fourth place behind Clark, Hill and Brabham – actually third place given Brabham's penalty – but then the BRM engine promptly threw a rod letting Richard Attwood's Lola-Cosworth through to third closely followed by the future 'King of the Palace' Jochen Rindt's Winkelmann Brabham-Cosworth.

Ahead of part two of this main race there was a rather disappointing 2-litre sports car race which saw Tommy Hitchcock take his 2-litre Brabham-Climax into the lead until Denis Hulme (in Sid Taylor's similar car) over took him and sailed away to victory. Third was Chris Amon in an Elva-BMW which finished well ahead of a four car dice for fourth which eventually went to John Hine 1,089cc Lotus 23. (Hine therefore won the 1150cc class ahead of Keith St. John's Elva-BMW, and the Lotus 23s of Jim Morley and Geoff Oliver.) Fastest lap went to Hulme with a time of 57.0 seconds dead – interestingly not too far off the times set by the Formula 2 cars on the same day.

The London Trophy Heat 2
After this the remnants of the first heat of the London Trophy emerged once more to do battle for the second heat, the winner being decided on the aggregate time of the two races. Unfortunately neither of the works Brabhams made it out onto the track again, neither did the two Tyrrell Cooper-BRMs.

Jim Clark made another of his textbook starts from pole and was soon pulling away from the field. Behind him a huge battle raged for second place between Rindt, Attwood and Hill, the latter winning over the Lola and the Brabham but unable to reduce the gap between himself and Clark's Lotus and eventually finishing 1.4 seconds behind. A similarly colossal dice went on for fifth place, Alan Rees (Brabham), Mike Spence (Lotus-Cosworth), Mike Beckwith (Brabham-Cosworth) and Trevor Taylor (Brabham-Cosworth) swapping places for much of the race before finally resolving the conflict and settling into the order Rees, Beckwith, Spence and Taylor.

Thereafter the final overall classification worked out to much the same order as in the first heat, which is to say Clark, Hill, Attwood, Rindt, Rees and Beckwith. The fastest lap time for the two races was set jointly by Clark and Stewart with a time of 55.8 sec, coincidentally exactly the same time as Hill had set in practice.

Saloon Cars End The Day
The main event over, the meeting wound up with the Anerley Trophy for saloon cars up to 1300cc. This provided a fairly easy win for John Rhodes in the works 1275 Mini-Cooper S who put on a splendid performance

Above
Jimmy takes his lap of honour. Having won both heats his overall margin over Graham Hill was more than ten seconds.

ahead of the similar car driven by John Lewis.
His was an impressive drive to take second was
made somewhat easier when John Handley and
Tony Lanfranchi collided on the first lap at North Tower,
the former continuing at reduced pace until his bent
bodywork burst a tyre, while Lanfranchi brought the
Alexander car in immediately and retired.

Elsewhere on the grid Chris Craft made up for the bad
start to come through into third place in his Ford Anglia
1200, while John Fitzpatrick finished fourth overall (and
won the under 1000cc class) in his Broadspeed Mini-
Cooper. Championship leader Warwick Banks in the
works 970 S also had a bit of a contretemps, collecting
John Cannadine in the Speedwell 1300 S on his second
lap when the latter tried to pass on the inside – again
at North Tower.

Gerry Marshall finished fifth in his 970 Mini-Cooper
but for once was not particularly popular with the crowd
having on the last lap collided at South Tower bend with
Campbell-Cole in a similar car which had hitherto been
leading him by a nose. All in all the carnage was pretty
high, with bent and broken cars all over the place, but
the crowd loved it and clearly went away happy just as
the first few drops of traditional Bank Holiday rain were
beginning to fall.

Above & right
Jimmy was the ultimate
professional and
always kept himself fit
and healthy. Even when
his schedule meant
several exhausting
transatlantic flights he
would arrive at a race
alert, cheerful and of
course, ready to win.

The London Trophy
Results – Part II

Pos.	Driver	No.	Car	Laps	Time	Speed
1st	Jim Clark	15	Lotus 35	25	23 min 40.8 sec	88.05 mph
2nd	Graham Hill	3	Brabham BT16	25	23 min 42.2 sec	
3rd	Richard Attwood	24	Lola T60	25	23 min 42.2 sec	
4th	Jochen Rindt	5	Brabham BT16	25	23 min 57.0 sec	
5th	Alan Rees	4	Brabham BT16	25	24 min 03.0 sec	
6th	Mike Beckwith	7	Brabham BT16	25	24 min 04.8 sec	
7th	Mike Spence	16	Lotus 35	25		
8th	Trevor Taylor	6	Brabham BT16	25		
9th	David Prophet	8	Brabham BT10	25		
10th	Chris Amon	11	Lola T55	25		
11th	Bill Bradley	9	Brabham BT10	23		
12th	Adam Wyllie	10	Brabham BT16	22		
dq	Peter Revson	21	Lotus 35		push start	
ns	Jack Brabham	1	Brabham BT16		clutch	
ns	Alan Rollinson	20	Brabham BT16		valve gear	
Pole Position		15	Jim Clark		(finished 1st in Part I)	
Fastest Lap		15, 3, 24	Clark, Hill, & Attwood		56.2 sec (89.03 mph)	

The London Trophy
Aggregate Results

Pos.	Driver	No.	Car	Laps	Time	Speed
1st	Jim Clark	15	Lotus 35	50	47 min 13.4 sec	88.62 mph
2nd	Graham Hill	3	Brabham BT16	50	47 min 24.4 sec	
3rd	Richard Attwood	24	Lola T60	50	47 min 46.8 sec	
4th	Jochen Rindt	5	Brabham BT16	50	47 min 57.2 sec	
5th	Alan Rees	4	Brabham BT16	50	48 min 15.6 sec	
6th	Mike Beckwith	7	Brabham BT16	50	48 min 16.8 sec	
7th	Mike Spence	16	Lotus 35	50	48 min 17.0 sec	
8th	David Prophet	8	Brabham BT10	49		
9th	Trevor Taylor	6	Brabham BT16	49		
10th	Chris Amon	11	Lola T55	49		
11th	Adam Wyllie	10	Brabham BT16	46		
12th	Bill Bradley	9	Brabham BT10	46		

Fastest Lap (overall - part I)   15 & 18   Clark & Stewart   55.8 sec (89.68 mph)

Chapter Nine
Silverstone
10th July

"CLARK SCORES HIS FOURTH SUCCESSIVE G.P. VICTORY"

At Silverstone Jim Clark took a commanding lead in the World Drivers' Championship. Clark ran away with the race, but in the closing stages his engine lost oil pressure and he was forced to switch off the engine on Woodcote corner on the last few laps. Graham Hill broke the lap record on the last lap but failed to catch the Lotus by less than 100 yards. John Surtees, driving the flat-12 Ferrari for the first time finished third....

Above right
Yet another victory celebration. Left to right Jim Clark, Leo Wybrott, Colin Chapman and Dick Scammell.

Timetable

Event: 18th R.A.C. British Grand Prix
Date: 10th July 1965
Location: Silverstone
Circuit Length: 2.927 miles

Time	Race	Laps	Distance
10:30 am	Senior Service International Sports Car Race	25	73.18 miles
11:45 am	Britax International Touring Car Race	20	58.54 miles
2:00 pm	18th R.A.C. British Grand Prix	80	234.24 miles
4:45 pm	International Formula III Race	20	58.54 miles

Silverstone Grand Prix Circuit – Existing Lap Records

Formula 1	John Surtees	Ferrari 158/63	1m 33.0 sec.	113.30 mph.
Formula 2	Cliff Allison	Lotus 12	1m 43.4 sec.	101.91 mph.
Formula 3	Piers Courage	Brabham BT10	1m 41.6 sec.	103.72 mph.
Sportscars over 2000cc	Bruce McLaren	McLaren M1A	1m 31.6 sec.	115.03 mph.
Sportscars under 2000cc	Jack Brabham	Brabham BT8	1m 37.2 sec.	108.41 mph.
Saloon Cars over 2000cc	Jack Sears	Ford Galaxie	1m 49.6 sec.	96.14 mph.
Saloon Cars 1301cc to 2000cc	Jack Sears	Lotus-Cortina	1m 53.2 sec.	93.09 mph.

R.A.C. British Grand Prix
Entry List

No.	Entrant	Car	Engine	C.C.	Driver
1	S.E.F.A.C. – Ferrari	Ferrari 158/63	Ferrari Flat12	1497	John Surtees
2	S.E.F.A.C. – Ferrari	Ferrari 158/63	Ferrari V8	1497	Lorenzo Bandini
3	Owen Racing Organisation	B.R.M. P261	B.R.M. V8	1498	Graham Hill
4	Owen Racing Organisation	B.R.M. P261	B.R.M. V8	1498	Jackie Stewart
5	Team Lotus	Lotus 33 (chassis R6/R11)	Climax V8	1496	Jim Clark
6	Team Lotus	Lotus 33 (chassis R9)	Climax V8	1496	Mike Spence
7	Brabham Racing Organisation	Brabham BT11	Climax V8	1496	Jack Brabham
8	Brabham Racing Organisation	Brabham BT11	Climax V8	1496	Dan Gurney
9	The Cooper Car Company	Cooper T77	Climax V8	1496	Bruce McLaren
10	The Cooper Car Company	Cooper T77	Climax V8	1496	Jochen Rindt
11	Honda Motor Company	Honda RA272	Honda V12	1499	Richie Ginther
12	Scuderia Centro-Sud	B.R.M. P578	B.R.M. V8	1498	Masten Gregory
14	Brabham Racing Organisation	Brabham BT7	Climax V8	1496	Denis Hulme
15	R.R.C. Walker	Brabham BT7	Climax V8	1498	Jo Bonnier
16	R.R.C. Walker	Brabham BT7	B.R.M. V8	1498	Jo Siffert
17	John Willment Automobiles	Brabham BT11	B.R.M. V8	1498	Frank Gardner
18	D.W. Racing Enterprises Ltd.	Brabham BT11	Climax V8	1496	Bob Anderson
19*	D.W. Racing Enterprises Ltd.	Lotus 33 (chassis R8)	Climax V8	1498	Paul Hawkins (dna)
20	Gerard Racing	Cooper T60	Climax V8	1496	John Rhodes
22	Reg Parnell	Lotus 25 (chassis R3)	B.R.M. V8	1498	Richard Attwood
23	Reg Parnell	Lotus 25 (chassis R7)	B.R.M. V8	1498	Innes Ireland
24	Ian Raby (Racing) Ltd.	Brabham BT3	B.R.M. V8	1498	Ian Raby
25	Gerard Racing	Cooper T71	Ford 4-cyl	1498	Alan Rollinson (dnq)
26*	Brian Gubby	Lotus 24 (chassis 943)	Climax V8	1498	Brian Gubby (dnq)

Four in a row for Clark

Held at Brands Hatch for the first time the previous year – hitherto the event had alternated between Aintree and Silverstone – in 1965 the British Grand Prix returned to traditional Northamptonshire home as the highlight of a four-race programme on a cloudy and intermittently damp day.

The proceedings opened with a 25-lap sports car race, the teams competing for the Senior Service Trophy although the field was somewhat depleted due as a consequence of John Surtees, Bruce McLaren and Team Lotus choosing not to accept the RAC's meagre starting money offer.

In practice Hugh Dibley in his Lola T70 was very clearly faster than John Coundley's McLaren-Elva. Third fastest was a second T70, Roy Pierpiont driving the Harold Young car whose usual driver – David Hobbs – was yet to be declared fully race-fit following a road accident a few weeks earlier. The drive had originally been offered to Roger Mac, himself injured at Reims, and then to Jack Sears who turned it down The task finally fell to Roy Pierpiont, an experienced driver who was fairly used to big bangers as both the manufacturer and driver of the Attila. On the outside of the front row was Bob Bondurant, driving the Willment team's recently acquired Lotus 30, with Tony Lanfranchi on the second row having posted a time of 1m 38s after the suspension broke on his Attila causing a big spin and requiring him to switch to Sid Taylor's 2-litre Brabham.

Despite Dibley's speed in qualifying it was Coundley who was first into Copse followed by Lanfranchi and John Dean's Lotus 30. Bondurant was meanwhile the last to get away after his own Lotus 30 needed a push which would eventually earn him a disqualification. Building on his advantage, Coundley began to pull away easily from Dean, while Trevor Taylor moved the bright yellow JC Bamford Lotus 30 past Lanfranchi into third place. Hugh Dibley by this time was lying fifth after his own bad start, Bondurant lying twelfth at the end of lap one but going like the wind. Pierpoint soon suffered a problem of his own, stopping at the end of his first lap, the car jammed in second, and remaining in the pits for some while before coming out only to retire shortly afterwards with overheating problems.

By lap five Dibley was showing some of his earlier promise, moving up into fourth (one place ahead of the astonishing Bondurant) until the next lap at Beckett's when his engine blew up depositing the contents of its sump all over the road. Taylor got past Dean to take second place, but then spun on Dibley's oil at Beckett's surrendering it to Bondurant who now faced the immense task of trying to catch Coundley's exceptionally well driven McLaren. Victor Wilson meanwhile retired his Lotus 30 with engine damage just as a shower of rain began to fall, and then on lap 20 Dean lost his fourth place altogether when the engine of his Lotus began to play up.

For a while Bondurant managed to close the gap, gaining one and a half to two seconds a lap until the whisps of smoke from his Lotus turned into a trail and he started to lose ground. Coundley was soon able to run out a comfortable winner from the yet-to-be-disqualified Bondurant with Trevor Taylor third,

Above
Qualifying sixth, Mike Spence equalled his best ever GP result with a fourth at Silverstone. His best ever finish would be a third at that years Mexican GP.

Above
The 1500cc 32-valve flat-crank Coventry-Climax FWMV engine gave around 205bhp and with a special megaphone exhaust, an unusual whistling note.

"The BRDC are to stage a party in honour of Jim Clark and Graham Hill after the first day's practice for the British Grand Prix on the evening of July 8th, at Silverstone. The two drivers will be presented with Gold Stars by the Hon. Gerald Lascelles, BRDC President, to commemorate their fine drives in winning the Indianapolis 500 and the Monaco GP.'

Lanfranchi fourth (and winner of the 2-litre class) and David Prophet fifth despite having to drive on the ignition switch for much of the race when the throttle on his Lotus 30 stuck open early on.

BMW Joins The Saloon Car Grid

The saloon cars were the next onto the grid, the field for the Britax Trophy a familiar mix of Mustang, Cortina, Minis and Anglias but now with the addition of Keith Greene driving a BMW 1800 TI. (Alan Hutcheson had his Galaxie out in practice, but a tyre burst at Copse on the Thursday had put the car hard into the bank and out of the race.)

Mike Salmon took an early lead in his Mustang followed by the works Lotus-Cortinas of Sears in E11 (run by Bob Sparshott) and Sir John Whitmore in E9 with Alan McCall in charge of running things. Baillie's Mustang was fourth, ahead of two more Lotus-Cortinas driven by Tom Fletcher and André Baldet, and John Fitzpatrick in the leading Broadspeed Mini.

Unfortunately Pierpoint was soon to retire his Mustang, pulling out on the first lap with an overheating engine due to a broken fan belt. The battling Cortinas managed to hold up Baillie for a couple of laps but then the Mustang got past and set off after Salmon. Fletcher held a lonely fifth place, Baldet being briefly harried by Fitzpatrick until the Mini's engine exploded as it passed the pits. Lewis then took over seventh spot to become the leading Mini and behind him all hell broke loose in the Mini/Anglia pack at Beckett's when Lanfranchi's Mini was shunted by Mike Young's Anglia causing the Mini to spin to halt although the Anglia was able to escape with a badly mangled front end.

In fact Mini retirements were extremely high, with Pilsworth, Banks, Neal and Campbell-Cole all retiring with engine problems while Costello went out with clutch failure, Anita Taylor pulled over to check a handling problem (traced to oil on the tyres) and Nellemann hit the inside wall at Stowe after another spin.

Up with the big boys Baillie eventually manged to pass Salmon, who was suffering from fuel starvation problems from midway through the race, and went on to take a comfortable win. Sears and Whitmore eventually dead-heated for third place, with Fletcher and Baldet finishing fifth and sixth respectively while John Lewis finished seventh to win the 1300cc class.

The Grand Prix

With entries from all the usual teams and a number of private owners who at this time were regularly able to make the start in major Formula 1 races, numbers one and two in the programme were the works Ferraris of Surtees and Bandini. The big difference here was that Surtees had at last managed to get his hands on a flat-12 engine although Bandini was still consigned to a V8. A similar engine had been brought along for Surtees too, just in case, and indeed he had been quicker in the eight cylinder car during practice, circling the track in 1m 31.4sec. – as opposed to 1m 31.7sec. in the flat-12 – although he decided to stick with the newer engine.

BRM fielded its two regular cars for Hill and Stewart, plus a spare in case of any problems, with Lotus also arriving with three cars, two fitted with flat crank engines (R6 and R9) and a late-arriving R11 with the 4-valve Climax unit. Once the last named was ready to

International Senior Service Sports Car Race
Results

Position	Driver	No.	Car	Laps	Time/Reason	Speed
1st	John Coundley	12	McLaren-Elva M1A	25	40 min 26.2 sec	108.58 mph
dsq	Bob Bondurant	19	Lotus 30	25	Push start	
2nd	Trevor Taylor	22	Lotus 30	25		
3rd	Tony Lanfranchi	14	Brabhan BT8	25		
4th	David Prophet	20	Lotus 30	25		
5th	Keith St.John	5	Elva-BMW Mk.7	24		
6th	Tony Sargeant	2	Merlyn Mk.6	24		
dnf	John Dean	17	Lotus 30	19	Engine	
dnf	Victor Wilson	21	Lotus 30	15	Engine	
dnf	Roy Pierpoint	16	Lola T70	7	Overheating	
dnf	Hugh Dibley	26	Lola T70	6	Engine	
Pole Position		26	Hugh Dibley		1 min 31.6 sec (115.03 mph)	
Fastest Lap (new record)		12	John Coundley		1 min 34.4 sec (111.62 mph)	
Class Winners			Coundley, Lanfranchi			

International Britax Touring Car Race
Results

Pos.	Driver	No.	Car	Laps	Time/Reason	Speed
1st	Gawaine Baillie	42	Ford Mustang	20	37 min 12.4 sec	94.40 mph
2nd	Mike Salmon	41	Ford Mustang	20	37 min 20.4 sec	
3rd	Jack Sears	36	Lotus-Cortina (E11)	20	37 min 51.8 sec	
3rd	John Whitmore	37	Lotus-Cortina (E9)	20	37 min 51.8 sec	
5th	Tom Fletcher	30	Lotus-Cortina	20	38 min 08.4 sec	
6th	André Baldet	33	Lotus-Cortina	20	38 min 51.8 sec	
7th	John Lewis	21	Austin Mini-Cooper S	20	38 min 57.4 sec	
8th	Rauno Aaltonen	7	Austin Mini-Cooper S	20	39 min 13.4 sec	
9th	Harry Ratcliffe	16	Morris Mini-Cooper S	19		
10th	Keith Greene	38	BMW 1800 T.I.	19		
11th	Mike Young	2	Ford Anglia	19		
12th	Chris Craft	3	Ford Anglia	19		
13th	Tony Lanfranchi	17	Morris Mini-Cooper S	19		
14th	Gordon Spice	18	Morris Mini-Cooper S	19		
15th	Tony Rutt	22	Morris Mini-Cooper S	19		
16th	David Wansborough	5	Austin Mini-Cooper S	19		
17th	Anita Taylor	11	Austin Mini-Cooper S	18		
18th	Ken Costello	10	Austin Mini-Cooper S	15	Clutch	
19th	Peter Pilsworth	9	Austin Mini-Cooper S	14	Engine	
20th	Warwick Banks	24	Morris Mini-Cooper S	13	Engine	
dnf	Christian Nelleman	19	Morris Mini-Cooper S	12	Accident	
dnf	John Nicholson	32	Lotus-Cortina	8		
dnf	Mike Campbell-Cole	6	Austin Mini-Cooper S	8	Engine	
dnf	Steve Neal	14	Austin Mini-Cooper S	6	Fan belt	
dnf	John Fitzpatrick	15	Morris Mini-Cooper S	6	Engine	
dnf	Roy Pierpoint	43	Ford Mustang	1	Fan belt	

Pole Position	41	Mike Salmon		
Fastest Lap (class record)	42 & 41	Baillie & Salmon	1 min 50.0 sec (95.79 mph)	
Class Winners		Baillie, Sears, Lewis,		

Clockwise from top left
Tommy Sopwith talks to
Jack Sears. Ritchie
Ginther doesn't look too
happy with the Honda.
Jackie Stewart tries to
loosen up with some
neck excercises. Chris
Parry (Firestone
Competitions Manager)
get serious with
Andrew Ferguson.

Clockwise from top left
Jimmy cuts it fine at
Becketts corner. As
Jimmy starts to slow
Sally Stokes looks
worried. Colin checks
the car over, while
Jimmy is back with his
regular helmet and
white peak.

"The Indy-winning Lotus 38 is being brought over the Atlantic to give the Silverstone spectators a treat at the British GP on July 10th. We wonder which way round Jim will drive it?"

go, Clark decided to stick with it, putting the Climax engine to good use and progressively reducing his times during the practice to take pole with a time of 1m 30.3sec.. (All this despite an incident earlier in the week when one of the new knock-off nuts being used by Lotus unwound itself during Thursday's practice; due to some very quick thinking Jimmy was able to bring the car to rest intact.) Lotus number 2, Mike Spence in R9, was on the second row alongside John Surtees in the Ferrari flat-12 which had turned in a time just under a second slower than Clark's.

The Brabham team came with three cars, for Brabham, Hulme and Gurney, and at the start of the weekend all three were fitted with two-valve Climax engines. By Friday night a 4-valve engine was ready and fitted into Dan Gurney's car for the race itself even though he hadn't practiced with it. (The team was convinced it would be quicker.) The Cooper team brought along their two normal cars for McLaren and Rindt to drive, plus a spare car which was fitted with a Hewland gearbox instead of the usual Cooper box.

Honda by this time had three of their RA272s built up and ready to go, but entered only one at Silverstone for Richie Ginther leaving his fellow American Ronnie Bucknum without a drive. Ginther however, finally got the car going well and in the third session was able to put up a very rapid time of 1m 31.3sec. to get himself on the front row of the grid.

Thereafter the field was completed with a number of privateers including the two Rob Walker Brabhams for Siffert and Bonnier, the Willment Brabham-BRM for

Frank Gardner, a pair of Parnell Lotus-BRMs for Richard Attwood and Innes Ireland, Bob Anderson's Brabham-Climax, the Gerard Racing Cooper-Climax for John Rhodes, and a Cooper-Ford for Alan Rollinson. Paul Hawkins was also on the entry list in his Lotus-Climax until a team member crashed it while it was being tested and it was unable to be repaired in time for the race.

As the mechanics prepared their cars for the 80-lap race, rain looked more likely than not. Several drivers, including Stewart at BRM, opted for the softer R7 tyre which was felt preferable to the harder R6 compound if things got wet. As ever, Colin Chapman called the shots for Team Lotus, telling both drivers that they would be using the harder tyres.

At the end of the warm-up lap there was some drama when Dan Gurney rushed his Brabham into the pit-lane with a suspected broken valve on the new engine. One of the team's mechanics unscrewed a plug to have a look inside but unfortunately the complete thread came out at the same time. As a very unhappy Gurney was being pushed away, team leader Jack Brabham sportingly offered him his own car and, although the somewhat taller Gurney was a little uncomfortable at being squeezed into the smaller cockpit, he took his place on the third row leaving an empty space on the second row ahead of the two works Brabhams.

As the flag dropped, Ginther in the transverse-engined V12 Honda used his extra horsepower to blast off the line thereby putting Honda into the lead of a Grand Prix for the first time. It didn't stay there long, however, and

Above and next pages
Jimmy, on pole position, looks both relaxed and serious for Peter before the start of the British Grand Prix. Jimmy and Lotus number two Mike Spence in the pit lane.

R.A.C. British Grand Prix
Grid

Pole Position

Jackie Stewart	Richie Ginther	Graham Hill	Jim Clark
B.R.M.	Honda	B.R.M.	Lotus-Climax
1 min 31.3 sec	1 min 31.3 sec	1 min 31.0 sec	1 min 30.8 sec

	Mike Spence	John Surtees	
	Lotus-Climax	Ferrari	
	1 min 31.7 sec	1 min 31.3 sec	

Bruce McLaren	Denis Hulme	Lorenzo Bandini	Dan Gurney
Cooper-Climax	Brabham-Climax	Ferrari	Brabham-Climax
1 min 32.8 sec	1 min 32.7 sec	1 min 32.7 sec	1 min 31.9 sec

Jo Bonnier	Frank Gardner	Jochen Rindt
Brabham-Climax	Brabham-B.R.M.	Cooper-Climax
1 min 33.5 sec	1 min 33.4 sec	1 min 32.9 sec

Jo Siffert	Bob Anderson	Richard Attwood	Innes Ireland
Brabham-B.R.M.	Brabham-Climax	Lotus-B.R.M.	Lotus-B.R.M.
1 min 34.2 sec	1 min 34.1 sec	1 min 33.8 sec	1 min 33.6 sec

John Rhodes	Ian Raby	Masten Gregory
Cooper-Climax	Brabham-B.R.M.	B.R.M.
1 min 39.4 sec	1 min 36.0 sec	1m 35.9 sec

"They were good times and there was much merriment and camaraderie between the people and the teams in Formula One." Sally Stokes remembers 1965 fondly.

by the time the cars had exited Copse at the end of the pit straight Clark had dived down the inside and resumed his customary position at the head of the field. As the cars crossed the start/finish line at the end of the first lap, Ginther lost another place to Hill, the Englishman taking off after Jimmy whilst Bandini retired his Ferrari with a broken exhaust and Masten Gregory pulled into the pit lane for a change of plugs.

With the field now reduced to just 17 cars, Clark and Hill were both pushing hard, smashing the lap record time after time although it was clear that Hill was having to fight really hard just to keep Clark in his sights. By lap 20 Clark was a full five seconds ahead of Hill, with Surtees in his Ferrari third and Stewart fighting with Spence in the number two Lotus for fourth place. The battle between these two was helping them close on Surtees, and by lap 24 Spence overhauled Stewart and started seriously to hound the Ferrari.

At half distance Clark was still continuing to extend his lead over Hill although his engine was beginning to sound noticeably less crisp than it had done at the start of the race. It seemed that Hill, who had hedged his bets by starting the race on a mix of tyres, was now struggling with front end grip from the softer R6s and, fearing that these might not last the full race distance, was taking it steady. The race accordingly settled down into something of a dull pattern with little serious prospect of any change between the running order up front.

There were problems further down the field too, with a number of the slower cars suffering a various

assortment of problems. The Cooper of John Rhodes stopped with gear selection difficulties, Hulme lost sixth place when the belt on his alternator broke, Bob Anderson had some gear selection problems of his own, and Innes Ireland pulled off at Becketts when the engine blew on his Reg Parnell-run BRM-powered Lotus 25. The final retirement came on lap 63 when Jochen Rindt's Cooper-Climax lost eighth place at Stowe, his engine expiring in a big way and leaving him rather a long walk back to the pits.

As the race began to draw to a close, and as Graham Hill fans resigned themselves to Clark's fourth and very comfortable British Grand Prix win in a row, things began to take a different direction. At the halfway stage, Jimmy was later to relate, his oil pressure had started to drop quite significantly as he went into the long sweeping Woodcote corner. By the time the cars entered the 70th lap he was suffering a similar problem on every corner, with several other drivers reporting seeing his Lotus blowing out fairly significant quantities of oil onto the track. It continued to do this until the very last few laps when Clark began to back off the throttle whenever he could, even switching off the ignition in the hope that he could nurse his engine through to the end of the race.

Little wonder then that, suddenly, the gap between Clark and Hill began to decrease dramatically. From more than 20 seconds ahead it was suddenly down to just 15 and still dropping by between three and four a lap. The BRM pit crew put out a signal to Graham that Jimmy was in trouble and, despite having brake trouble requiring him to pump the pedal three or four

Above
As Jimmy, the car and most of the Lotus crew boarded the flatbed trailer for a victory lap, (headed of course by a Lotus Elan) the crowd swarmed onto the track to get a better view.

R.A.C. British Grand Prix
Results

Pos.	Driver	No.	Car	Laps	Time/Reason	Speed
1st	Jim Clark	5	Lotus 33	80	2 hr 05 min 25.4 sec	112.02 mph
2nd	Graham Hill	3	B.R.M. P261	80	2 hr 05 min 28.6 sec	
3rd	John Surtees	1	Ferrari 158/63	80	2 hr 05 min 53.0 sec	
4th	Mike Spence	6	Lotus 33	80	2 hr 06 min 05.0 sec	
5th	Jackie Stewart	4	B.R.M. P261	80	2 hr 06 min 40.0 sec	
6th	Dan Gurney	8	Brabham BT11	79		
7th	Jo Bonnier	15	Brabham BT7	79		
8th	Frank Gardner	17	Brabham BT11	78		
9th	Jo Siffert	16	Brabham BT7	78		
10th	Bruce McLaren	9	Cooper T77	77		
11th	Ian Raby	24	Brabham BT3	73		
nc	Masten Gregory	12	B.R.M. P587	70		
nc	Richard Attwood	22	Lotus 25	63		
dnf	Jochen Rindt	10	Cooper T77	62		
dnf	Innes Ireland	23	Lotus 25	41		
dnf	John Rhodes	20	Cooper T60	38		
dnf	Bob Anderson	18	Brabham BT11	33		
dnf	Denis Hulme	14	Brabham BT11	29		
dnf	Richie Ginther	11	Honda RA272	26		
dnf	Lorenzo Bandini	2	Ferrari 158/63	2		

Pole Position		5	Jim Clark		1 min 30.8 sec (116.12 mph)	
Fastest Lap (record)		3	Graham Hill		1 min 32.2 sec (114.29 mph)	

Left
The start of the Formula three race. Left to right, Roy Pike on Pole in the Chequered Flag Brabham, Peter Gethin (Charles Lucas Brabham), Peter Revson with his hands in the air (Ron Harris Type 35) and David Cole on the outside, also in a Brabham.

Below
Clockwise from top left. A rogues gallery, Leo Wybrott, Bob Sparshott, Arthur Birchall and Alan McCall with Dick Scammell on his left.

Left
Four in a row for JC.
This was Jimmy's fourth
consecutive British
Grand Prix victory, a
sequence which had
started at Aintree in '62.

times at every corner, Hill quickly responded with some very fast laps of his own.

With four laps left Hill was just over 12 seconds down on Clark. A lap later it was only 10.7 and at the start of the penultimate lap it was just 7.7 seconds. As the cars started the final lap the crowd were suddenly on their feet and Graham, now just over four seconds adrift, was driving as hard as he could, sensing that victory was within his grasp. As he set off down the pit straight he could see Jimmy entering Copse corner ahead of him and spurred on by this he put in the fastest lap of the race – 1m 32.2sec. at 114.29mph. – a new track record for the full Silverstone Grand Prix circuit.

As the two cars came into Woodcote for the last time, however, Jimmy's skill not just behind the wheel but also in preserving his car in such dire circumstances looked to have paid off. Ever hopeful, he gave the car one last burst of throttle and managed to make it across the line less than 100 yards ahead of Hill who passed Jimmy moments after the two of them had taken the chequered flag. From a somewhat processional race, and when it was least expected, the fans had witnessed a genuinely thrilling end.

Formula Three To Finish The Day

As in the days of old when the little 500cc cars had concluded the big Silverstone meetings, the day finished with a 20-lap F3 race. Roy Pike in the Chequered Flag Brabham was on pole position and from the start went off into a lead he was never to relinquish. Fellow front row starter Peter Revson never even made it off the line when his engine lost all oil pressure. Although pressed

for a for a few laps by the Brabhams of David Cole and Peter Gethin, Pike succeeded in shaking them off, leaving them to a race-long duel which eventually resolved itself in Gethin's favour when Cole dropped back to finish tenth. Chris Irwin in the second Chequered Flag car got up to third place at one stage, but then smoke began pouring from the cockpit and he retired with a broken engine. Tommy Hitchcock in his Brabham then took over Irwin's third place but he spun coming out of Woodcote and slid into the pit wall causing plenty of damage to the car but thankfully emerging unscathed.

For a few laps there was another huge dice – between Dean's and Blokdyk's Brabhams, Ray Parsons' Lotus 35, Throddson's Brabham and Stiller's Lotus 27 – which eventually ended up with Dean finishing third ahead of Blokdyk and Stiller. Parsons collided with Bibb's Cooper whilst lapping him at Becketts but again, neither driver was hurt.

Six Out Of Six For Jimmy

In managing to keep his increasingly sick Lotus in the lead, Clark thoroughly deserved his fourth British Grand Prix victory in a row. Extending his lead over Hill in the title race he went on to secure his second World Championship just two races later, victory in the German Grand Prix making a perfect 'six out of six' in the six races a driver could put towards their championship score in 1965. Even better, by the time Clark clinched the Championship in Germany, he could also claim to have won every single GP he had contested that year, the sole exception having been the Monaco GP when he had been otherwise occupied, winning the Indy 500.

International Formula III Race
Results

Position	Driver	No.	Car	Laps	Time/Reason	Speed
1st	Roy Pike	10	Brabham BT16	20	34 min 25.8 sec	102.02 mph
2nd	Peter Gethin	9	Brabham BT10	20	34 min 25.8 sec	
3rd	Tony Dean	29	Brabham BT15	20	34 min 25.8 sec	
4th	Trevor Blokdyk	2	Brabham BT16	20	34 min 25.8 sec	
5th	Harry Stiller	19	Lotus 32	20	34 min 25.8 sec	
6th	Jim Sullivan	7	Brabham BT15	20	34 min 25.8 sec	
7th	Denis O'Sullivan	8	Brabham BT10	20	34 min 25.8 sec	
8th	Bob Bondurant	32	Cooper T76	20	34 min 25.8 sec	
9th	Teddy Dawson	24	Lotus 31	20	34 min 25.8 sec	
10th	David Cole	6	Brabham BT15	20	34 min 25.8 sec	
11th	Keith St.John	5	Brabham BT9	20	34 min 25.8 sec	
12th	Ken Bass	28	Merlyn Mk.9	20	34 min 25.8 sec	
13th	Sverrir Thoroddsson	14	Brabham BT15	19		
14th	Graham White	3	Brabham BT9	19		
15th	Len Gibbs	23	Lotus 31	19		
16th	Rollo Fielding	31	Cooper T76	19		
17th	Tony Goodwin	27	Lola Mk.5A	18		
18th	Charles Crichton-Stuart	12	Brabham BT10	18		
dnf	Ray Parsons	20	Lotus 35	15	Crash	
dnf	Thomas Bibb	33	Cooper T72	14	Crash	
dnf	Melvyn Long	15	Lotus 27	10	Oil filter	
dnf	Tommy Hitchcock	4	Brabham BT16	7	Accident	
dnf	Malcolm Payne	16	Lotus 31	6	Oil pressure	
dnf	Derek Bell	18	Lotus 31	4	Bearing	
dnf	Chris Irwin	11	Brabham BT16	3	Oil pressure	
dnf	Richard Burton	22	Lotus 31	2	Big end	
dnf	Peter Revson	17	Lotus 35	0	Engine	
dnf	Frank Williams	21	Cooper T71	0	Engine	
Pole Position		10	Pike		1 min 40.4 sec (105.03 mph)	
Fastest Lap (record)		10	Pike		1 min 41.4 sec (103.92 mph)	

Chapter Ten
Brands Hatch
30th August

"SURTEES WINS AT BRANDS BANK HOLIDAY MEETING"

Driving a brand new Lola T70 fitted with a 5.8-litre Chevrolet engine, John Surtees won both 30-lap parts of the Guards Trophy at Brands hatch on August Bank Holiday. Averaging 95.79mph in the first part and 96.43mph in the second part, he also put up a new sports car lap record....

Above right
Tea Break, or rather 'Pepsi time'. Bob Dance, Alan McCall and Bob Sparshott take a few minutes out from their busy weekend.

Timetable

Event: Guards International
Date: 30th August 1965
Location: Brands Hatch
Circuit Length: 2.65 miles

Time	Race	Laps	Distance
12.00 pm	The Redex Trophy	20	52.97 miles
1.15 pm	The Guards International (Part I)	30	79.50 miles
2.30 pm	The British Eagle International Trophy	20	52.97 miles
3.35 pm	The Guards International (Part II)	30	79.50 miles
4.45 pm	The Ilford Films Trophy	20	52.97 miles

Brands Hatch, Long Circuit – Existing Lap Records

Formula 1	Jim Clark	Lotus-Climax	1m 35.4 sec.	100.00 mph.
Formula 2	Graham Hill	Repco-Brabham	1m 43.4 sec.	92.26 mph.
Formula 3	Brian Hart	Lotus-Ford	1m 45.6 sec.	90.34 mph.
Sportscars over 2000cc	Hugh Dibley	Repco-Brabham	1m 42.6 sec.	92.98 mph.
Sportscars under 2000cc	Frank Gardner	Brabham-Ford	1m 44.0 sec.	91.73 mph.
Saloon Cars over 2000cc	Jim Clark	Ford Galaxie	1m 54.4 sec.	83.39 mph.
Saloon Cars 1301cc to 2000cc	Jim Clark	Lotus-Cortina	1m 54.8 sec.	83.10 mph.

Guards International
Entry List

No.	Entrant	Car	Engine	C.C.	Driver
1	Harold Young Ltd.	Lola T70	Chevrolet V8	5967	David Hobbs
2	Stirling Moss Auto Racing Team	Lola T70	Chevrolet V8	5525	Hugh Dibley
4	Team Surtees Ltd.	Lola T70	Chevrolet V8	5967	John Surtees
5	Team Surtees Ltd.	Lola T70	Chevrolet V8	5359	Jackie Stewart
7	Bruce McLaren Motor Racing Ltd.	McLaren M1A	Oldsmobile V8	4918	Bruce McLaren
8	Team Lotus	Lotus 40	Ford V8	5754	Jim Clark
10	John Willment Automobiles	Lotus 30	Ford V8	4727	Frank Gardner
11	Ashmore Brothers	Lotus 30	Ford V8	4727	Gerry Ashmore
12	John Dean Racing	Lotus 30	Ford V8	4727	John Dean
14	Tony Kilburn Racing	Lotus 30	Ford V8	4727	Simon de Lautour
15	J.C. Bamford (Excavators)	Lotus 30	Ford V8	4727	Trevor Taylor
16	Mecom Racing Team	Lola T70	Ford V8	4727	Walt Hansgen
17	D.R.Good	Lola T70	Ford V8	4727	Roy Pierpoint
18	All American Racers	McLaren-Elva M1A	Ford V8	4727	Dan Gurney
19	David Prophet Racing	McLaren-Elva M1A	Ford V8	4727	David Prophet
21	John Coombs	McLaren-Elva M1A	Oldsmobile V8	4450	Graham Hill
22	John Coundley Racing Partnership	McLaren-Elva M1A	Oldsmobile V8	4450	John Coundley
23	R.Nathan	Brabham BT8	Oldsmobile V8	4450	Roger Nathan
24	Maranello Concessionaries	Ferrari 365P2	Ferrari V12	4390	Mike Parkes
25	David Piper (Auto Racing)	Ferrari 365P2	Ferrari V12	4390	David Piper
31	Bruce McLaren Motor Racing Ltd.	Elva Mk.8	B.M.W. 4-cyl	1991	Chris Amon
32	Radio London Racing	Elva Mk.7	B.M.W. 4-cyl	1991	Keith St.John
34	Chris Williams	Elva Mk.7	B.M.W. 4-cyl	1991	Peter Gethin
35	Chris Williams	Lotus-Brabham	B.M.W. 4-cyl	1991	Chris Williams
36	Sidney Taylor Racing	Brabham BT8	Climax 4-cyl	1973	Denis Hulme
37	Celerity Inc.	Brabham BT8	Climax 4-cyl	1973	Tommy Hitchcock
38	Kay Racing International	Brabham BT8	Climax 4-cyl	1973	Peter Revson
41	Racing Partnerships (Jersey) Ltd.	Merlyn Mk.6	Ford 4-cyl	1594	Tony Sargeant

Surtees Wins Twice

The BRSCC gathered together a first-class entry of both cars and drivers for a series of races organised over the long circuit at Brands Hatch for the August Bank Holiday Monday. A record crowd of more than 60,000 spectators packed into the circuit to see the day's racing, a large number of them staying on to listen to a jazz session by Chris Barber and his band. A huge enthusiast for Lotus and for racing in general, Barber had earlier in the day entered a pair of Lotus Elans for Mike Beckwith and John Hine in the GT race.

Ahead of the main event, the day started at noon with a 20-lap race for 'Appendix J (1965) Group 3 GT' cars, the drivers competing for the Redex Trophy. Even before the race got underway hopes were high for a good battle between Bob Bondurant, driving the Chequered Flag Team's open Cobra, and Jack Sears driving the Willment Cobra Coupé. In fact right from the off the white open Cobra developed clutch slip so that although Bondurant initially took the lead he gradually fell back, finishing the race but only after just about everyone else had passed him.

Sears was therefore completely on his own although the bunch of Lotus Elans that were following behind put up some good racing among themselves, with outstanding drives from Ray Parsons in the Team Lotus entry and Jackie Oliver in the DR Fabrications car. The two finished second and third respectively. Boley Pittard in the Walker-Day Racing Alfa-Romeo Giulia TZ also did well to keep ahead of the other nimble Cheshunt cars, making it home in fourth ahead of another phalanx of Elans driven by Edmonds, Wayne, Calvert and Liddell.

The Cars Line Up For The Guards

The dicing Elans having got everyone into a holiday mood, the big event of the day kicked off with the first heat of the Guards Trophy, an important 30-lap race for Appendix 'C' sports cars with prize money of £300 for the entrant of the winning car overall. As was only to be expected, the line-up mustered a huge amount of both brute force and talent with John Surtees, Jackie Stewart, David Hobbs, now with a Chevrolet engine rather than the smaller capacity Ford and fully fit after a road accident just 6 weeks before in which he had broken his nose, cheeks, jaw and left arm, Hugh Dibley, Walt Hansgen, and Roy Pierpoint all driving Lola T70s.

They were joined by Bruce McLaren in his own works M1A, John Coundley, George Wintersteen, Graham Hill, Dan Gurney and David Prophet in Elva-built production examples of the same car, Jim Clark with – at last – the brand new Lotus 40, and Frank Gardner, Gerry Ashmore, John Dean, Trevor Taylor and Simon de Lautour at the helm of several Lotus 30s. Joining them from Italy were a pair of Ferrari 365P/2 models, both with 4.4-litre V12 engines, driven by Mike Parkes and David Piper, and to complete the field a couple of privately-built cars. Driven by Bob Johnson and Roger Nathan, these were Ford V8-engined in a Cooper-Monaco and an Oldsmobile V8-engined Brabham BT8.

The organisers estimated the total at something in excess of 120,000cc and 10,000 horsepower, to which must be added a number of 2.0-litre cars including the three fast 4-cylinder, Climax-powered Brabham BT8s for Denis Hulme, Peter Revson and Tommy Hitchcock, and Chris Amon in the Bruce McLaren-entered Elva BMW.

Above
Ray Parsons finished second to Jack Sears in a Cobra in the 'Redex Trophy' sports car race.

Redex Trophy
Results

Pos.	Driver	No.	Car	Laps	Time/Reason	Speed
1st	Jack Sears	101	Shelby Cobra Coupé	20	36 min 35.6 sec	94.94 mph
2nd	Ray Parsons	131	Lotus Elan	20		
3rd	Jackie Oliver	134	Lotus Elan	20		
4th	Boley Pittard	138	Alfa-Romeo Giulia TZ			
5th	Jeff Edmonds	139	Lotus Elan			
6th	Malcolm Wayne	136	Lotus Elan			
7th	John Calvert	141	Lotus Elan			
8th	Eric Liddell	137	Lotus Elan			
9th	Keith Burnard	123	Abarth-Simca 2000			
10th	Patrick McNally	103	Shelby Cobra			
11th	Jim Mackay	154	Lotus Eleven GT			
dnf	William Bradley	151	Triumph Spitfire			
dnf	Bob Bondurant	102	Shelby Cobra			
dnf	Mike Campbell	124	Elva Courier			
dnf	William Nicholson	126	MGB			
dnf	R. Bertorelli	157	Lotus Eleven GT			
Pole Position		102	Bob Bondurant			
Fastest Lap		101	Jack Sears		1 min 47.2 sec (88.99 mph)	
Class Winners			Sears, Burnard, Parsons, Mackay			

Far left
Mike Spence and
Jimmy talk to Geoff
Murdoch (ESSO
Competitions Manager).

Left
Jackie Stewart climbed
onto the roof of the
ESSO hospitality trailer
and proudly displayed
his rival 'Shell'
sponsorship badge.

The day was clearly to belong to John Surtees, however, putting to very good use the 5.9-litre Chevrolet V8 in his brand new Lola T70 by winning both 30-lap sections of the Guards Trophy feature race, averaging 95.79mph in the first part and 96.43mph in the second part, and putting up a new sports car lap record in the latter at 1m 36.0sec. indicating an average speed of 99.37mph. Second in both parts was Bruce McLaren in a works 5.0-litre Oldsmobile-engined McLaren M1A, with the victor's team-mate Jackie Stewart in third place driving the older Lola-Chevy with which Surtees had previously won a number of race during the same season. Denis Hulme, driving the TT-winning 2.0-litre Brabham-Climax, finished fourth overall ahead of Feter Revson in the immaculate Kay Racing Brabham BT8. Elsewhere mechanical troubles beset many drivers, Jim Clark spinning twice in the first part with the new Lotus Type 40 and in the second part at Clearways when his engine seized.

The start had seen Surtees in pole position with Hill and McLaren joining him on the front row, followed on row two by Gurney and Hobbs, with, respectively, Chevrolet 5.9-litre, 4.5-litre Oldsmobile, 4.9-litre Oldsmobile, 4.7-litre Ford, and 5.9-litre Chevrolet engines. Such a line up certainly suggested sufficient horsepower to satisfy the crowd, but somehow the start was not as impressive as one might have expected perhaps because the cars carried a good deal of weight. Indeed the cars' independent rear suspension, and their very wide-treaded Firestone, Goodyear and Dunlop tyres, helped get the power down on the track so well that there was very little in the way of wheelspin, smoke, noise and the general pandemonium that had been expected.

Surtees was in great form, however, and driving a brand new Lola-Chevrolet with almost paper-thin fibreglass bodywork, he simply ran away from the opposition, his bright red car holding the road beautifully and looking very stable compared to some of the other cars. Bruce McLaren tried very hard to keep up, but it was soon obvious that even with equivalent of possibly superior roadholding his 4.9-litres couldn't combat with the leader's 5.9-litres. Hobbs meanwhile was going well in third place although Stewart, hounding him in the other Lola-Chevrolet, eventually passed him by.

Dan Gurney had unfortunately made a nonsense of his own start by taking off in third gear so that by the time he reached Paddock Bend almost the entire field had passed him. Try as he might he could not make up distance, although at one point he did get as high as fourth.

Jim Clark meanwhile had done barely five minutes of official practice, the Lotus 40 having been finished late. (Contrary to reports, this was its first race appearance as the car driven in Austria by Spence was actually a Lotus 30.) The lack of practice meant Clark was way back on the seventh row at the start and the poor gear shift in the Lotus made it barely raceworthy. Somehow he managed to work his way up to eighth place, but twice spun after selecting neutral instead of the required gear.

That said, Graham Hill had an even worse race, the Oldsmobile engine in his John Coombs-entered McLaren dying on the opening lap, apparently because of something electrical. Thereafter it refused to function properly even after he had limped back to the pits, and

British Eagle International Trophy
Grid

		Pole Position
Denis Hulme	Jim Clark	John Surtees
Brabham-Cosworth	Lotus-Cosworth	Lola-Cosworth
1 min 39.4 sec	1 min 38.6 sec	1 min 38.4 sec
	Jack Brabham	Graham Hill
	Brabham-Cosworth	Lotus-B.R.M.
	1 min 39.4 sec	1 min 39.4 sec
Richard Attwood	Mike Beckwith	Mike Spence
Lola-Cosworth	Brabham-Cosworth	Lotus-Cosworth
1 min 37.4 sec	1 min 39.6 sec	1 min 39.6 sec
	Alan Rees	Brain Hart
	Brabham-Cosworth	Lotus-Cosworth
	1 min 39.8 sec	1 min 39.8 sec
Bob Anderson	Peter Revson	Chris Amon
Brabham-Cosworth	Lotus-B.R.M.	Lola-Cosworth
1 min 41.4 sec	1 min 40.8 sec	1 min 40.2 sec
	Piers Courage	Dennis O'Sullivan
	Brabham-Ford (F3)	Brabham-Cosworth
	1 min 42.4 sec	1 min 41.6 sec
John Fenning	David Prophet	Roy Pike
Cooper-Ford (F3)	Brabham-Cosworth	Brabham-Ford (F3)
1 min 43.2 sec	1 min 42.4 sec	1 min 42.4 sec
	Peter Gethin	Chris Irwin
	Brabham-Ford (F3)	Brabham-Ford (F3)
	1 min 44.0 sec	1 min 43.4 sec
Boley Pittard	David Cole	John Cardwell
Lotus-Ford (F3)	Brabham-Ford (F3)	Lotus-Ford (F3)
1 min 45.0 sec	1 min 44.0 sec	1 min 44.0 sec
	Ray Parsons	C. Crichton-Stuart
	Lotus-Ford (F3)	Brabham-Ford (F3)
Etc.	1 min 45.2 sec	1 min 45.0 sec

"Sir John Whitmore and Jack Sears, sharing a Lotus-Cortina, have won the Nurburgring 500 Kilometers race for touring cars, at an average speed of 78.6mph, after a photo-finish with Roy Pierpoint and Jochen Neerpasch in their Ford Mustang."

though back on the track after after a certain amount of remedial attention he was well and truly out of the running. As was Hobbs whose gearbox packed up.

Surtees then won this first Heat with ease and efficiency, making an excellent start to the day for Lola especially when Stewart brought his car home third. Officially the cars had been entered by Team Surtees, but both were in effect 'works' entries having been supplied and prepared by Eric Broadley and his men. Otherwise it went almost without saying that Denny Hulme won the 2-litre class, driving Sidney Taylor's beautifully prepared Brabham-Climax to fifth place overall. Against such opposition the two heavy Ferraris were completely outclassed on the compact Brands circuit with Mike Parkes (in the Maranello Concessionaires car) managing a rather unimpressive sixth place while Piper was effectively still learning to drive his green, privately owned 'P2' having only collected it from the factory only the day before practice.

F3 Cars Mix It With The F2 Boys

From the bellowing of big capacity push-rod V8 engines to the high-pitched drone of 1000cc overhead cam four-pots, the pitch of the day changed dramatically for the next event with nearly every well-known racing driver taking part in a 20-lap Formula 2 race for the British Eagle Trophy. Bizarrely the organisers had decided to thorw equal numbers of F3 cars into the mix, apparently in a bid to spice things up a bit although the result was little more than to throw the F2 boys an additional hazard when it came to lapping the much slower cars several times. This race had £100 going to the winner (F2) and £40 to the best finisher in the Formula 3 class.

Jim Clark nevertheless made up for his earlier debacle with the Lotus 40, driving a Ron Harris Lotus-Cosworth Type 35 F2 car to a very convincing victory despite being chased relentlessly by Hulme and Brabham in the two works Brabham-Cosworths, and by John Surtees in the Midland Racing Partnership Lola T60. (Having felt that the Honda engines that the team had been helping develop throughout the season weren't giving the horsepower they had at the start of the year, during the summer the Brabham team had taken the decision to temporarily revert to Cosworth power. With a 1-2 in the F2 race in Sweden and a 2-3 here at Brands, it was clearly a decision that had paid off.)

In a sense, for Surtees, the race was the complete antithesis of his performance in the earlier event, the action over the 20 laps seeing him dropping back to seventh after spinning then catching up with Hill again and passing him to take fourth only to crash on the last lap taking the nose off his Lola. This late demise enabled Hill in the end to finish fourth, driving John Coombs' new Lotus 35 which had replaced his regular Brabham BT16, just ahead of Alan Rees in the Winkelmann Brabham and another Lola driven by Richard Attwood.

In the F3 section, and not for the first time, Roy Pike was quite outstanding in Graham Warner's Chequered Flag Brabham-Ford BT15, winning easily after his only serious rival Piers Courage retired his Charles Lucas Brabham on the first lap. The race for second was close, however, with plenty of jostling between Peter Gethin in one of three Lucas Engineering Brabham-Fords and John Cardwell in an older Ron Harris works Lotus 32s running in F3 specification.

Above
The Guards Trophy race was another disaster for David Hobbs in the Harold Young Lola T70. He retired from the first heat with gearbox failure and the team were unable to fix it in time for the part II.

"Jack Brabham's victory in the Formula 2 race at Karlskoga was reported in the Daily Express under the Heading 'Jim Clark loses'."

Right
Jimmy wore the Harrods cardigan that Sally bought him almost all the time, here he talks to Jim Endruweit.

Below
Jimmy would always try to take the 'T' car out for at least a few laps in practice. Here he heads John Fitzpatrick's 970cc works Mini-Cooper S.

Above
In the British Eagle
Trophy F2 race Jimmy
was dominant, leading
home the works
Brabham-Cosworth duo
of Denny Hulme and
Jack Brabham himself.

British Eagle International Trophy
Results

Pos.	Driver	No.	Car	Laps	Time/Reason	Speed
1st	Jim Clark	60	Lotus 35	20	33 min 29.6 sec	94.94 mph
2nd	Dennis Hulme	52	Brabham BT16	20	33 min 32.6 sec	
3rd	Jack Brabham	51	Brabham BT16	20	33 min 32.8 sec	
4th	Graham Hill	53	Lotus 35	20	33 min 49.4 sec	
5th	Alan Rees	54	Lotus 35	20		
6th	Richard Attwood	67	Lola T60	20		
7th	Mike Spence	61	Lotus 35	20		
8th	Brian Hart	65	Lotus 25	20		
9th	Bob Anderson	70	Brabham BT16	20		
10th	Mike Beckwith	56	Brabham BT16	20		
11th	Dennis O'Sullivan	59	Brabham BT16	20		
12th	David Prophet	57	Brabham BT10	20		
13th	Roy Pike	74	Brabham BT15 (F3)	19	35 min 07.2 sec	90.55 mph
14th	Chris Irwin	69	Merlyn Mk.9	19		
15th	John Surtees	66	Lola T60	19		
16th	Peter Gethin	73	Brabham BT10 (F3)	19		
17th	John Cardwell	79	Lotus 32 (F3)	19		
18th	Morris Nunn	64	Lotus 22	19		
19th	David Cole	78	Brabham BT15 (F3)	19		
20th	Ray Parsons	80	Lotus 35 (F3)	19		
21st	Tommy Hitchcock	87	Brabham BT16 (F3)	19		
22nd	Jim Sullivan	88	Brabham BT15 (F3)	19		
23rd	Ken Bass	90	Merlyn Mk.9 (F3)	18		
dnf	Chris Amon	68	Lola T60 (F3)	13		
dnf	Harry Stiller	77	Brabham BT16 (F3)	10		
dnf	John Fenning	85	Cooper T76 (F3)	10		
dnf	Charles Crichton-Stuart	76	Brabham BT10 (F3)	8		
dnf	Malcom Payne	84	Lotus 31 (F3)	8		
dnf	Peter Revson	62	Lotus 35	6		
Pole Position		66	John Surtees		1 min 38.4 sec (96.95 mph)	
Fastest Lap		60	Jim Clark		1 min 39.4 sec (95.98 mph)	

Heat II: Surtees Again

With no break, the sports cars were out for Heat two of the Guards Trophy almost as soon as the open-wheelers had been cleared from the track. Survivors of the first heat lined up on the grid in order of finishing, so that now the front row comprised Surtees (Lola), McLaren (McLaren) and Stewart (Lola), with Gurney (McLaren) and Hulme (Brabham 2-litre) in row two.

This time Stewart jumped into an early lead, but Surtees soon re-established his authority leaving Stewart for a time to hold up Gurney who keen to compensate for his earlier mistake was desperate to get after Surtees. Eventually he got by the number two Team Surtees Lola, but not before Surtees himself was too far ahead to be caught. Worse still, for Gurney, after holding a solid second place for a number of laps he finally parked smartly on the grass shortly after Clearways Bend when a bolt came out of the rear suspension leaving a rear wheel at a rather alarming angle.

In fact the performance given by Surtees was essentially a repetition of Heat one, the sort of impeccable show that was expected now that Eric Broadley had got the Lola T70 really sorted. Bruce McLaren came in second (again) with Stewart in third place followed by Hansgen in the Mecom Team Lola-Ford V8. Clark was way back, still in trouble, his car really not to his liking. At one point he was sitting as high as fifth place, but eventually a violently locking front brake caused a spin into the ditch at Clearways Bend and he climbed out of his unraceworthy machine apparently keen to be rid of it. Thereafter fifth belonged to the quiet and unassuming Hulme in the immaculately prepared Sid Taylor car,

John Coundley making it up to sixth place after a poor run in the first heat after picking up a nail and sustaining a puncture.

The overall result was obtained by adding the times recorded in each heat but clearly little understanding of mathematics was required to work out the first three places. Further down the ranks it was more complex, however, so that due to the strange way of recording the event as two separate races (up to 2000cc and over 2000cc) Hulme officially got no credit whatever for finishing fourth overall and was instead merely classed as winner of the under 2.0-litre class.

And Finally 20 Laps For Saloon Cars

A busy day finished with another busy race, this time a further 20 laps with the usual variety of different saloon cars competing for the Ilford Films Tropy. Once again the four classes dictated a field comprising Ford Mustangs and Lotus-Cortinas, BMC Minis of 1275cc (along with the odd Anglia) and yet more Minis of 970cc with the occasional pocket exotic from Abarth, John Anstead in the Radbourne Motors 1000TC.

True to form the works Cortinas of Jim Clark (E9) and Jack Sears debuting a new leaf-spring E12 took the initial advantage until Jack Brabham driving Alan Brown's orange Ford Mustang used his brute power to get by along the straight after South Bank Bend. At Westfield Bend the yellow flags were waved when Sears ran into the back of the new World Champion and spun him round, and at the end of the first lap Brabham was leading Sears until Roy Pierpoint in another Mustang snatched second place along the Top Straight.

Above left
"I know the engine is here somewhere," Mike Spence and Bob Dance look concerned about something on the Type 40. So does Jack Sears on the right.

Above right
The Maranello Concessionaries V12 Ferrari 365P2 of Mike Parkes was reliable if not fast and finished the two-part race in 6th.

"On July 14th BARC Gold Medals were presented to Colin Chapman and Jim Clark to recognize their achievement as constructor and driver in winning the Indianapolis 500. This was Clark's second such award and Chapman's first."

Behind him were Mike Salmon's Mustang, Clark who had managed to get E9 up and out again, and Frank Gardner in the Willment Lotus-Cortina. Further back still it was very much a battle of the Minis, the two Superspeed Anglias having failed to start after another problem in scrutineering and John Anstead in the little Fiat Abarth complaining of lack of urge.

On the fourth lap Clark went straight on at Bottom Bend, coming into the pits from the wrong side in order to have a flat tyre replaced. Though out of the running, he nevertheless came out for some more action and spent the rest of the race doing 'acrobatics' with his Cortina even cornering on two wheels. Unfortunately his progress was halted twice more, the first when a mechanic had to replace the ignition terminal by the side of the track at South Bank Bend, and a second when he stopped at the pits to complain of faulty steering.

Despite all this the officials decided to let him stay out to entertain spectators and in the event he went on to set a new outright saloon car record for the circuit of 1m 54.2sec.. (He was of course excluded from the results on two counts: that he had reversed the wrong way down the pit lane; and because a mechanic had worked on the car outside the pits.)

Back in the real race, with Brabham drawing well away from his pursuers, Pierpoint and Salmon gave chase in their Mustangs. Sears and Gardner were next in line, then Sir Gawaine Baillie's Mustang, and then on lap 16 Salmon was black flagged with a violently wobbling near side rear wheel afterwards traced to a broken hub.

Towards the end Pierpoint managed to close the gap on Brabham, but he left his challenge too late and so finished 2.2 seconds behind.

There was drama and frustration in the 1.0-litre class too, John Fitzpatrick's Broadspeed Mini leading until his seat broke and Warwick Banks in the works car took command. Mike Campbell-Cole and David Miller enjoyed their own glorious dust-up for second place, the latter losing it at Hawthorne Bend on lap 7, spinning and collecting Campbell-Cole on the way out. Miller rolled but Campbell-Cole somehow got away with nothing more than some superficial front end damage.

In the larger class, and with John Rhodes delayed while a coil lead was replaced, Paddy Hopkirk briefly took command for the works Cooper team before he too had a tyre go at Clearways handing the class win to John Cannadine from Gordon Spice. Elsewhere in the running order Tony Lanfranchi's Alexander Mini suffered both a disintegrating clutch and a broken carburettor on lap two, while another failed clutch did for John Handley's Broadspeed entry.

Eventually the day drew to a close, and those spectators eager to get home rushed for their cars only to sit in a traffic jam that stretched nearly to London. The sensible ones stayed on to 'drink to their successes, drown their sorrows' and gathered around the main grandstand to listen to Chris Barber and his band until darkness. It was a pleasant and fitting end to a crowded, busy and happy August Bank Holiday race meeting.

Above
Early in the Ilford Trophy race. With Jack Brabham's Mustang already out front, Pierpoint heads Sears and Salmon in the fight for second place.

The Ilford Trophy
Results

Pos.	Driver	No.	Car	Laps	Time/Reason	Speed
1st	Jack Brabham	174	Ford Mustang	20	38 min 36.0 sec	82.31 mph
2nd	Roy Pierpoint	172	Ford Mustang	20	38 min 38.2 sec	
3rd	Jack Sears	182	Lotus-Cortina (E12)	20	38 min 56.2 sec	
4th	Frank Gardner	183	Lotus-Cortina	20		
5th	Gawaine Baillie	173	Ford Mustang	20		
6th	John Cannadine	195	Austin Mini-Cooper S	20	40 min 00.0 sec	
7th	Gordon Spice	206	Austin Mini-Cooper S	20		
8th	Andrew Hedges	192	Austin Mini-Cooper S	20		
9th	Peter Pilsworth	196	Austin Mini-Cooper S	20		
10th	John Nicholson	184	Lotus-Cortina			
11th	Geoff Mabbs	200	Morris Mini-Cooper S			
12th	Warwick Banks	211	Austin Mini-Cooper S 970			
13th	Tony Rutt	201	Morris Mini-Cooper S			
14th	Ken Costello	215	Morris Mini-Cooper S 970			
15th	Laurie Goodwin	208	Ford Anglia Super			
16th	Peter Clarke	202	Morris Mini-Cooper S			
17th	Harry Martin	218	Morris Mini-Cooper S 970			
18th	John Rhodes	198	Morris Mini-Cooper S			
19th	Tom Simpson	187	Lotus-Cortina			
20th	John Anstead	210	Abarth 1000 TC			
nc	Mike Campbell-Cole	213	Austin Mini-Cooper S 970		Accident	
dnf	Mike Salmon	175	Ford Mustang	16	Broken rear hub	
dnf	John Handley	191	Austin Mini-Cooper S		Clutch	
dnf	Paddy Hopkirk	197	Austin Mini-Cooper S		Puncture	
dnf	David Miller	212	Austin Mini-Cooper S 970	7	Accident	
dnf	John Fitzpatrick	214	Morris Mini-Cooper S 970		Broken seat	
dnf	Tony Lanfranchi	199	Morris Mini-Cooper S	2	Clutch	
dsq	Jim Clark	181	Lotus-Cortina (E9)		Outside assistance	

Pole Position — 174 Jack Brabham
Fastest Lap (record) — 181 Jim Clark — 1 min 54.2 sec (83.54 mph)

Guards International
Results – Parts I & II

Pos.	Driver	No.	Car	Laps	Time/Reason	Speed
1st	John Surtees	4	Lola T70	30	49min 47.8 sec	95.79 mph
2nd	Bruce McLaren	7	McLaren M1A	30		
3rd	Jackie Stewart	5	Lola T70	30		
4th	Dan Gurney	18	McLaren-Elva M1A	30		
5th	Denis Hulme	36	Brabham BT8	29		
6th	Mike Parkes	24	Ferrari 365 P2	29		
7th	Peter Revson	38	Brabham BT8	29		
8th	Jim Clark	8	Lotus 40	28		
dnf	David Hobbs	1	Lola T70		Gearbox	

| **Pole Position** | | 4 | John Surtees | | 1 min 36.0 sec (99.37 mph) | |
| **Fastest Lap** | | | | | | |

Pos.	Driver	No.	Car	Laps	Time/Reason	Speed
1st	John Surtees	4	Lola T70	30	49min 28.6 sec	96.43 mph
2nd	Bruce McLaren	7	McLaren M1A	30		
3rd	Jackie Stewart	5	Lola T70	30		
4th	Walt Hansgen	16	Lola T70	29		
5th	Denis Hulme	36	Brabham BT8	29		
6th	Peter Revson	38	Brabham BT8	29		
7th	David Piper	25	Ferrari 365 P2	29		
8th	Mike Parkes	24	Ferrari 365 P2	29		
dnf	Dan Gurney	18	McLaren-Elva M1A		Wheel fell off	
dnf	Chris Amon	31	Elva Mk.8		Sticking Throttle	
dnf	Jim Clark	8	Lotus 40		Accident	

| **Pole Position** | | 4 | John Surtees | | (first in part I) | |
| **Fastest Lap** | | 4 | John Surtees | | 1 min 36.0 sec (99.37 mph) | |

Guards International
Aggregate Results

Position	Driver	No.	Car	Laps	Time/Reason	Speed
1st	John Surtees	4	Lola T70	60	1 hr 39 min 16.4 sec	96.10 mph
2nd	Bruce McLaren	7	McLaren M1A	60	1 hr 40 min 35.2 sec	
3rd	Jackie Stewart	5	Lola T70	60	1 hr 41 min 21.2 sec	
4th	Denis Hulme	36	Brabham BT8	58		
5th	Peter Revson	38	Brabham BT8	58		
6th	Mike Parkes	24	Ferrari 365 P2	58		
7th	David Piper	10	Ferrari 365 P2	57		
8th	John Coundley	22	McLaren-Elva M1A	56		
9th	Walt Hansgen	16	Lola T70	54		
10th	Tony Sargeant	41	Merlyn Mk.6	54		
11th	Geoffrey Oliver	43	Lotus 23	54		
12th	Peter Gethin	34	Elva Mk.7	50		
nc	Hugh Dibley	2	Lola T70			
nc	Roy Pierpoint	17	Lola T70			
nc	David Hobbs	1	Lola T70			
nc	Jim Clark	5	Lotus 40			
nc	Dan Gurney	18	McLaren-Elva M1A			
nc	Graham Hill	21	McLaren-Elva M1A			
Fastest Lap (overall)		4	John Surtees		1 min 36.0 sec (99.37 mph)	
Class Winners			Surtees, Hulme			

Chapter Eleven
Oulton Park
18th September

"OULTON PARK GOLD CUP GOES TO JOHN SURTEES"

John Surtees had successful weekend at circuits some 3,000 miles apart when he won the Formula 2 Gold Cup at Oulton Park in a Lola-Cosworth and, after a hectic air dash to Canada, won the Players Trophy at the Mont Tremblant circuit in his Lola-Chevy....

Above right
Jimmy celebrates with John Surtees. Although John took the Gold Cup, Jimmy's sixth place was enough for him to take the British F2 Championship.

Timetable

Event: International Gold Cup Meeting
Date: Saturday 18th September 1965
Location: Oulton Park
Circuit Length: 2.761 miles

Time	Race	Laps	Distance
2:00 pm	Formula 3 race	19	52.5 miles
3:10 pm	Formula 2 race	40	110.5 miles
2:00 pm	Saloon Car race	19	52.5 miles

Oulton Park – Existing Lap Records

Formula 1	Jim Clark	Lotus 25-Climax	1m 39.2 sec.	100.20 mph.
Formula 2	G.Hill & J.Rindt	Brabham BT16	1m 41.4 sec.	98.02 mph.
Formula 3	Roy Pike	Brabham-Cosworth	1m 46.2 sec.	93.59 mph.
Sportscars over 2000cc	Bruce McLaren	McLaren M1A	1m 39.0 sec.	102.89 mph.
Saloon Cars over 2000cc	Dan Gurney	Ford Galaxie	1m 53.2 sec.	87.80 mph.
Saloon Cars over 1301cc to 2000cc	Jim Clark	Lotus-Cortina	1m 57.0 sec.	84.95 mph.
GT Cars upto 2500cc	Jim Clark	Lotus Elan	1m 52.8 sec.	88.12 mph.
Grand Touring Cars 2500cc to 3000cc	Innes Ireland	Ferrari 250	1m 53.0 sec.	87.96 mph.

Gold Cup
Entry List

No.	Entrant	Car	Engine	Driver
1	Midland Racing Partnership	Lola T60	Cosworth SCA	John Surtees
2	Midland Racing Partnership	Lola T60	Cosworth SCA	Richard Attwood
3	Midland Racing Partnership	Lola T60	Cosworth SCA	Paul Hawkins
4	Ron Harris Team Lotus	Lotus 35	Cosworth SCA	Jim Clark
5	Ron Harris Team Lotus	Lotus 35	Cosworth SCA	Mike Spence
6	Ron Harris Team Lotus	Lotus 35	B.R.M.	Peter Revson
7	John Coombs	Brabham BT16	B.R.M.	Graham Hill
8	Brabham Racing Developments	Brabham BT16	Honda	Jack Brabham
9	Brabham Racing Developments	Brabham BT16	Cosworth SCA	Denis Hulme
10	Brabham Racing Developments	Brabham BT16	Cosworth SCA	Chris Irwin
11	Tyrrell Racing Organisation	Cooper T75	B.R.M.	Jackie Stewart
12	Tyrrell Racing Organisation	Cooper T75	B.R.M.	Bob Bondurant
14	Merlyn Racing	Merlyn Mk.9	Cosworth SCA	John Cardwell
15	D.W. Racing Enterprises	Brabham BT16	Cosworth SCA	Bob Anderson
16	D.W. Racing Enterprises	Brabham BT16	Cosworth SCA	Alan Rollinson
17	Roy Winkelmann Racing	Brabham BT16	Cosworth SCA	Alan Rees
18	Roy Winkelmann Racing	Brabham BT16	Cosworth SCA	Jochen Rindt
19	David Prophet Racing	Brabham BT10	Cosworth SCA	David Prophet
20	David Prophet Racing	Brabham BT10	Cosworth SCA	Bill Bradley
21	Normand	Brabham BT16	Cosworth SCA	Mike Beckwith
22	Ian Raby (Racing) Ltd.	Merlyn Mk.9	Cosworth SCA	Ian Raby
23	Aurora Gear (Racing) Rotherham	Brabham BT16	Cosworth SCA	Trevor Taylor
24	E.Offenstadt	Cooper T75	B.R.M.	Eric Offenstadt
25	Brian Hart	Lotus 35	Cosworth SCA	Brian Hart
26	B.Collomb	Lotus 35	Cosworth SCA	Bernard Collomb
27	Bob Gerard	Cooper T73	Cosworth SCA	John Taylor
28	Race Proved by Willment	Lotus 35	Cosworth SCA	Frank Gardner

"John Harris (Lotus Elan) is the new 'Autosport' champion. He took the title by winning his class in both two-hour heats of the final at Snetterton on September 12th."

Formula Two At Its Finest

In the very best traditions of the mid-60's Formula 2 racing, spectators to Oulton Park for the 1965 International Gold Cup Race witnessed a finish in which a mere only 0.6s separated the first three cars. Driving at his brilliant best in the Midland Racing Partnership Lola Type 50, John Surtees won the race having held the lead for the final 15 laps. Denny Hulme, in the works Brabham-Cosworth, finished a painfully close second, having also led at one stage, with the third-placed Graham Hill in the Coombs Lotus 35-BRM close behind him. Hill had never managed to take the lead, but – signifying some very exciting racing – both the Winklemann Brabhams of Rindt and Rees had at one point, as had the Lotus of Jim Clark in what was almost certainly the best spectator race of the entire season.

Practice First

Official practice had been confined to the Friday before the race, the Formula 2 cars being the first out and in unusually large numbers with not a s ngle non-starter in sight which must constitute some kind of a record. The Brabham Racing Developments team was there in force, with four cars for Jack himself, Denny Hulme, and an 'AN Other'. The crowds were soon flocking round the transporter, especially once word got out that Jack's car was once again to be Honda-powered and that the three Japanese mechanics had once again travelled from Tokyo to attend. The three remaining Brabhams had the more conventional Cosworth units, but one of these, the T car-chassis no. F2-28-65, was actually a brand new machine with slightly revised rear suspension. The mystery driver for the third car was soon revealed to be Chequered Flag Formula 3 star Chris Irwin.

Ron Harris-Team Lotus brought along only three Type 35s for its three drivers, Clark and Spence using Cosworth-powered cars whilst Peter Revson's had a BRM unit fitted, the suspicion being that if something went wrong in practice the lack of a spare car would mean Revson (probably) would be going home unhappy. MRP meanwhile fielded three Lola Cosworths, all Type 60s, for John Surtees, Dickie Attwood and Paul 'Hawkeye' Hawkins.

A number of two-car teams also made the cut, including Winklemann Racing with a pair of characteristically immaculate Brabham-Cosworths for Jochen Rindt and Alan Rees. Tyrrell Racing fielded two not quite so clean looking Cooper-BRMs for Jackie Stewart and Bob Bondurant, David Prophet arrived with a pair of Brabham-Cosworths for himself and Bill Bradley, and DW Racing Enterprises had two Brabham-Cosworths for Bob Anderson and Alan Rollinson. (The second of these was still under the supervision of Frank Lythgoe Racing but using DW's name apparently helped to obtain entries.)

Among the 'singletons' Trevor Taylor had the Aurora Gear Racing Brabham Cosworth, Mike Beckwith a similar Normand entry, while Brian Hart entered a Lotus 35 with Cosworth motivation for himself. John Coombs similarly fielded the ex-Parnell Lotus 35 for Graham Hill, while Willment produced yet another 35 for Frank Gardner. Chris Irwin's defection to Brabham meant that John Cardwell took over the works Merlyn Cosworth Mk.9 (Ian Raby entered a similar car) while Bob Gerard bought a Cooper T72-Cosworth for John Taylor who also had his own Brabham. Finally, there were a couple of foreign

Gold Cup
Grid

Pole Position

Denis Hulme	Jochen Rindt	Graham Hill	Jim Clark
Brabham-Cosworth	Brabham-Cosworth	Brabham-BRM	Lotus-Cosworth
1m 41.0 sec	1m 41.2 sec	1m 41.2 sec	1m 41.4 sec

Alan Rees	Mike Spence	Trevor Taylor
Brabham-Cosworth	Lotus-Cosworth	Brabham-Cosworth
1m 41.6 sec	1m 41.6 sec	1m 42.0 sec

Jack Brabham	Jackie Stewart	John Surtees	Chris Irwin
Brabham-Honda	Cooper-BRM	Lola-Cosworth	Brabham-Cosworth
1m 42.0 sec	1m 42.4 sec	1m 42.4 sec	1m 43.0 sec

Brian Hart	Richard Attwood	Bob Anderson
Lotus-Cosworth	Lola-Cosworth	Brabham-Cosworth
1m 43.4 sec	1m 43.4 sec	1m 43.8 sec

Mike Beckwith	Ian Raby	Alan Rollinson	John Cardwell
Brabham-Cosworth	Merlyn-Cosworth	Brabham-Cosworth	Merlyn-Cosworth
1m 44.2 sec	1m 44.4 sec	1m 44.6 sec	1m 45.6 sec

David Prophet	Bill Bradley	Paul Hawkins
Brabham-Cosworth	Brabham-Cosworth	Lola-Cosworth
1m 45.6 sec	1m 46.4 sec	1m 47.0 sec

Bob Bondurant	Frank Gardner	Peter Revson	Eric Offenstadt
Cooper-BRM	Lotus-Cosworth	Lotus-BRM	Cooper-BRM
1m 47.4 sec	1m 47.6 sec	1m 47.8 sec	1m 48.8 sec

John Taylor	Bernard Collomb
Cooper-Cosworth	Lotus-Cosworth
1m 55.8 sec	2m 03.0 sec

Opposite
Mike Spence dropped
out of the Gold Cup on
lap 23 when he crashed
at Knicker Brook.

entries in Eric Offenstadt who brought along a Cooper-BRM and Bernard Collomb with a Cosworth powered Lotus 35.

Fortunately – perhaps especially for Revson – there were no major incidents in practice. Surprisingly none of the top cars managed to better the Formula 2 lap record set up at the Spring meeting by Hill and Rindt, although an indication of the closeness of the battle which was to take place the following day can be seen in the times.

In fact the 12 fastest cars were within two seconds of each other, Hulme heading the list with 1m 42sec., Rindt and Hill coming just 0.2 seconds behind, Clark 0.2 slower again, and just another fifth of a second separating the Lotus number one from team mate Spence and Alan Rees. Trevor Taylor and Jack Brabham were the next up with 1m 42.0sec., Brabham and Hulme both trying the new car and both achieving 1m 46.0sec., while Irwin – after putting in more practice laps than anyone else – eventually posted a very respectable 1m 42.8sec.. The eventual winner, Surtees, did a comparatively slow 1m 42.4sec., as it happens exactly the same time as Stewart in his Tyrrell car. Peter Revson who qualified near the back with a rather slow 1m 47.8sec. was nevertheless pleased to see his teammates survive without incident and just hoped that his down-on-power BRM engine would up its game for the race.

Later in the day a second session for the Formula 2 cars was well and truly rained off. A few cars did venture out but no one achieved anything of note and the grid was

not affected by any of the times. On returning to the paddock the cars and drivers that had gone out found it reduced to a sea of glorious mud. Revson was still happy though, he was in the race.

Things were markedly different in the Formula 3 practice session which took place before the rains came down. Here no less than five cars came in under Roy Pike's lap record of 1m 46.2sec., Irwin's Chequered Flag Brabham BT16 the fastest at 1m 44.8sec., and the surprise of the session being John Fenning in the Stockbridge Cooper T76 just four-tenths of a seconds slower. Others to break the existing record were Pike himself, Peter Revson (who was now out in F3 version of the Lotus 35 and getting plenty of track time) and Piers Courage in a Lucas Brabham BT10.

Peter Gethin was less fortunate, bringing the Charles Lucas Lotus 35 into the pits with its clutch hydraulic pipe smouldering on the exhaust system, so that for the race he had to take over the team's Brabham which Lucas had practiced in. Graham White in his 1963 Brabham BT6 came unstuck in an even bigger way at Knicker Brook, somersaulting the car but surprisingly uninjured and the car a very definite DNS even though it was apparently far from being written off.

Equally surprising, perhaps, was that in practice for the saloon car race Frank Gardner in the Willment Lotus-Cortina was fastest overall with his time of 1m 57.0sec. equalling Jim Clark's class lap record. As for Team Lotus, they had three of their four car squad available for the weekend, the new leaf-sprung E12 being run by Sid Carr after a brief run Brands Hatch. Unfortunately it still had

Above
At the end of the first lap Hulme led from Rindt, Clark Taylor, Rees and Hill.

Opposite top
Ready for the off. From left to right: Chris Irwin (row 3), Clark, Hill, Rindt, Rees (hidden), Brabham (row 3) and Hulme (far right).

Opposite lower
Jim Clark made one of his rare mistakes when leading the Gold Cup. On lap 8 he spun at Cascades and had to get out of the car to push it back into the right direction.

"Jim Clark wore an average of less than 1.5mm off each tyre tread during his winning drive in the German GP. Like most competitors, he spent a lot of time airborne over the bumps!"

brake and handling problems, and after another brief run in practice was hastily consigned to the transporter for the rest of the weekend. With E10 being left back at the workshop, E9 (run by Alan McCall) was redesignated as Clark's race car while Bob Sparshott prepared E11 for Jack Sears.

Formula 3s Take To The Track
Rain was still falling on Saturday morning but a strong wind meant the track was more or less dry by the time the racing started although it denied the crowd a chance to see the Red Devils parachuting onto the infield.

To allay their disappointment the Formula 3 cars lined up promptly, with Irwin in pole position although when the flag dropped it was Fenning who made the best start and took Old Hall first. He was followed by Pike, Irwin, Dean, and the Swiss Jurg Dubler in a Brabham. By the time they swept through into the second lap Pike had taken the lead from Fenning, Piers Courage was lying fourth followed by Revson, David Cole (Brabham), Boley Pittard (Lotus 35), Harry Stiller (another Brabham), and Morris Nunn in a Lotus 22.

The leading trio was soon absolutely locked together in combat, and by lap three Irwin held the lead from Pike, the Chequered Flag boys driving brilliantly as a team and managing to holding off Fenning. Further down the field spins soon became the order of the day, with Courage putting on a show on lap three and again three laps later at Cascades, Tony Dean spinning off on lap two before rejoining, and then more spins from Cole, Costin and Gethin. Maybe the track wasn't quite as dry as everyone thought.

The half distance positions showed Irwin fractionally leading Pike, with Fenning third, the Ron Harris cars of Revson and Cardwell next behind them, and then a bunch with Pittard just leading Nunn, who was going well, then Dubler and Ray Parsons. Lap 13 proved unlucky for Irwin, however, who had pulled away from his team mate only to collide with Natalie Goodwin whilst lapping her. It will be remembered that at the previous year's Gold Cup meeting he had also led for much of the race in a Merlyn, holding off Jackie Stewart in the process. Fenning briefly took the lead but by the end of the lap Pike was past him. The Harris cars lay third and fourth and then came the Willment cars of Pittard and Parsons. Nunn retired his Lotus with engine trouble while Dean was up to ninth.

At the end of the 19 laps Pike had triumphed, crossing the line with Fenning six seconds behind, then the Holbay powered Lotuses of Revson and Cardwell, Pittard behind him and Dean splitting the Willment pair to put Parsons back to seventh. Gethin had worked his way up to eighth, but it was nevertheless still something of a disappointing day for the Lucas team. Of the foreigners that took part, Dubler retired on lap 16, the Frenchman Patrick Dal Bo with the Pygmée was 12th, and from Germany Henning Bock in a Cooper T72 was pathetically slow, finishing a full four laps behind.

The Gold Cup
In years gone by, when the Gold Cup was a Formula One race, the drivers were paraded around Oulton Park before the start of the race in Land Rovers or something similar. For 1965 they were content to do a quick warm-up tour before reassembling on the grid, a few

Above
Jack Brabham once again had Honda power in the back of his BT16 but had little chance to show its capabilities. He retired on the first lap with clutch failure.

Gold Cup
Results

Pos.	Driver	No.	Car	Laps	Time	Speed
1st	John Surtees	1	Lola T60	40	1 hr 08 min 44.0 sec	96.40 mph
2nd	Denis Hulme	9	Brabham BT16	40	1 hr 08 min 44.2 sec	
3rd	Graham Hill	7	Brabham BT16	40	1 hr 08 min 44.6 sec	
4th	Trevor Taylor	23	Brabham BT16	40	1 hr 09 min 03.2 sec	
5th	Alan Rees	17	Brabham BT16	40	1 hr 09 min 18.6 sec	
6th	Jim Clark	4	Lotus 35	40	1 hr 09 min 25.4 sec	
7th	Brian Hart	25	Lotus 35	40	1 hr 09 min 58.6 sec	
8th	Ian Raby	22	Merlyn Mk.9	39		
9th	Paul Hawkins	3	Lola T60	39		
10th	Bill Bradley	20	Brabham BT10	39		
11th	David Prophet	19	Brabham BT10	39		
12th	John Cardwell	14	Merlyn Mk.9	39		
13th	Alan Rollinson	16	Brabham BT16	39		
14th	Bernard Collomb	26	Lotus 35	36		
15th	Eric Offenstadt	24	Cooper T75	34		
16th	Jochen Rindt	18	Brabham BT16	31		
17th	Jackie Stewart	11	Cooper T75	29		
dnf	Mike Spence	5	Lotus 35	23	Accident	
dnf	Peter Revson	6	Lotus 35	8	Oil loss	
dnf	Richard Attwood	2	Lola T60	5	Gearbox	
dnf	Mike Beckwith	21	Brabham BT16	4	Accident	
dnf	Chris Irwin	10	Brabham BT16	4	Accident	
dnf	Bob Anderson	15	Brabham BT16	4	Engine	
dnf	Jack Brabham	8	Brabham BT16	1	Clutch	
dnf	Frank Gardner	28	Lotus 35	1	Ignition	
dnf	Bob Bondurant	12	Cooper T75	0	Accident	
Pole Position		9	Denis Hulme		1min 41.0 sec (98.76mph)	
Fastest lap (record)		4 & 9	Clark & Hulme		1min 41.2 sec (98.22mph)	

Left
Bob Bondurant in the
Tyrrell Cooper-BRM
was out of the Gold Cup
by the first corner. After
touching wheels with
Mike Beckwith he shot
off the track and ended
up in the ditch.

mechanics busy cleaning the last traces of the muddy paddock off their cars and then the grid clearing with two minutes to go leaving the drivers on their own.

As the flag dropped the cars made a very clean start with all eyes trained on Old Hall where Rindt managed to snatch the lead from Surtees. Few noticed Bondurant shooting off at a tangent and landing in the bank just past the gate opposite the end of the pits. He had apparently touched Beckwith, and although the car was not damaged his race was run almost before it started. Gardner similarly pulled straight into the pits and retired with what was later described as plug trouble.

Meanwhile down the Avenue, round Cascades up to Island and into Esso the cars jostled and swapped positions and the order as they flashed by the pits at the end of the first lap was Hulme, Rindt, Clark, Taylor, Rees, Hill, Surtees and Attwood. The next time round Rees was in front of Taylor, Surtees and Spence had displaced Hill, and then came Attwood, Anderson, Irwin, Rollinson, Hart, Revson, Beckwith, Raby, Hawkins, Cardwell, Bradley, John Taylor, Prophet, Offenstadt, Collomb, Stewart (clearly in trouble) and finally Brabham who pulled into the pits to retire with clutch problems.

For a while the leading bunch were running so close that some sort of trouble was inevitable: soon the pits were busy, with Irwin and Beckwith both stopping for good, the former having spun at Lodge to the detriment of the car, and Beckwith probably as a result of his bump at the start. Stewart was also in, having some electrical difficulties attended to and losing six laps before he was underway again. With five laps gone, the positions

settled down with Clark in the lead (but only just) with Hulme behind him then Rindt, Rees, Surtees, Hill, Taylor, Spence, Attwood who retired the following lap, Rollinson battling with Hart, and Revson and Raby bringing up the rear.

The first four were inseparably close, Taylor was also keeping in touch, the former number two Lotus GP driver pulling away from the present one. Everyone was expecting another Clark benefit but then, on lap eight and under extreme pressure, he made on of his rare mistakes and spun going into Cascades ending up facing the wrong direction and having to jump out of the car to manoeuvre it round. By the time he had got going again he was down in sixteenth; Jochen Rindt was the new leader with Hulme second, Rees third, Surtees now fourth in front of Hill, an all five cars running within about a second of each other.

Lap 10 saw Rees take the lead from Rindt, a position he held for the next ten laps at which point, having hounded him from second place, Surtees slipped through to take the lead with Rindt and Hulme right behind and all constantly swapping places to the crowd's evident delight. At half distance the order was Surtees, Rees, Hulme, Hill, Rindt, followed by Taylor, Spence, Hart, Clark (already back up to ninth), Raby, Hawkins, Bradley, Prophet, Cardwell, Rollinson now slower after a spin the previous lap, Collomb, Offenstadt and Stewart; the last two having pitted, Revson had retired the BRM-engined Team Lotus entry.

Still the leading battle raged and in the words of the race commentator "*the gap between first, second and third*

is so close as to be quite insignificant." Spence went off at Knicker Brook on lap 23 and was unable to rejoin the race, and two laps later Hulme thought he had better have another stint in the lead but could only hold on to it for three laps. After a small mistake on lap 26 he too dropped back (to fifth) with Surtees taking the lead once more, followed by Rees, Hill and Rindt.

The next excursion was made by Rees who spun at Druids on lap 29 so dropping to sixth place behind Taylor. Two laps later Hulme passed Rindt to get back into third place but then the following lap the Austrian retired with a broken rubber doughnut in his drivetrain. That put Clark in sixth but despite bringing the lap record down to 1m 41.2sec. – a feat equalled by Hulme – he'd simply lost too much time to catch the leaders. With just five laps to go the order was Surtees, 2.2 seconds in front of Hill who was in turn just 1.8 seconds ahead of Hulme. Taylor was next, then Rees, Clark, Hart, Raby, Hawkins with Bradley snapping at his heels, Prophet, Cardwell, Rollinson, Collomb, and Offenstadt and Stewart who had both pitted for a second time.

The leading positions were still in doubt however, and with two laps to go Hulme passed Hill and kept in front right to the flag. As he crossed the line the New Zealander was only a fifth of a second behind Surtees with Hill 0.4 seconds further down after 40 quite furious laps. For once Yorkshireman Trevor Taylor's luck held, and looking really happy he finished an excellent fourth.

With Rees in fifth, Clark's battling sixth place had at least earned him a vital point in the Championship putting him one point ahead of Hill at the head of the table. Having

already clinched the Formula 1 Drivers Championship, and the four race European Formula 2 series with wins in Pau and Rouen (and another to come at Albi), the Autocar British Formula 2 Championship was the Scotsman's third title of the year – plus of course the Indy 500.

Plenty Still To Come

The Gold Cup meeting was rounded off with a 50-mile Touring Car race, itself the final round of an exciting British Touring Car Championship. The leader of the competition, Roy Pierpoint, badly needed a win to pull off the championship. If he failed to do this, Warwick Banks was right behind him in the smaller-engined Cooper S; he too could be champion, as long as he won his own up to 1000cc class, making the last race of the day as interesting as any which preceeded it.

Despite Gardner in pole it was Jim Clark who was first into Old Hall, racing ahead of Pierpoint in the white and blue Mustang which seemed to be going wide. Suddenly the car fishtailed from side to side, knocking cars all over the place and blocking the track when it stopped in what could best be described as something of a motorway pile-up. Most of the cars managed to restart, including the Mustang, but unfortunately the Minis of Mike Cambell-Cole (who had been fastest in class in practice) and John Lewis were both out for good. Tony Lanfranchi reappeared from deep in the undergrowth, Warwick Banks' engine died but he was able to restart it, Chris Craft had tyre marks down the side of the Super-speed Anglia, and Middlehurst (Mini) and Harry O'Brian in his Lotus-Cortina were also out of the running.

Formula 3 Race
Results

Pos.	Driver	No.	Car	Laps	Time	Speed
1st	Roy Pike	31	Brabham BT16	19	34 min 00.8 sec	92.53 mph
2nd	John Fenning	41	Cooper T76	19	34 min 06.2 sec	
3rd	Peter Revson	33	Lotus 35	19	34 min 21.4 sec	
4th	John Cardwell	34	Lotus 35	19	34 min 30.4 sec	
5th	Boley Pittard	59	Lotus 35	19	34 min 54.9 sec	
6th	Tony Dean	46	Brabham BT15	19	34 min 59.6 sec	
7th	Ray Parsons	60	Lotus 35	19	35 min 09.0 sec	
8th	Peter Gethin	37	Brabham BT10	19	35 min 18.0 sec	
9th	Harry Stiller	56	Brabham BT16	19	35 min 18.4 sec	
10th	Malcolm Payne	50	Lotus 31	19	35 min 19.6 sec	
11th	Melvyn Long	49	Lotus 35	19	35 min 20.4 sec	
12th	Patrick Dal Bo	45	Pygmee 135	19	35 min 26.4 sec	
13th	Keith St.John	62	Brabham BT15	19		
14th	Roger Brash	68	Merlyn Mk.9	18		
15th	Mike Gill	55	Brabham BT15	18		
16th	Jim Sullivan	47	Brabham BT16	18		
17th	Natalie Goodwin	39	Brabham BT15	18		
18th	Briar Hough	66	Cooper T76	18		
19th	John Spurgeon	65	Lotus 27	17	nrf	
20th	Tim Featherstone	64	Lotus 31	17		
21s	Henning Bock	54	Cooper T72	16		
dnf	Jurg Dubler	58	Brabham BT15	14		
dnf	Roy Cook	63	Lotus 31	13		
dnf	Chris Irwin	32	Brabham BT16	11	Accident	
dnf	Morris Nunn	44	Lotus 22	10		
dnf	Teddy Dawson	52	Lotus 22	10		
dnf	Piers Courage	38	Brabham BT10	9		
dnf	David Cole	57	Brabham BT15	3		
Pole Position		32	Chris Irwin		1m 44.8 sec (95.11 mph)	
Fastest lap		31	Roy Pike		1m 45.2 sec (94.48 mph)	

At the end of lap one then, the order was Clark, Brabham in the Alan Brown Mustang, then Sears, Gardner and Fitzpatrick just ahead of Rhodes. In the smallest class Bob Smith was in the lead, the Group 3 saloon car record holder for the circuit leading the sub-1.0-litre cars with his Vitafoam entry. John Terry in the Broadspeed 1275 S had had a small moment at Esso before retiring, while John Handley in the team's 970 S fought hard to make up time after taking the escape road at Cascades.

On lap two Brabham surged by Clark and was never headed again. Gardner, however, was soon to retire having held down fourth place for some while before a couple of adventures at Cascades. At half distance Brabham led from Clark and Sears with Sir Gawaine Baillie's Mustang moving up to fourth ahead of John Rhodes. Jack Newman was sixth, his Cortina being hounded by the battered Pierpoint, then came Steve Neal in the immaculate Arden car. Warwick Banks and John Handley were similarly dicing for the lead in the class (both having passed Smith) while fourth in that class was the Swede Jan-Eric Andreason. John Fitzpatrick had retired as early as lap four, his differential having failed while he was leading the 1300cc class.

From then on the real interest centered on Roy Pierpoint's progress, and of course the Banks/Handley class battle which would decide the title. Pierpoint could only make it up to fourth place, i.e. second in class, while Banks seemingly took the title by winning his class by just a fifth of a second. In the last few laps Baillie retired whilst Jim Clark rounded off a good day by setting yet another new class record in the Cortina.

Then, a week later, it was all change. Jack Brabham's Alan Brown Mustang was disqualified from the race due to valve spring infringement. That made Clark the race winner, a 1-2 for Team Lotus in fact, and meant that Pierpoint, as the new Class D winner, was also the new BRSCC British Saloon Car Champion after all.

It had been, in other words, quite a day. Few would have tipped Surtees to win the Gold Cup in the Lola, but he had done so nonetheless. Formula 3 race had, yet again, provided really tremendous value, and the saloons, well, they provided drama not just on the day but well into the next week as well.

For Sally Stokes there was also drama on the way home. "*We were getting a ride home with Jack Brabham in his plane, returning to Panshanger Airport in Essex, close to where Colin lived and not too far for Jimmy and I to return to central London. We took off heading south and after a short while Jack started saying he was a bit low on fuel and was wondering if we would make it home. He and Colin discussed the problem and hastily decided to go into Coventry to refuel. The engine started sputtering and we were put on a speedy 'final approach' into the airport. I was quite frightened as to whether we would make it but got no sympathy from a young David Brabham sat next to me. "Don't worry Sally, Daddy often does this....just read your book" I was told. As it turned my fears were justified. The guys fuelling up said "How much petrol does this plane hold....we are putting in a lot" and Colin replied "I think we just landed on fumes!" Jack was quite unruffled about the whole thing and we were told he was famous for taking chances!"*

Above left
Despite his best efforts, Jimmy just couldn't hold the Mustang of Jack Brabham at bay.

Above right
The Mini of Warwick Banks and Bob Smith battle it out for class honours. Banks took the class win and though he had won the championship as well. For a week at least.

Saloon Car Race
Results

Pos.	Driver	No.	Car	Laps	Time/Reason	Speed
dsq	Jack Brabham	114	Ford Mustang	19	37 min 16.6 sec	84.44 mph
1st	Jim Clark	105	Lotus-Cortina (E9)	19	37 min 20.8 sec	
2nd	Jack Sears	106	Lotus-Cortina (E11)	19	37 min 59.2 sec	
3rd	Roy Pierpoint	111	Ford Mustang	19	38 min 12.8 sec	
4th	Jack Newman	101	Lotus-Cortina	19	38 min 48.4 sec	
5th	John Rhodes	84	Morris Mini-Cooper S	19	38 min 48.6 sec	
6th	Steve Neal	91	Austin Mini-Cooper S	19	39 min 18.2 sec	
7th	Mike Young	82	Austin Mini-Cooper S	18		
8th	Chris Craft	81	Morris Mini-Cooper S	18		
9th	Robin Smith	102	Lotus-Cortina	18		
10th	Warwick Banks	71	Austin Mini-Cooper S 970	18		
11th	John Handley	75	Austin Mini-Cooper S 970	18		
12th	Bob Smith	77	Morris Mini-Cooper S 970	17		
13th	Jan-Erik Andreasson	72	Morris Mini-Cooper S 970	17		
dnf	Frank Gardner	107	Lotus-Cortina	8	Accident	
dnf	John Fitzpatrick	90	Austin Mini-Cooper S	3	Accident	
dnf	John Terry	92	Austin Mini-Cooper S	2	Accident	
dnf	Mike Campbell-Cole	74	Austin Mini-Cooper S 970	0	Accident	
dnf	John Lewis	93	Austin Mini-Cooper S	0	Accident	
dnf	Tony Middlehurst	89	Morris Mini-Cooper S			
dnf	Harry O'Brien	108	Lotus-Cortina			
dnf	Gawaine Baillie	112	Ford Mustang			

Pole Position		107	Frank Gardner	
Fastest Lap (record)		114	Jack Brabham	1 min 55.2 sec (86.28 mph)
Class Winners			Brabham, Clark, Rhodes, Banks